The Man Question

The Man Question

Male Subordination and Privilege

Nancy E. Dowd

NEW YORK UNIVERSITY PRESS
New York and London

NEW YORK UNIVERSITY PRESS
New York and London
www.nyupress.org

Library of Congress Cataloging-in-Publication Data

Dowd, Nancy E., 1949–
The man question : male subordination and privilege / Nancy E. Dowd.
p. cm.
Includes bibliographical references and index.
ISBN-13: 978-0-8147-2005-9 (cl : alk. paper)
ISBN-10: 0-8147-2005-6 (cl : alk. paper)
ISBN-13: 978-0-8147-2094-3 (ebook)
ISBN-10: 0-8147-2094-3 (ebook)
1. Men—Legal status, laws, etc. 2. Sex and law. 3. Masculinity.
4. Fatherhood. 5. Feminist theory. I. Title.
K645.D69   2010
305.31—dc22   2010011998

New York University Press books are printed on acid-free paper,
and their binding materials are chosen for strength and durability.
We strive to use environmentally responsible suppliers and materials
to the greatest extent possible in publishing our books.

Manufactured in the United States of America

10 9 8 7 6 5 4 3 2 1

To Zack

Contents

Preface

This book owes its origin in the first instance to my students in Gender and the Law at the University of Florida Levin College of Law. After many years of teaching the course, which focused entirely on women and the law as well as feminist theory, I decided to add readings about men, men's issues, and masculinities, particularly because of my interest in issues related to fathers and fatherhood. The effect was electric; the class was both threatened and energized by the readings, resistant and yet open to rethinking their assumptions about gender equality and gender issues. Expansion of the readings about men and masculinities led to a proposal to NYU Press for a reader to supplement courses in feminist theory and gender and the law. At the final stage of review, the editors asked if I would write a book on the place of masculinities in feminist theory. At that stage my colleague Barbara Bennett Woodhouse (now at Emory University) strongly urged me to research and write the book. It began a process of further immersion in this subject for several years. I am grateful for her support and encouragement throughout this project, as well as her comments and feedback as the book took shape. I have also benefitted from the feedback of Professor Shani King, another colleague at the University of Florida, on various pieces of this work. Many other colleagues at the University of Florida have been influential in my thinking, over several years of conversations about the book. Richard Collier has been a source of dialogue throughout this project and visited briefly at the law school during the book's development and presented some of his work on masculinity. Two other significant influences as I worked on this volume were Ann McGinley and Frank Rudy Cooper, both of whom have influenced me with their own work on masculinities and have been very supportive of this project.

In the course of working on this volume I was ably assisted by the librarians at the College of Law, who retrieved volumes from many disciplines and helped track down sources from various journals. I have also been strongly supported with summer research grants from the college as I worked on the manuscript over several summers. Dean Robert Jerry, then Associate Dean George Dawson, and Senior Associate Dean Bill Page have all been wonderfully supportive of this project. Stephanie Bates Galligan, JD '10, has been a dynamic and fantastic research assistant who brought this research project to fruition at its final stages. I also have been assisted in this project by wonderful research assistance from Kelly Reese, Emily Banks, and Renee Allen. Cindy Zimmerman provided incredible support in the early stages of this project, and Debbie Willis also provided wonderful support in the preparation of the manuscript.

Portions of the book have been presented at various conferences, including the conference celebrating the twenty-fifth anniversary of the Feminism and Legal Theory Project of Professor Martha Fineman held at the University of Wisconsin; a workshop on comparative family law in early 2009 as well as a workshop on masculinities and feminism in the fall of 2009, both at Emory University; the fourteenth LatCrit conference in 2009; the University of Baltimore Feminist Legal Theory conference in spring 2010; and the spring 2010 symposium "Feminist Perspectives in Masculinities" sponsored by the *Harvard Journal of Law and Gender*. An edited and revised version of chapter 3 was published by the *Wisconsin Women's Law Journal* in 2008, and the research presented in chapter 6 was the basis for an essay published in the *Korean Law Journal*'s special issue on comparative family law in 2009.

Deborah Gershenowitz, my editor at NYU Press, has shaped this project from its inception and supported it strongly in every possible way. She is simply fabulous to work with on any project.

My children once again have been understanding that "Mom is working on another book." My daughter, Zoe, now in college, as well as my son, Zack, are amazing and wonderful. My sister, Patricia McDermott, has been my daily source of feedback and support. My father remains as much in my mind as if he were still here. To them in particular I give my deepest thanks.

Throughout the period when this book was written two men have had a major impact on my thinking. One is my son, Zachary Dowd, who is seventeen as this book is completed. Living through his teenage years as I delved into this literature brought the personal and the professional closely together. Hopefully it helped me understand better the pressures he faces; clearly he helped me better understand the realities of becoming a man. The other man is Ted Shaw, who engaged in endless discussions about the book as I delved into the research and writing. Dr. Shaw is a licensed psychologist and founding partner of the ITM Group in Gainesville, Florida; he has several affiliations with the University of Florida. He has testified more than three hundred times in federal, circuit, civil, and family court and has logged more than fifteen thousand face-to-face hours evaluating and treating sex offenders. He has authored articles and book chapters related to adult and adolescent offenders and has presented throughout the United States and in Europe, Canada, and South America. His expertise, along with his interest and support, ultimately led to a recognition that his work with sex offenders has some fascinating intersections with my work and thus to a joint chapter in this volume. In every possible way he has been my unfailing support in this project.

Introduction

Feminist legal theory began by asking "the woman question." Feminists persistently asked why women were missing, what justified their subordination, differentiation, and inequality. Feminists affirmatively called for valuing that which was woman-identified. Antiessentialist critics of feminism required feminists to "ask the other question" or questions—questions of race, class, and sexual orientation. Feminists had to acknowledge differences among women and the intertwining of privilege with inequality, including instances of women's subordination of other women.

Antiessentialism inevitably led to noticing how the intersections of gender, race, class, and sexual orientation dissolve any notion that only women are subordinated. And that fact inexorably pushes us to ask "the man question." The man question is how gender functions to subordinate some or all or most men, as well as how men consciously and unconsciously accept privilege with its patriarchal dividend as well as its costs. Asking the man question strengthens the promise of feminist analysis to challenge and fight inequality and injustice. It may also increase the potential for alliances between women and men. In this volume I begin that task by exploring masculinities scholarship and what it can bring to feminist legal theory.

Feminists have studied men, patriarchy, and masculine characteristics as sources of power, domination, inequality, and subordination. Various theories of inequality have been developed by feminists to challenge and reveal structures and discourses that reinforce explicitly or implicitly the centrality of men and the identity of the top of a hierarchical power and economic structure as male. Feminists have examined, for example, inequalities in work, wealth, family, privacy, reproductive rights, victimization from violence, and state intervention. In law, feminists have exposed women's absence from legal rules, statutory structures, and constitutional doctrines and protections. They have exposed women's silence, or their concentration, in particular areas of law that expose women's relegation to the private sphere. Even where women are formally equal, feminists have sought to explain their ongoing real inequality. Thus, they have exposed how even the process of reform can contain the seed of reconstituted inequality. So, for example, gender neutrality, while persuasive in theory, hides asymmetrical realities, such as the disproportionate caretaking responsibilities of women or women's disproportionate victimization from sexual assault and domestic violence.

One can argue this focus makes sense. Two stories that Michael Kimmel, a leading masculinities scholar, relates in his work would support such a view. Kimmel describes a study that asked, what would both boys and girls do if they woke up the next morning the opposite sex? The girls "thought about the question for a while, expressed modest disappointment, and then described the kinds of things they would do. . . . Become a doctor, fireman, policeman, or baseball player were typical answers. The boys, by contrast, took virtually no time before answering. 'Kill myself' was the most common answer" (2004, 46).

The second story expresses the link between masculinity and power, particularly violent power, as a source of pride and ultimate power. "After he had successfully tested a nuclear bomb in November 1952, . . . Edward Teller, the Nobel Prize–winning nuclear physicist, wrote the following three word telegram to his colleagues: 'It's a boy.' No one had to point out to Teller the equation of military might—the capacity for untold violence—and masculinity" (Kimmel 2004, 273–74).

Yet at the same time, failing to look at men, in both their power and burdens, may hide key aspects of male experience. The expectation that men are stoic and emotionally strong makes it difficult to respond to their emotional traumas, as evidenced by the challenges in treating soldiers. The term "shell shock" emerged out of World War I to describe male soldiers who "acted like women," meaning they exhibited hysterical behavior thought only to be associated with women. The term was coined to describe hysteria in "the rougher sex," but its victims were viewed as "subnormals, psychic weaklings, malingerers, and draft evaders" (Lunbeck 1994, 253). It was not until the post–Vietnam War era that this phenomenon was understood as a response to trauma, exacerbated by the threat it posed to the individual's and society's view of manhood.

One of the fascinating ways in which power, privilege, and the burdens of masculinity are apparent is in language. In a funny, but also sad, book, Peter Murphy explores the terms we use for and about men, and what they suggest about our views about men. As he points out, "the insidiousness of language in the tragedy of contemporary manhood. . . . [illustrates] how it works against us while appearing to empower us" (2001, x). Although arguably the controllers of language, men use a language of hatred, according to Murphy: "The overwhelming emphasis on performance and the portrayal of the penis as a mechanical device, whether tool or weapon or machine in need of manipulation and repair, reduces masculinity to values of harness, power and control" (137–38). Murphy calls for men to re-create the language of masculinity "informed by equality, not rivalry, caring about other human beings, not subordinating as many people as possible" (144).

By focusing on women, feminists have constructed men largely as uni-dimensional. This focus is understandable and arguably was necessary, but with the development of scholarship on men *as* men, rather than as the assumed subject, the unstated norm, that work may bring additional insights to feminist theory for the benefit of women's equality, as well as uncovering to a greater extent men's inequalities and disadvantages within patriarchy.

The study of masculinities derives directly from feminist theory, emerging in the 1970s and 1980s to explore the construction of manhood and mascu-linity, to question the real circumstances of men, to explore how privilege is constructed, and to examine what price is paid for privilege. One of the most intriguing and troubling aspects of men's gender privilege is the price men pay. For example, men are disproportionately the victims of violence at the hands of other men, violence that is integral to the very definition of masculinity. This definition of what it means to be a man begins with boys and is defined most strongly by bullying. A second, closely related example is military service, an obligation strongly tied to the definition of manhood as linked to strength and violence, which connects to an explicit expectation of military service exclusive to men. Men are required to register for the draft, a gender-specific obligation dictated by an assumption grounded in the defini-tion of masculinity even amid radical changes in the position of women in the military. Men's bodies are expendable in a way that women's bodies are not. Women's bodies may be expendable in other, particularly sexual, ways, but men's bodies are expendable most explicitly in war.

The construction of masculinity also limits and undermines fathers. Fatherhood is an area that exposes the price of patriarchy by its construction of parenting as being an economic provider rather than a caregiver. The chal-lenges of a work/family structure for fathers are therefore interrelated with those of mothers, but they are significantly different. While women are iden-tified as mothers whether they have children or not, and are expected to care for their children whether they choose to or not, men are not expected to care for children but rather are expected to support their families economi-cally. Men's difficulty in being engaged caregivers is linked to socialization as well as workplace structure, reinforced by a legal structure that assumes male breadwinning. In addition, the norms of success at the workplace and the behaviors that are rewarded with success may be contradictory to the nurture needed by children. Linked to this is the expectation, despite enshrined norms of gender neutrality and equality, that men will not care for their children. Redefining fatherhood in order to claim a different role for fathers frequently is couched in claims that link to men's privilege rather than arguments grounded in recognition of the limitations imposed by the construction of masculinity and the institutionalization of those norms. The fathers' rights movement, for example, is dominated by claims of uniqueness and essentialism, and resistance to feminist analysis. Far from being grounded in cooperative, mutual, complementary models of parenting, the movement is a shrill voice attempting to reclaim patriarchal privilege. The movement constructs its claims grounded on the argument that a man in the house is necessary for children's successful development.

Masculinities study also challenges the portrait of men as essentialist. Instead of seeing men as a single entity, and only described in terms of dominance and power, the study of masculinities reveals ways in which the dominant gender system subordinates and differentiates among men. Race frequently trumps gender privilege, most notably in the lives of black boys and men. This is evident in their rates of educational attainment and employment status, as well as in the disproportionate presence of black males in the juvenile justice and adult criminal justice systems. The rate of involvement with the criminal justice system and incarceration rises to the level of emergency for black communities and seriously undermines any claim of justice and equality of our criminal justice system. It also leads ineluctably back to the educational realm and the link to employment opportunities. The continued racialization of education in concert with the differential treatment of boys and girls sets up the subordination carried out in the criminal justice system. At the same time, antiessentialism also means exposing affirmative differences among men that challenge dominant definitions of masculinity. The lives of men of color suggest models of masculinity without privilege, particularly with respect to their role in families. Masculinities analysis exposes how those alternative models are constructed as well as quashed by the dominance of a preferred, singular gender model that ultimately limits men's freedom as well as resisting women's equality.

The interplay of masculinity and race provides a different perspective to consider how these factors combine to deny privilege, as well as to expose how those *with* privilege acquire and sustain it. The study of masculinity, therefore, brings a rich additional perspective to how gender functions and the centrality of race in constructing gender. By approaching the study of masculinities from an explicitly antiessentialist perspective, that is, borrowing the feminist insight that not all women are similarly situated and that systems of hierarchy intersect and interrelate in complex ways, we enrich the understanding of the complex interplay particularly of race, class, and gender.

Finally, the study of masculinities exposes the range of masculine models, not only with respect to race and class but also with respect to sexual orientation. Queer theory presents one of the most sustained critiques of the privileged masculinity norm that defines manhood as heterosexual. This analysis has enriched gender theory by challenging the implied heterosexual norm of feminist analysis. In the context of masculinities, it exposes again how all men are limited. The limitation of marriage to opposite-sex couples is an obvious example of this. A more subtle but equally powerful example is the requirement that all men behave like straight men at the workplace or suffer harassment, irrespective of their sexual orientation. The corollary for women is that they must not act like a man or invade traditionally male occupations, or they will suffer harassment for this challenge to traditional gender roles.

The study of masculinity not only reveals a more complex portrait of men but also enhances the understanding of the construction of gender for women. Women's subordination *and men's subordination* are intertwined in the system of male privilege. At the same time, masculinity study offers another insight into the construction of power and privilege, with the aim of undermining it. It exposes in particular the odd reality that most men feel powerless rather than powerful, yet that powerlessness does not lead to alignment with other subordinated groups but rather to a defense of potential or actual privilege, even if it is privilege that particular men do not enjoy.

The aim of this book is to explore how masculinities studies can enrich and further inform feminist theory. In part 1, I look at this issue from a theoretical perspective and ultimately suggest how masculinities scholarship can enrich feminist theory. Chapter 2 explores the traditional place of men in feminist theory as the essentialist holders of privilege. It links the development of masculinities theory and research to two trends. First, it was a logical outgrowth of feminist inquiry into women and gender. Bringing it into feminist theory fits into the antiessentialist movement in feminist theory generated by Critical Race Theory, Critical Race Feminism, Global/Postcolonial critiques of feminist theory, and Queer Theory. Antiessentialism is now a core component of feminist theory, although it is not always easily implemented in fact. Second, masculinities analysis links to interdisciplinary research explicitly concerned with boys and men as gendered subjects, as opposed to analysis of the lives of boys and men as if gender were irrelevant and privilege unintended or incidental. The chapter explores the history and development of masculinity studies as an outgrowth of feminist and queer theory, particularly in sociology and psychology, beginning in the 1970s. Finally, the chapter highlights the challenge of studying men and masculinity with the goal of achieving greater freedom and equality, not a revitalized, reoriented patriarchy.

Chapter 3 provides an overview of masculinities scholarship, particularly scholarship that has focused on theory. Most of the theoretical work has been done outside the legal academy, so this section is multidisciplinary, with particular contributions from sociology and psychology. As Michael Kimmel has so eloquently pointed out, "gender is everywhere, and yet masculinity is oddly invisible" (1997a, 183). The theoretical perspectives and questions explored in this chapter include masculinity as social construction, whether men can be feminists, resisting male privilege, the concept of hegemonic masculinity, the impact of masculinity on boys and young men, and strategic suggestions for reorienting masculinity in a pro-woman direction. The chapter also explores the role of culture, and especially media, in producing and reproducing gender, and the complex threads of rebellion and ongoing reproduction of power.

With this theoretical overview as a base, in chapter 4 I weave together the themes, theories, and strategies that masculinities scholarship suggests for feminist theory. I focus on (1) why the man question needs to be asked, and thus the importance of understanding the construction of masculinity, or masculinities, in order to identify both privilege and subordination; (2) how masculinities function intersectionally, particularly with race, and thus why race is an essential feminist issue, but also class and sexual orientation; (3) what this suggests for feminist analysis, that is, what looking at men can tell us about how we analyze and strategize with respect to women; and (4) what this suggests for all lines of inequality and our understanding of the process of subordination and strategies to achieve equality and freedom. Included in this chapter is a discussion of the challenges of incorporating masculinities analysis without undermining women and of bringing to the center the most disadvantaged and subordinated men as a way of uncovering the privilege of some women as well as the hierarchy among men.

One thing that is clear from masculinities scholarship is how different much of this scholarship is from feminism, because the emancipatory project is not as clear. The position from which men begin as a group as compared to women as a group does not rest on equivalency. In both reality and theory, there is strong asymmetry. There is no masculinism equivalent to feminism because it immediately seems to slide toward dominance instead of equality or liberation. Masculinities studies do not offer a parallel or balance but rather offers something else.

First, it offers insight into the construction of masculinity, which can have an impact on degendering structures and cultures. Feminists have long claimed that structures and cultures are "male," which disadvantages women as well as men who do not meet masculinity norms. Masculinities studies offer less, however, in terms of destabilizing privilege or achieving equality. The most promising alternatives may well be found by examining the masculinities of alternative, nondominant men.

Second, it exposes the ways in which men are oppressed by the same gender system that oppresses women. Men are oppressed in a different way, as a price for privilege and in order to achieve manhood. Within this perspective one can begin to try to understand why so many of the powerful (men as a group) feel so powerless, which seems to flow most strongly from what it takes to accomplish masculinity and the relationships of men to one another, more than men's relationships to women.

Finally, it seems clear that as much as feminism can benefit from masculinities research, it also can challenge the scholarship. The agenda and goals need to be pushed toward achieving equality and liberty, rather than narcissistic self-examination. Acknowledging hegemonic power needs to be coupled with a renewed determination to challenge it, to identify successful strategies and structural change. All of this requires a stronger sense of the model or models of a different manhood or manhoods.

In parts 2 and 3, I move from theory to application, using specific contexts to suggest how masculinities analysis can inform and enrich feminist analysis. I focus on boys and men, because they have largely been left out of feminist analysis. At the same time, I suggest how the infusion of masculinities analysis can contribute to feminist analysis in a host of ways, not solely as a gender-specific means of analysis. In part 2, I focus on boys in the areas of education and juvenile justice; in part 3, I focus on men in the contexts of fatherhood and as adult survivors of child sexual abuse.

Part 2 begins with chapter 5, on boys and education, an area where there has been much recent writing on the issues confronting boys. There has been a significant amount of research on the emotional and psychological development of boys, as well as on their learning styles, which has implications for education. There are documented difficulties, academic and behavioral, of boys in school. Those difficulties are different from those experienced by girls. In addition, the challenges of success may be even more complex for young men of color, who may have to negotiate peer norms that require them to "cover" their desire to excel academically with more acceptable masculinity. Masculine norms in the educational process have been explored to challenge the cultural barriers to women hidden by formal policies of inclusion, but they have not as often been explored for the way they discipline and limit men and construct a model of hierarchy and subordination toward women. Education is an area that is rich with analysis of both girls and boys, exposing gender as a barrier for both, but it is also rife with the temptation to think of solutions as requiring prioritizing only girls or boys, rather than including both.

Chapter 6 looks at boys and juvenile justice. A trip to the courthouse in virtually any jurisdiction would suggest that this is a system of boy justice, because of the disproportionately male pattern of children in the system. This pattern links to the similar pattern in the adult criminal justice system. Race also powerfully constructs those in the juvenile justice system and whether children quickly reform from youthful indiscretions or persist and head for the "deep end" of the juvenile justice system. Disproportionately the harshest legal treatment of juveniles is reserved for boys, especially minority boys.

In part 3, I apply masculinities analysis to two contexts involving men. In chapter 7, I consider men and fatherhood. Fatherhood is one of the critical life roles for men, but one that is significantly at odds with core concepts of masculinity. As fatherhood has evolved from an authoritarian patriarch to an expectation of shared parenting and nurture, men have struggled with the concept of fatherhood and have complained of significant bias in the legal system. This chapter explores concepts of fatherhood and the constraints of masculinity. Masculinity essentializes fatherhood rather than supporting men's nurture and care. Men's powerful emotional and physical responses to fatherhood can be turned into new claims of hierarchy rather than explored for their relational connection to children. At the same time, stereotypes of men's inadequacy as parents persist, even at the highest levels of our courts.

The definition of fatherhood persists as an economic role rather than a nurturing role, which particularly harms the most fragile families. I include information derived from the Fragile Families project, which has collected data and evaluated public policy options for fragile families, defined as nonmarital families with limited resources. One in three children is born into a nonmarital family, so nonmarital fathers are particularly important to masculinity analysis of fatherhood. The Fragile Families findings belie our ste-reotypes of nonmarital fathers, as overwhelmingly fathers are present and desire to be involved in the lives of their children but have great difficulty doing so.

In chapter 8, together with Ted Shaw, a forensic psychologist who is an expert on sex offenses, I explore adult male victims of child sexual abuse. Men are rarely considered as victims of sexual abuse or assault, but an explo-ration of data on child sexual abuse makes clear that they are frequently victims. Just as the scars of childhood trauma affect adult women, so too they affect adult men. Masculinities analysis suggests that trauma is experi-enced in ways that are both similar to and different from the consequences for women. Feminists have been instrumental in elevating the issue of child sexual abuse to public consciousness; this chapter suggests that model could work even more effectively if men are included in our concepts of victims. Working proactively, it suggests an even broader issue of developing a healthy model of sexuality for men and for women, as well as supporting all victims.

This chapter also suggests that there are other areas of victimization that we ignore or render invisible because we have constructed men as offenders rather than victims. Other forms of child abuse, especially physical abuse, often disproportionately affect boys. Men are disproportionately the victims of prison rape, which occurs largely unchecked in juvenile and adult jails and prisons. Domestic violence affects boys directly and indirectly, and adult males can be victims of domestic violence from their partners.

Finally, in chapter 9, I draw some conclusions from these examples of specific applications of masculinities analysis. The example of education sug-gests the pattern of a swing from a male-centered system to reform based on feminist critique on behalf of girls and women, followed by an exami-nation of boys as gendered subjects that can be read as backlash or as cri-tique of the initial, underlying system. Education suggests the "both/and" approach to gender analysis, an approach that does not require equivalence but rather keeping both groups in view. Masculinities analysis also suggests or reinforces the importance of keeping hierarchy within gender in view, lest equality mean only the equality of the privileged of each sex. It suggests very powerfully how much race must be a feminist priority.

The juvenile justice chapter indicates the importance of careful analysis of systems where there is gender asymmetry. When one sex is disproportion-ately represented, there is the danger of seeing this as some naturally occur-ring pattern, rather than questioning the socially constructed norm. Asking why there is disproportion is critical, as well as how that informs the structure and goals of the system. The justice system inevitably has some concept of the "good boy" or the "good man." The racialized pattern in the system suggests "good" means "white." The combination of willingness to punish boys and blackness is toxic. Again, the racial pattern reinforces why race must be a feminist priority.

The chapters on men have interesting parallels and suggestions as well. Fatherhood is not simply asymmetrical; it is totally male by definition. Being a father is a critical piece of being a man. But being a father, acting as a parent, is incredibly different from the patterns for being a mother. In that respect the juvenile justice and fatherhood chapters are linked, reinforcing the importance of looking at structural and cultural answers where the sexes are unequal or one sex is virtually or totally excluded. Fatherhood also poses a direct confrontation between core values of masculinity and emerging redefinition of fatherhood. Not only is care not a masculine norm, but the structure of breadwinning makes it difficult for even the most devoted father to give care.

Finally, the exploration of men as victims of child sexual abuse exposes men's vulnerability and hidden victimization. Just as girls are targeted as girls, so too are boys targeted as boys. The presence of that unacknowledged harm means a silencing that harms individuals and their relationships, and thus their communities. Reimagining a sexuality of equality must include recognition of these realities.

In all these areas, and many others, masculinities scholarship has much to offer. Theory can be enriched by asking the man question; applications of gender analysis can be informed by a more complex understanding of how gender inequality works, as well as strategies for change. Feminist theory has much to offer to masculinities theory as well. In each of these specific applications it is critical that an examination of boys and men not be done at the expense of girls and women. It also must acknowledge the generally privileged position of boys and men, as that intertwines with their disadvantage in unique ways. Masculinities analysis must consistently be linked to this reality of privilege. The goal of equality must always include this broader view of gender justice. Asking the man question must include returning to the woman question.

Part I —

Theory

2

Men, Masculinities,
and Feminist Theory

Why have men, as a focus of discussions regarding gender bias, gender equality, and gender-specific concerns, been absent from feminist theory? There are two obvious answers to this question. First, women have been the focus of feminist theory, *and rightly so*: their inequality, oppression, and unjust status as a group generated the inquiry and also exposed their absence and invisibility in virtually all academic disciplines. Thus feminist analysis explored not only women's inequality but also how the construction of knowledge has been influenced to a significant extent, theoretically and empirically, by the perspective, concerns, and presumed centrality and universality of men as representative of what is "human."

Second, men *have* been included in feminist analysis. Indeed they have been central to feminist analysis. Feminists have sought to explain and understand women's subordination and the persistence of patriarchy despite frontal legal, social, and cultural challenges, and to devise strategies to define and accomplish gender equality and justice. Feminists have focused on men's power and dominance, how it is conferred and reinforced, how it operates through a complex set of institutions, social norms, cultural constructs, and formal legal rules.

But men have been largely absent from feminist theory as an object of gender analysis, and thus they have tended to be viewed in an essentialist, universal, undifferentiated way. Men have been viewed as a class or group, as a basis for comparison (demonstrating women's unequal position, such as their economic position); as the source of subordination by virtue of gender privilege or abusive power (directly harming women, such as in violence in the form of sexual harassment, domestic violence, or sexual assault); as beneficiaries of gender privilege by virtue of norms that presume men as the subject (advantaging men in areas such as health care study and treatment based on exclusively male subjects for research, by the promotion of male standards and culture at work, and defending male "turf" in male domination of particular jobs or the highest ranking jobs). While this placement of men in feminist analysis is not unjustified, it reflects an acceptance of men, in most instances, as undifferentiated and as largely privileged by the gender system.

What feminist analysis has not generally done, however, is to study men as men. By that I mean that men have not been studied in at least three ways. First, men have not been analyzed as a group other than for how they benefit from the gender system; their disadvantages, the price paid for privilege, has not gotten significant attention. Nor have men been studied as a group to determine how they gain and sustain privilege. Second, men's relationship with women has been examined primarily standing from the position and perspective of women. What has not been considered is how men experience this relationship and what barriers prevent them from collaborating with women when it would seem to be in their best interests. Third, men's relationship with men has gone almost totally unexplored, leaving an undifferentiated picture of men as a group, an essentialist picture that fails to consider intersections of race, class, and sexual orientation and how those characteristics interact with presumed undifferentiated male privilege and power.

The potential that "asking the man question" in feminist theory suggests, particularly by exploring masculinities scholarship, is to enrich feminist theory by clarifying, reorienting, and further contextualizing how and why inequality exists. It would benefit women as a group and would add men as a group as an object of inquiry, but with due attention to their generally different position. At the same time, it would include those places where men are disadvantaged, where women may have privilege as part of their subordinated status, and it would connect the interactions of men and women in the gender system rather than presuming that their interests are oppositional in all situations. At the same time, feminist analysis challenges masculinities scholarship to remain focused on inequality, power, subordination, and oppression as critical to any meaningful study of men. To the extent masculinities scholarship has moved toward rendering women invisible, by focusing on men as men or men in relation to other men, feminism underscores the importance of keeping women's inequality in view.

In this chapter I explore the traditional view of men in feminist theory, the emergence of masculinities scholarship as a field of study, and the challenges of that field. In the chapter that follows I explore in detail the theoretical perspectives of masculinities scholarship.

Traditional View of Men in Feminist Theory

The focus of feminist legal theory has been to "ask the woman question." Women have been the object of inquiry and the necessary focus of gender inequality, because they have been the subjects of subordination and inequality as a class. On virtually every empirical measure, when compared to men, women are unequal, and feminists' goal has been to lessen or eliminate those inequalities. Law has acted both explicitly, with differential treatment grounded in gender stereotypes and presumed inferiority, and also implicitly, through its adoption of rules premised on masculine norms and its inattention to subjects that are important on the basis of women's lived experience. In addition, law uses the research and knowledge of other disciplines in a variety of ways, such as in expert testimony, in the legislative history of statutes, or as a basis for argument.

Feminists have developed a range of theories to explain inequality and to use as a basis for strategies to achieve equality. Formal equality theory, or liberal theory, argues that in most respects women and men are the same, and therefore formal legal differences in the treatment of women and men are unjustified. Ironically, in many of the most famous cases brought to establish this simple principle, men were the plaintiffs, asking to be treated the same as women in statutory schemes that gave women favorable treatment. In other cases, women asked to have the same responsibilities and rights as men—to vote, to serve on juries, to attend schools funded by the state irrespective of the curriculum. Liberal theory has been remarkably successful in striking down many of the formal barriers that have limited women's lives. But this approach meant men were the standard for equality. Equality meant having what men had, being able to do what men do.

On the other hand, some feminists argued that women's differences had to be taken into account in order to achieve equality. Pregnancy is the classic difference that feminists pointed out had been marginalized and unsupported by a host of structures, including employment and health insurance. By failing to support pregnancy, the system made it inevitable that pregnant women were forced to retreat into the private sphere, to remain dependent, and to be set apart as having a medical condition unlike any other. If difference were taken into account, on the other hand, it would require affirmative support for pregnancy. Difference feminists were willing to argue beyond physical differences to social and cultural differences. Some, such as Christine Littleton, argued for equality as acceptance and support of life courses traditionally associated with women, such as the care of children and others, as essential to real equality. In difference arguments, all men and all women were divided along a binary line. Equality would mean recognizing and valuing things associated with women. Everything "male" was assumed to be already valued.

Yet other feminists, most notably Catharine MacKinnon, argued that equality is not about sameness and difference, but rather is about power and subordination. Evaluate the situation in terms of power, according to this view, and it will tell you whether there is inequality present. Power is male, individually and systemically. MacKinnon also emphasized the role of sexuality in subordination and how inequality was embedded in concepts of passion and desire. She exposed and named the way sexuality was used to subordinate women at work by calling it sexual harassment, a concept that evolved to include the notion of gender policing and protection as well as uninvited sexual advances.

In these theoretical approaches and others feminists have sought to understand the nature of inequality as well as to imagine what equality looks like and to suggest strategies to achieve equality. Feminists have challenged existing legal categories and named new ones. They have identified structures and culture as male identified or male biased. Feminists recognize that equality efforts may be partial and contextual, not universal or eternal. The situation may reconfigure to require further steps or even reversal of a prior course of action.

Whether exploring and uncovering gender bias—express or hidden—exposing silences, grappling with inequality, or arguing for reforms, feminists have largely treated men and masculinity as a universal category. Men have been something that women have been argued to be the same as, to be different from, to have generated a culture or set of values distinctive from men's, to be socialized differently than men. Feminists have argued that women can do what men do, that they have unique differences that must be taken into account, that their life course and socialization requires differences be taken into account, that structures and organizations reflect male models and values to the disadvantage of women, and that social disapproval of women taking on male characteristics creates a catch-22 for women in that they cannot simply take on male-identified characteristics or skills in order to succeed. Overwhelmingly, men have been a singular, unified group largely represented as privileged and dominant by virtue of gender. In models of equality, men are rendered as essentially powerful so that achieving women's equality is measured against an essentialist view of men.

This is not to say that at least some feminist analysis has not noticed that at least some men are disadvantaged by the gender system, and sometimes just as strongly as women are. Angela Harris (2000) raised the issue of masculinities in her classic article a decade ago analyzing the Abner Louima case. In 1997 Louima was arrested in New York City, and while at the police station he was sodomized with a broomstick by three police officers. The incident was widely viewed as another instance of racial brutality by white officers of a black victim. Harris explored the gendered meanings of the actions in this case and its relationship to a culture and training of hypermasculinity in police work that affects police relationships with all citizens. Harris's analysis exposed the ordinariness, the normalcy of gendered conduct in a racially charged setting, but it also suggested the presence of such gendered meanings even where race is not such a visible factor. The reaction of other officers who were in the vicinity is linked to a code of conduct among men as well as a code among police officers. Harris's call was to incorporate analysis of gender violence among men into feminist analysis of violence and critical race analysis of the vexed relationship between communities of color and police.

There have been places where men have become more visible in feminist analysis. These include same-sex sexual harassment, bullying and school violence, the rights of fathers in family law, some work on prison rape and domestic violence, and emerging work applying masculinities scholarship to work and employment issues, as well as some criminal justice areas. It is remarkable, however, the extent to which gender is read as female. When men are the subject of disadvantage, gender is often not considered in the equation. Black men are almost never considered as men; they are raced but not gendered. Gay men are identified by sexuality but not by masculinity.

We can learn from masculinities scholarship in two ways: it can teach us about the construction of male privilege in order to dismantle privilege and power, and it can teach us how privilege comes with a price. If we ignore that price, we ignore how the system of male power also harms men. We may also miss the opportunity for collaboration. To the extent that systems of power must be dismantled, it tells us more about how they are constructed and operate rather than simply about what they produce.

Development of Masculinities Scholarship

Masculinities as an identifiable field of study, or men's studies, emerged as a result of feminist analysis as well as gay and lesbian studies and queer theory (Adams and Savran 2002b; Buchbinder 1994; Kimmel 2002a, 2002b). Although men have been dominant in who and what was studied in many fields (as epitomized by feminist historians' critique that traditional scholarship has been his-story and by the use of the term "malestream" to describe the domination of men's concerns in mainstream sociology), men were not studied as men, as gendered beings (Hearn and Morgan 1990b). The feminist challenge to ask the woman question in every discipline inevitably led to a small group of scholars asking the man question, and therefore to scholarship focused on men as gendered beings. But in looking at men as gendered subjects, the question or questions asked have often been different, and the theorizing is therefore quite different from feminist theory. In addition to feminist theory, gay and lesbian rights and queer theory have strongly influenced masculinities scholarship. Brod and Kaufman (1994a) suggest three reasons for this: first, because heterosexism is so critical to masculinity; second, because gay men have unique insight on masculinity; and third, because of the historical relationship between the two fields.

Beginning in the early 1970s, in the context of the emergence of feminist analysis, some scholars and activists began to argue that men also were harmed by sexism (Adams and Savran 2002a; Buchbinder 1994). Several leading academics, clearly profeminist, began to challenge the models in their disciplines. Joseph Pleck and Jack Sawyer edited *Men and Masculinity* in 1974, and a parallel movement was occurring in the United Kingdom (Buchbinder 1994). Joseph Pleck published his landmark critique of psychological and sociological models in this period (Pleck 1981; see also Pleck and Pleck 1980). In other disciplines as well, a critique emerged of existing academic models and new explorations began of men as gendered beings (Buchbinder 1994). Men's studies courses emerged in the late 1980s at several universities, and roughly two hundred courses connected to men's studies were in existence by 1989 (Buchbinder 1994). The 1990s was the decade when masculinities studies spread rapidly in many disciplines, as represented in courses, conferences, and publications (Adams and Savran 2002a). On the popular side, the men's movement emerged in the early 1990s, energized by Robert Bly's *Iron John* (1990). Bly argued that men needed to reconnect with their essential nature by regaining male-male bonds in the purified setting of the wilderness. Other men both in the men's movement and in academic work critiqued the essentialist and antifeminist nature of Bly's vision (Adams and Savran 2002a).

Sociology was the initial home of masculinities studies, and that disciplinary perspective still dominates, although much work has also come from psychology (Beynon 2002; Buchbinder 1994; Haddad 1993a). As the dominant discipline, the sociological perspective looks particularly at the way gendered individuals interact with gendered institutions, and it therefore focuses on identities and structures from the perspective of difference and domination (Kimmel, Hearn, and Connell 2005a). Theoretically, the perspectives of masculinities scholars include "positivism, cultural relativism, psychoanalysis, interpretivism, critical theory, neomarxism, feminisms (of various forms and kinds), poststructuralism, postmodernism, and postcolonialism" (ibid., 4). The empirical research of the 1980s and 1990s explored masculinity in specific settings, especially education and the workplace, as well as historical research on ideas about masculinity. In addition, there has been applied research in the areas of education, health, violence, fathering, and counseling where masculinity work has changed policies or practices (Connell 2005b).

At the same time, work on lesbian/gay/queer studies was emerging in the 1970s and influenced the emerging study of men and masculinity. Michael Foucault's *The History of Sexuality* was published in 1976 and began a critique of psychoanalysis and other scholarship that followed a rigid view of sexuality (Foucault 1980 [1976]).

One scholar characterizes the earliest work in the '70s as fairly uncritical and self-serving, focusing on the limits of men's gender role. "Concepts such as 'frustration,' 'crisis,' 'fears,' and 'vulnerabilities' were consistently used and manipulated to portray men as victims of the social construction of masculinity" (Haddad 1993a, xi). By the 1990s, however, the research turned to explore issues of men's power and control of others, including women, children, and other men (ibid.). In addition, history and ethnography demonstrate that masculinity is not fixed and is diverse (Kimmel, Hearn, and Connell 2005a).

The claim of "crisis" is a persistent one in masculinities study, sometimes in the form of backlash, sometimes accurately noting the change in some of the ideological or material bases of traditional masculinity (shifts away from justifying patriarchy or male workplace dominance) or the adoption of changed consciousness (equality in parenting or relationships) that nevertheless challenges old ways of thinking (Beynon 2002; van Hoven and Horschelmann 2005a). Indeed, Beynon argues that crisis may be even "constitutive of masculinity itself" (2002, 76). It accurately reflects some of the empirical data about men and boys. By many measures, including health, crime, stress, and emotional well-being, boys and men are not doing well (ibid., 76–79).

The term or concept "masculinity" or "masculinities" in its current form was first used in the mid-1980s, although it had been used in psychology prior to that (Brod 1994). In 1985 a classic article by Carrigan, Connell, and Lee was called "Toward a New Sociology of Masculinity"; two years later a collection edited by Brod was called *The Making of Masculinities*, and by 1989

Hearn referred to "masculinities" as a term describing issues and research about men. As Brod points out (1994), it was a natural progression from feminist analysis to begin to look at male relationships and gender constructions, and that led to examining male-male relationships. Initially there was a clear recognition of the necessity not to undermine the work of feminists, which had focused so much on issues of power. At the same time, this work exposed the power dynamics between and among men. While masculinities as originally conceptualized was connected to the issues of power between men and women as well as between men and men, over time the concept for some scholars lost the focus on power. "As it became popularized in the hands of others, masculinities sometimes seemed to lose the dimension of power and simply signify plurality or diversity" (ibid., 86). Brod also identifies a second tendency in the development of masculinities studies: the danger of separatism. Separatism, Brod argues, "focuses only on male-male relations and leaves women out of the picture" (88). He cites as particularly of concern the mythopoetic men's movement of the early 1990s that exemplified separatism and distancing from, even ignoring of, women's issues.

Although sociology has been the dominant discipline, the earliest work on masculinities was in psychology. Psychology developed the concept of masculinity embodied in the idea of a *male sex role*. This shifted from a biologically based or determined role to the concept of a social role under the influence of sex difference research, which found few psychological differences between men and women. Feminists challenged the view of the female sex role and criticized it as oppressive and subordinating. In the early 1980s Joseph Pleck published his critique of the male sex role, demonstrating the lack of empirical data supporting the concept of masculinity and concluding that the role was a form of gender politics (Connell 2005b; Pleck 1981).

Nevertheless, the notion of a biological, embedded masculinity remains powerful. Kimmel (1994) summarizes classic notions of masculinity as well as the problems with this concept. As Kimmel explains, this leads us to think of manhood and masculinity as something timeless and universal, deep in the heart of men. It is an essence, a quality; you either have "it" or you do not. Most significantly, it is something created in opposition: to "racial minorities, sexual minorities, and above all, women" (124). He states the four key phrases of Robert Brannon (1976) that define manhood: No Sissy Stuff, Be a Big Wheel, Be a Sturdy Oak, Give 'Em Hell (Kimmel 1994, 125–26). Not being feminine is a rejection that Kimmel claims is "angry and frightened" (127). The consequence, especially of rejecting the mother, is to push away the actual mother, to reject those characteristics associated with mothers/

women, and finally to devalue all women. Being a man is a lifelong task: "When does it end? Never. To admit weakness, to admit frailty or fragility, is to be seen as a wimp, a sissy, not a real man" (128). A key part of manhood, then, is constantly to be measured by other men. The core emotion is fear, and the desire not to be humiliated in front of other men, with homophobia as the key organizing principle. "In one survey, women and men were asked what they were most afraid of. Women responded that they were most afraid of being raped and murdered. Men responded that they were most afraid of being laughed at" (133).

Masculinities scholarship has challenged essentialist, biological notions of masculinity most strongly by demonstrating that masculinity changes and shifts historically and personally, as it is socially constructed and created. In the process of exploring masculinities, the scholarship has evolved to the point of developing the healthy dialogue and differences between theorists and empiricists, between disciplines, and over its defining characteristics, which creates a rich scholarship (Kimmel, Hearn, and Connell 2005a). Like feminist scholarship, it has developed in waves from initial explorations and discovery to more sophisticated analyses and intellectual debates (Whitehead 2002; Whitehead and Barrett 2001).

Challenges

In the following chapter I explore in detail masculinities theory, but first it is important to highlight some of the challenges of masculinities theory and its differences from feminist analysis. First is the tendency to make gender analysis a zero-sum game: either you examine women or men, girls or boys, so exploring one, talking about one, is immediately assumed to dismiss the other or renders the other invisible. One sees this tendency in the argument that focusing on women and girls has been to men's disadvantage, and thus, to be fair, men and boys deserve exclusive focus for a while. This binary, either/or thinking assumes only one gender can be the focus and that their needs and positions can (or must) be viewed in isolation. It makes it easy to be dismissive of the claims of either feminist or masculinities scholarship. A good example of this is the debate around education, which has taken first girls and then boys as its focus and treats them as either/or rather than both/and. I explore this problem further in chapter 4.

A second challenge is making the position of men as a class equivalent to that of women as a class (or boys and girls). The inclusion of men in gender analysis does not make their position equal or equivalent as a group as oppressed as women. Men and boys need to be taken seriously, but their position is quite different. The asymmetry rests in their differential position as a group. "Masculinity studies analyze a dominant and oppressive class that has, arguably, always been the primary focus of scholarly attention" (Adams and Savran 2002a, 7).

Finally, a third challenge is that resistance to feminist analysis makes masculinities scholarship an easy place to feed antifeminist or antifemale backlash in the guise of sympathy for men and boys. A good example of this is the fathers' rights movement, as an outgrowth of research on fathers and fatherhood. Fathers were simply not studied for a long time, and they remain understudied in comparison with mothers, reflecting the assumption that mothers care for children while fathers do not. Research about fathers has demonstrated their ability to care and their important role for children. As I explore in detail in chapter 7, the construction of masculinity is a major factor that hurts and undermines fathers' care of children. It simply makes nurture inconsistent with masculinity and identifies it as female. In a context where masculinity continues to define itself most importantly as "not being a girl," anything woman-identified must be avoided at all costs. In order to embrace care as a norm, some researchers and advocates have embraced fathers' essential difference and uniqueness as a way to "masculinize" father care, but frequently it is coupled with an antimother, antifemale critique. Masculinities scholarship has contributed to our knowledge about fathers and fatherhood, but it may directly or indirectly contribute to this kind of backlash.

In addition to these challenges, scholars within the field have suggested two other areas of needed development for masculinities scholarship. One is essentialism, particularly expressed as the need to "globalize" masculinity study while at the same time noting that globalization has tended to support the export of a Western-oriented hegemonic masculinity as a world masculinity. Connell criticizes the export of a dominant Euro-American style of masculinity (2002b; see also Connell 2005a). At the same time, Connell argues that there has been a countertrend, strongest in Islam, of the men of the metropolitan countries versus the men of the Third World (2002b). In a variety of contexts Connell has pushed more than any other scholar for the importance of studying masculinity other than in American and European contexts, as well as to understand how a global hegemony is being built as a result of globalization. There is also a link with the history of imperialism, which was a gendered, masculine-led enterprise. "The cult of masculinity rationalized imperial rule by equating an aggressive, muscular, chivalric model of manliness with racial, national, cultural and moral superiority" (Krishnaswamy 2002, 292). It is also interesting to note that in addition to the construction of a specific British masculinity deemed superior, the masculinity of colonized men, in this example Indian men, was characterized as effeminate (ibid.).

The second challenge, noted by Kimmel, is reconnecting the field to other analyses of dominance. The "core intellectual project . . . of the next decade [is] constructing bridges between the different axes of power and to illuminate how those systems both reinforce each other and also may contradict each other. For it is in the seams of power that those structural weaknesses are exposed, where resistance is born and coalitions are built" (2002b, xi).

With these caveats in mind, in the next chapter I describe the theoretical approaches and insights of masculinities scholars. This more detailed look at masculinities scholarship suggests a range of ways that feminist analysis might be enriched.

3

Masculinities Theory and Practice

Understanding masculinities, manhood, and men is critical for feminist theory. First, men are not universal or undifferentiated, and seeing men and boys in a more complex, real way helps to identify inequalities more clearly. Second, the intersections of masculinity with other critical identity factors or traits, especially race, class, and sexual orientation, tell us more about the interaction of privilege and disadvantage, an interaction that operates for some women as well and that operates differently for men than for women. We can learn from those intersections more about resistance and change, as well as the pull of privilege. Third, men pay a price for privilege, and those gender burdens should be exposed and addressed. This may create alliances between women and men, rather than identifying men solely as beneficiaries of gender privilege or men and women as adversaries struggling in a zero-sum game. At the same time, the power and privilege attached to masculinity must insistently be kept in view even as male disadvantage is acknowledged and added to the agenda. Finally, dismantling male privilege and restructuring masculinity requires understanding how masculinities are constructed as well as identifying and envisioning new masculinities. Masculinities scholarship may help to prove long-held feminist claims of the incorporation of male standards and concepts in structures and institutions. Research about the production and reproduction of masculinities in areas such as workplace discrimination could be especially helpful in countering cultural and structural discrimination.

Overview of Masculinities Theory

An overview of masculinities theory may be useful to keep the broad parameters in view before exploring in greater detail this body of scholarship. A starting point is noticing its name. It is not "masculinism" or "masculinist theory," which would parallel feminism and feminist theory. This asymmetry of naming reflects the asymmetry of the focus and content of masculinities theory as compared to feminist theory. "Masculinism" or "masculinist" are awkward terms that suggest the glorification of male power and privilege. "Masculinities" reflects the focus of many scholars in the field on understanding, first and foremost, how male identity is constructed and sustained. While there is a commitment to the goal of fighting inequality, the focus of much of the scholarship has not been on how to undermine or reduce patriarchal power. Feminism and feminist theory, by contrast, remain focused on issues of inequality far more than on issues of identity.

Theoretical work has developed several core concepts that pervade masculinities scholarship. Masculinities are viewed as socially constructed, rather than biologically given, and therefore as changeable and fluid. There is not a singular masculinity but rather multiple masculinities. Among these masculinities, many scholars agree that there is a dominant hegemonic masculinity, although other scholars are critical of this concept. Masculinities are as much about men's relationship to other men as they are about men's relationship to women. A primary orientation of masculinity is negative definition: it is critical not to be a woman and not to be gay. Finally, although masculinity is associated with power, many men feel powerless.

According to masculinities theory, masculinity, in any form, is not a biological given, not a thing that one has; rather, it is socially constructed, a set of practices that one constantly engages in or performs. In that sense, it is interactive: the individual relates to the social/cultural construction, but the individual also remakes and changes it, potentially, rather than simply following the script. It is fluid, not fixed, neither universal nor timeless, but rather changeable and malleable. Seeing masculinity as a social construct rejects and critiques the notion of a set or stable sex role that one acquires, or the notion of masculinity as an inevitable phase of development from child to adult, from boy to man. Indeed, this perspective even rejects the notion that only males perform masculinities: because it is a social construction, while it is dominantly used or performed by men, it does not require a biologically male body. Women can be masculine also. There are female masculinities, and those can expose masculinity in some unique ways.

The approach is closest to cultural feminism, yet the underlying dynamic is different. The focus of masculinities scholarship is on identity and practices, in the sense of exposing what masculinities are and how they function and are felt. The purpose of cultural feminism is to identify things associated with women and argue that they should be equally valued, that inequality is linked to the lack of value or support attached to the qualities associated with women and the practices of their lives. Inherent in this claim is that female-associated qualities and practices are valuable. The critique of cultural feminism is that it might unintentionally reinforce the limitation of women to those identities, qualities, practices, and life courses associated with women, that it reinforces limits. Within masculinities study, because men as a group are not subordinated and things associated with men are not devalued, the examination of what constitutes masculinities— the acquisition, sustenance, and practices of masculinities—lacks a clear goal, even when there is an express concern about equality and social justice. Much of what is associated with men is deemed of value, so it is not a matter of claiming value. Those things that are not valued, or that we might want to detach from masculinity because it is a negative (violence, for example), raise a unique issue and might point in the direction of analyzing how those qualities are acquired and how they might be discouraged (or other more positive values encouraged), but this has not been the focus of much of the analysis. What also might be helpful from this approach is identifying what is male/masculine in structures and institutions, so that dominance/hierarchy or sexual advantage can be identified (and presumably eliminated).

A key piece of masculinity theory is that masculinity is not unitary; hence the name of the field is masculinities, plural. There are multiple masculinities, although some scholars would also point out that there are some critical links between them, suggesting some universality. Multiple masculinities do not, however, mean that all masculinities are equal. Rather, many scholars argue that there tends to be a preferred, dominant masculinity. Hegemonic masculinity identifies the most empowered, those at the top of the male hierarchy. In relation to hegemonic masculinity, there are subordinate masculinities and also subversive masculinities. Not surprisingly, the subordinate masculinities are defined especially by race and class. Also important to remember is that within race and class identities there are multiple masculinities (not a singular "black male masculinity" or "gay male masculinity" but rather a range of masculinities subsumed under race and sexual orientation identities). Subordinate or subversive masculinities hold the promise of resistance and new models but also the concern that denial of power will translate into the oppression of others who are situated lower in the hierarchy, rather than collaboration or solidarity with others who are subordinated. Antiessentialism is recognized as critical to the development of masculinities theory, yet masculinities scholarship reflects difficulties carrying out that insight, which mirrors difficulties in implementing antiessentialism in feminist theory as well.

There are two common pieces to defining masculinities: masculinity means being not feminine and not homosexual. It is this negative defining that is so critical, it seems, to issues of power and hierarchy. Race and class add to the key definitional pieces of who are the top men.

Masculinity is as much about men's relation to other men as it is about men's relation to women. Indeed, it seems that competition and hierarchy with other men may be a more intense component of masculinity. In addition, one's standing and place is never secure; masculinity is often described as something never attained but rather something that must be consistently achieved on a daily basis. The importance of men's relationship to other men is brought home particularly by thinking about the different spaces and places that men and women occupy in their daily lives and what spaces are male only, or dominantly male, as compared to homosocial female environments. Within homosocial environments, men are constantly evaluated and tested.

This sense of constant testing may be linked to men's experience of power. Ironically, men, although powerful and empowered as a group, feel powerless. Some men are indeed powerless; others are powerless because the demands of masculinity are that it must be constantly proven; it can never simply be achieved and claimed. It is easy to be a woman; it is a constant struggle to be a man. The boundaries placed on men are significant, and the expectations to meet dominant norms disserve men in relationships with both women and men. It may be that the significance of men's relationships to men explains why women disappear frequently in masculinities analysis. In the same way that men are unidimensional and essentialized in feminist theory, so too is the same tendency present regarding women in masculinities theory.

Leading Theorists: Sociologists

The roots of modern masculinities scholarship lie in psychology, but it is sociologists that have led modern developments. In the following sections I separately explore the work of leading sociologists and psychologists who have developed theories of masculinities, but scholars in the field regularly cross disciplinary lines and include other disciplines as well.

R.W. Connell, one of the leading theorists in the field, in a rich body of work develops a broad perspective on gender as well as specific insights on masculinity. On gender, Connell emphasizes our attachment to the concept of gender difference, despite the similarities between women and men: "Women and men are psychologically very similar, as groups. We should long ago have been calling this field 'sex similarity' research" (2002a, 42). Connell identifies four structures of gender relations: power relations, production relations, emotional relations, and symbolic relations. Men's dominance is reinforced by the state, yielding what Connell calls the *patriarchal dividend*, the benefit all men claim from their dominance in the gender order, or "the advantage to men as a group from maintaining an unequal gender order" (142). The pervasiveness of dominance means that it is taken-for-granted oppression, leading to assumptions that patterns are natural or given.

Connell argues that we need to focus on "processes and relationships through which men and women conduct gendered lives. Masculinity . . . is simultaneously a place in gender relations, the practices through which men and women engage that place in gender, and the effects of these practices in bodily experience, personality and culture" (2005b, 71). Connell, then, focuses on how masculinity is created and practiced and in particular how it embodies inequality and dominance.

Connell's core concept, and one that has been embraced by many other masculinity scholars, is the concept of *hegemonic masculinity*: "the configuration of gender practice which embodies the currently accepted answer to the problem of the legitimacy of patriarchy, which guarantees (or is taken to guarantee) the dominant position of men and the subordination of women" (2005b, 77). Dominance is achieved by authority, not by violence. Hegemony means cultural dominance and support, and rarely dominance that is violently claimed. There is complicity by those who do not meet the hegemonic standard: as Connell notes, few men meet the definition of hegemonic masculinity, but most men benefit, reaping the patriarchal dividend even if they do not fulfill the definition (ibid.). There are other masculinities, subordinate and resistant. Not all men benefit similarly from hegemonic masculinity, and particularly the benefit varies by race, class, and age. Hierarchy and multiplicity are key parts of this core concept, as is the notion that the dominated support their own subordination.

Modern masculinities, according to Connell, are defined by their response to various challenges and crises: the collapse of patriarchy and widespread support for the emancipation and equality of women; women's participation in paid labor; and the challenge to sexuality with greater acceptance of gay masculinity (2005b). What is critical, however, according to Connell, is that masculinity has been responsive to change, redefining patriarchy. Patriarchy has not collapsed; only the idea of patriarchy or its acceptance has: "What has crumbled, in the industrial countries, is the *legitimation* of patriarchy" (226). In order to move this dismantling of patriarchy further, Connell's agenda includes "contesting men's predominance in the state, professions and management, and ending men's violence against women, . . . changing the institutional structures that make elite power and body-to-body violence possible in the first place, . . . ending the patriarchal dividend in the money economy, sharing the burden of domestic work and equalizing access to education and training, . . . ending the stigma of sexual difference and the imposition of compulsory heterosexuality, and reconstructing heterosexuality on the basis of reciprocity not hierarchy" (229–30).

According to Connell, you cannot achieve equality without dismantling hegemonic masculinity (Connell 2005b). This would include "reembodiment" for men, "a search for different ways of using, feeling and showing male bodies" (233). The model must be gender specific and distinctive because of men's position: "the model of a liberation movement simply cannot apply to the group that holds the position of power" (235; see also Connell 2000b).

A second leading theorist of masculinities, Michael Kimmel (2004), focuses on issues of inequality, power, and difference. Kimmel points out that structures create differences between men and women, using, for example, Rosabeth Kanter's research on corporate organization and culture. Kimmel argues against the use of the concept of gender difference, stating that difference is a product of gender inequality and is used to legitimate inequality. As an example, he points to how we conceptualize and describe sex differentiation. In fetal development, all embryos begin as "female" and then differentiate; similarly, in puberty, sex hormones change bodies, causing the development of secondary sex characteristics. How we think about those two events says a great deal about our thinking about difference and hierarchy (see also Fausto-Sterling 1995). Kimmel (2004) argues that the focus should be on reducing gender inequality; only then can difference be celebrated rather than used to justify injustice.

Kimmel emphasizes the invisibility of gender to men, as well as the invisibility of men as objects of gender study: "we continue to act as if gender applied only to women. Surely the time has come to make gender visible to men. As the Chinese proverb has it, the fish are the last to discover the ocean" (2004, 6). As one consequence of this invisibility, we ignore what Kimmel exposes as men's lack of a sense of power, despite their clear gender advantage. While social constructionist approaches identify gender as power relations, the assumption that all men recognize, feel and use that power is false. Rather, "although men may be in power everywhere one cares to look, individual men are not 'in power,' and they do not feel powerful. . . . Men as a group are in power (when compared with women), but do not feel powerful"

(100). Power is an attribute of group life, not of individual life; "it can neither be willed away nor ignored" (100; see also Kaufman 1994). Kimmel notes that a definition of masculinity as striving for power comes from women's perspective; from men's perspective, they commonly see themselves as powerless. Out of this sense of powerlessness comes the desire for control. Masculinity thus is about fear and shame and emotional isolation (see also Coltrane 1994). This is consistent with David Leverenz's insight that manhood is about defense against humiliation; underlying everything is *fear* (1986). The sense that masculinity is a constant struggle, never achieved but always needing to be proved, is a powerful piece of this sense of powerlessness (Faludi 1999).

Kimmel also focuses on the construction of gender by the interaction of people and institutions. We "do" gender not in a vacuum but in the context of institutions constructed with gender in mind: "Our social world is built on systemic, structural inequality based on gender; social life reproduces both gender difference and gender inequality" (2004, 113). Those institutions include school, work, and families. Kimmel looks for what correlates with more or less inequality. For example, he finds that fathers' involvement in childrearing and women's control of property are central to status and equality (ibid.). He also sees as critical the need to examine the relationships between different systems of power in order to destroy inequality (2002b, xi).

Jeff Hearn is a third important masculinities theorist whose work is explicitly from a framework that considers power the critical gender issue (2004). Hearn would distinguish men's studies from critical studies on men, with the former focusing on the descriptive and the latter insisting that power issues are critical, as well as explicitly connecting to feminist and queer theory. Hearn suggests a shift in theorizing from masculinity to men, and focusing on the *hegemony of men*. Hearn argues that masculinities research has focused too narrowly on gender relations: "It is time to go back from *masculinity* to *men*, to examine the hegemony of men and about men. The hegemony of men seeks to address the double complexity that men are both a *social category formed by the gender system* and *dominant collective and individual agents of social practices*. . . . The deconstruction of the dominant and the obvious, the social category of men, remains urgent. What indeed would society look like without this category, not through gendercide but through gender transformation?" (59). Hearn embraces the concept of hegemony but focuses not on the construction of masculinity but rather on the construction and sustaining of male power. In the process, he particularly examines "taken-for-granted power," which is where hegemony sustains itself by support from those who are dominated.

Hearn's insistence on staying focused on power unravels and reorients theory in a significant way. Power is a part of social relations, actions, and experience. Much of it is taken for granted, which renders it invisible. Hearn points out that the concept of hegemony is helpful, since the concept includes the active consent of the dominated. He raises an excellent question: is dominance tied most essentially to the gender system or to the economic system? (2004).

Lynne Segal in her classic work on the subject of masculinities is unequivocal that the economic system is critical: "masculinity gains its meanings, its force and appeal, not just from internalized psychological components or roles, but from all the wider social relations in which men and women participate which simply take for granted men's authority and privileges in relation to women" (1990, 294). Dismantling male power, in Segal's view, requires "the pursuit of change in the economy, the labor market, social policy and the state, as well as the organization of domestic life, the nature of sexual encounters and the rhetoric of sexual difference" (294). Fundamentally, she sees the goals as those of socialist feminism: "the world of caring, sharing and co-operation ideally characterizing family life" (318). Others would also answer Hearn's question by noting the importance of the work environment and the expression of masculinities in the workplace: "On the one hand, men often collaborate, cooperate and identify with one another in ways that display a shared unity and consolidate power between them. Yet on the other hand, these same masculinities can also be characterized simultaneously by conflict, competition and self-differentiation in ways that highlight and intensify the differences and divisions between men" (Collinson and Hearn 2001, 162).

Hearn's approach means looking at men in relation to each other, and in relation to women and children, and looking at how government categorizes men (2004, 60). His approach is gender specific but asymmetric: he takes the position that critical study of men and masculinities means support of feminism but that the study of men does not have parity with the study of women (Hearn and Morgan 1990a). According to Hearn, the critique should be "anti-sexist, anti-patriarchal, pro-feminist, and gay-affirmative. . . . [And] the underlying task . . . is to change men, ourselves, and other men" (Hearn and Morgan 1990a, 204). He captures the dominance of men in sociology with the term *malestream*, a substitution for mainstream, denoting how the discipline historically almost exclusively focused on men, but not as gendered beings. This is akin to noting how feminists critiqued history as "history" (Hearn and Morgan 1990b, 7). Hearn's vision is the "possibility of the abolition of 'men' as a significant social category of power" (2004, 66).

Others who have contributed to an examination of male power that complements Hearn's work include John Remy and Sylvia Walby. Remy (1990) discusses the concepts of androcracy, patriarchy, and fratriarchy and the institution of the male hut (associated with male bond and fraternity). What is particularly striking about Remy's work is his focus on homosocial environments or areas of homosocial or dominantly homosocial power, and the policing of entry to only some men and no women. Remy defines androcracy as "rule by men," divided into patriarchy, or "rule of the fathers," and fratriarchy, or "rule of the brothers/rule of the brotherhood." Both forms are based on an institution that he calls the men's hut. German social scientists identified a key aspect of androcracy as *Mannerbund* or "men's league." The place of power in androcracy is the men's hut or men's house: "This is the place where those males who have earned the right to call themselves *men*, or are in the process of attaining this emblem of privilege, gather" (46). In order to enter the hut, men must go through a rite of passage, which usually includes some tests.

Sylvia Walby (1990) focuses on power as expressed in the concept of patriarchy, which justifies the domination of women as a group. She identifies six critical structures where patriarchal power is expressed: household production, wage work, the state, male violence, sexuality, and cultural institutions. Practices create structures. The movement over time has been from private to public patriarchy, according to Walby.

Two other critical theoretical voices are James Messerschmidt and Don Sabo, both of whom bring insights from masculinities and crime. Messerschmidt (1993) criticizes both criminology and feminism for their analyses of crime. Criminology generally has not studied men as men, and when it has, it tends to see men in an essentialist, biological way grounded in sex differences and inevitable male behavior (Daly and Maher 1998b; Naffine 1996; Walklate 2004). Feminism, while refocusing on women as victims and perpetrators, has tended to portray men still as unidimensional perpetrators and rarely notices men as victims of crime. Messerschmidt sees the dominance of men as victims and perpetrators of crime as explained by crime being merely another way of doing gender: "Crime by men is not simply an extension of the 'male sex role.' Rather, crime by men is a form of social practice invoked as a resource, when other resources are unavailable, for accomplishing masculinity" (1993, 85). The content of men's practices varies by race and class. Reducing inequality, in his view, is the best long-term way to reduce crime.

Sabo similarly sees prison as an extension of normal patterns of masculinity and argues that imprisonment reinforces violent masculinities: "The prison code is very familiar to men in the United States because it is similar to the male code that reigns outside of prison" (Sabo, Kupers, and London 2001a, 10). If we could challenge the mentality that supports prisons, it might lead to thinking in terms of our broader social prisons. "Perhaps the most essential problem of men's liberation is getting men to understand themselves individually as victims of sexual inequality without losing sight of why they are the collective oppressors of women. We believe it is necessary to rethink and reshape our understandings of the prison itself as an element within the larger gender order" (17).

David Gilmore's fascinating cross-cultural anthropological work (1990) adds a different perspective to masculinities, exposing similarities in concepts of masculinity and manhood. Although Gilmore's work is frequently cited in support of the view that manhood is a universal and timeless essence, he makes it clear that masculinity is learned and constructed, not inherent. He also points out that cross-culturally manhood is seen as something to be attained that is not easy, and he contrasts this with how femaleness and womanhood are viewed. "Manhood is a test in most societies," according to Gilmore, confirming that it is stressful and never fully achieved (220). Gilmore also finds manhood is consistently associated with three things: "One must impregnate women, protect dependents from danger, and provision kith and kin" (223).

Another interesting take is that from the discipline of geography, or geographies, in an edited collection by van Hoven and Horschelmann (2005b; see also Thorne 1993). What is so interesting about this approach is thinking about space as representing gender: pubs, sports areas, workplaces are all places where masculinities are made and performed. As with other disciplines, this is one that is male oriented, and only recently has it considered masculinity, again emphasizing the asymmetrical nature of masculinities and feminist theory. Daphne Spain (1993) talks about gendered spaces, separating architectural space (within a building) and geographic space (between and among different buildings). She explores how spaces reinforce gender stratification. It is fascinating to consider how men and women move differently through space, especially those spaces that are singularly male versus singularly female. What happens in spaces that are exclusively or dominantly male is suggested by work on the military, where the resocialization of recruits is based on a masculinity norm of "physical toughness, the endurance of hardships, aggressiveness, a rugged heterosexuality, unemotional logic, and a refusal to complain, coupled with continual testing to assure that these qualities are maintained" (Barrett 2001, 81). The military is the epitome of a "gendered institution" that creates "gendered identities" (ibid., 97).

Leading Theorists: Psychological Perspectives

A second disciplinary focus in masculinity theory and scholarship originates in psychology. It is quite different from the sociological perspective. On the one hand, the concept of masculinity seems more rigid and stereotypical, particularly with respect to trying to "measure" masculinity. Because psychologists often evaluate mental health against an assumed norm, the tendency toward essentialism is dramatic. Another respect in which there are differences is that a definition of masculinity is used clinically, to treat someone who has a psychological disorder. This is masculinities "on the ground" and affords an insight into the impact of masculinities on individual lives as well as on society. A third difference is that the focus for some psychologists is describing human development and articulating what is "normal" when it comes to gender, which again inherently tends toward a singular concept of masculinity (Lunbeck 1994).

Psychologists have been interested in boys as well as men. The patterns they identify link the development of the two. A common connecting link is the lack of emotional, empathetic, and relational development. Among the issues identified by one researcher are men's lack of early childhood contact with adult males and frequently an adult dissatisfaction with their relationships with their father; the suppression of emotion taught from an early age, which has lifelong psychological, physical, and social implications; difficulty in creating and sustaining intimate relationships and a general lack of healthy, robust relationships with others; significant mental health issues connected to divorce or the breakup of adult relationships, contrary to the social model of independence; a disproportionate involvement in violence and a disproportionate representation in prisons; and a shorter average lifespan than women (Kilmartin 2000).

One scholar provides three psychoanalytical models of masculinity (Richards 1990). First, there is Freud's, in which identifying with the father is defensive and includes castration anxiety. Second, there is the model of Chodorow and others, in which the threat is not the father but the mother, who may engulf the boy, and the task is resisting dependency. So these first two models define masculinity as a negative, defensive task. The third model is of identification with the father as a loving adult, an identification that is important to selfhood. It is only in this third model "that we have an image of masculinity as a benign, indeed necessary, quality of psychic life in men" (164).

Oddly, of course, it is primarily men who have developed psychological theories, yet they have done so without thinking about men as men. As late as the early 1990s, research was sparse. Gender-aware work began with fathers and then emerged in psychotherapy for men. The classic notion was that there is a male gender role, and the process of psychological development is learning or attaining that role. This was seen as involving two basic steps, called "disidentification" (Blazina 2004). Boys first have to sever their ties with their caregiver mothers and then have to take the second step of identifying with their father. "These developmental tasks have been held as necessary steps toward emotional autonomy, psychological separation, and most important here, securing the development of the masculine self" (151). As this description indicates, inherent in this view is a model of masculinity that includes autonomy, separation, and a "masculine self." As Blazina indicates, this classic model has been unhealthy for men, leading to what he calls the "fragile masculine self" that either avoids healthy emotional relationships or is overdependent (153). He argues that the need for change requires less restrictive gender roles for boys and healthier relationships for adult men. Particularly important to this revised model is moving away from what has been identified by Bergman (1995) as "relational dread," that is, teaching boys that relational interaction should be avoided by requiring separation from their mothers. Concern with the emotional tasks of boys and their relationship with mothers is a strong theme picked up by psychologists who have focused their work on boys, and the emotional issues of adult men are a pervasive theme among all psychologists.

Assumed in the disidentification process is a "masculine self" that must be attained. This assumes a kind of innate "maleness" or "masculinity" with a biological base that must be achieved (Phillips 2006). Social constructionists challenge the biological basis of this gender role and argue that it is socially and culturally constructed and taught, rather than biologically based. Further, the masculinities theorists in the psychological field have seen the role not as positive but as problematic. This shift is critical because it is a shift from the individual focus to a societal focus: "There is a very large and consequential difference between understanding masculinity, gender, identity, and development as innately predetermined and influenced by society and understanding them as socially produced through pervasive and insidious norms of identity, development, and behaviors. The former view focuses the disciplinary and clinical gaze primarily on man. . . . The latter view is more complex, multidimensional, and difficult as the focus is on the societal level as well as the individual as a social being" (ibid., 421).

Joseph Pleck is the leading scholar who has challenged and reoriented the concept of gender role (1981). Most importantly, Pleck argues that men violate much of their gender role, so that it is a model of strain rather than a role that is achieved and practiced easily (Phillips 2006). "The replacement paradigm proposes that contemporary gender roles are contradictory and inconsistent; that the proportions of persons who violate gender roles is high; that violation of gender roles leads to condemnation and negative psychological consequences; that actual or imagined violation of gender roles leads people to overconform to them; that violating gender roles has more severe consequences for males than for females; and that certain prescribed gender role traits (such as male aggression) are too often dysfunctional" (Levant and Pollack 1995a, 3).

Pleck identifies three core ideas from his model of gender role strain: "A significant proportion of males exhibit long-term failure to fulfill male role expectations. . . . This dynamic is 'gender role *discrepancy*' or 'incongruity.' Second, even if male role expectations are successfully fulfilled, the socialization process . . . is traumatic, or the fulfillment itself is traumatic. . . . This is the 'gender role *trauma*' argument. . . . Third, . . . the successful fulfillment of male role expectations can have negative consequences. . . . This is the 'gender role *dysfunction* argument'" (1995, 12). Pleck sees as critical to this strain and negative outcome the role of masculine ideology. Pleck sees similarities between his work and the core concept of social constructionism but argues that it is part of the ideology of masculinity that it has to be constantly proved, not because it is men's essential nature.

Pollack (1995) takes a very different tack, focusing on the process of emotional development and its lifelong consequences. Pollack's theory utilizes Nancy Chodorow's work to create object relations theory grounded particularly in the experience of boys and its consequences for adult men (Phillips 2006). He sees the development of empathy as critical for men and connects the lack of empathy to the forced separation of boys at a young age from their mothers; this enforced separation leads men both to seek isolation and to desire relatedness and intimacy (Pollack 1995). The favorite emotion of men is anger, Pollack argues, because that is an emotion that is allowed. Pollack argues for a redefined masculinity that retains concepts of difference and celebrates positive male traits: "redefining a new, postfeminist masculinity, . . . creating a masculinity that distills what is historically, proactively, and positively male-gendered yet remains respectful of women's specialness as well, . . . a redefinition, from a critical, psychoanalytic perspective, of boys' early developmental struggles for gendered selfhood. . . . As boys, men suffer a traumatic abrogation of their early holding environment, that is a premature psychic separation from both their maternal and paternal caregivers"

(35). Pollack characterizes male gender identity as problematic because of male identification with mothers: boys must separate while also valuing their connection with their mothers. He sees socialization models that require separation as "a gender-specific vulnerability to *traumatic abrogation* of the early holding environment, an *impingement* in boys' development" (41).

Pollack calls for greater empathy toward men in order for men to learn to be more empathetic. He also sees engaging in nurture as critical to repairing and reorienting men, so that men can transform themselves (1995). His particular focus has been on the emotional life of boys, discussed in further detail later in this chapter, and he identifies the educational system as well as families as the essential environments within which boys develop and are socialized.

Bergman is the third leading psychological theorist, and he focuses on the importance of development of self in relation, power-with instead of power-over and autonomy, and sees this as most likely to occur in midlife, when autonomy so clearly fails (1995). Instead of focusing on identity, Bergman focuses on the relational piece: greater relationship and intimacy is what creates a powerful person. The goal is the "relationalization" of men and women, with the goal of establishing creative and collaborative relationships.

Bergman agrees that a critical component for men is separation from their mothers, and in general, from relationship, as an essential step in becoming a man (1995). In contrast to classic theorists who saw this separation as essential to identity, Bergman sees relationship as essential to identity: "Rather than identity before intimacy, relationship *informs* identity in a continuous, ongoing process—the more connected, the more powerful" (73). Bergman describes the development of boys as identifying relationship as bad because it is being like mother, while fathers fail to create a strong emotional relationship with their sons. In addition, boys learn male violence and power. The toll this takes on relationships and the need to reorient only comes for many men in midlife, when the desire for connection outweighs socialization to the contrary.

Bergman argues for a vision of "non-self-centered, mutual relationships" and of "grow[ing] in connection, . . . collaborative, co-creative" (85). "What is being suggested here is not the feminization of men but the relationalization of all, men and women both, . . . moving into a power-with way of living. . . . In shifting the paradigm from self-other to relationship, we are entering the realm of the common good" (88–89).

One other psychological perspective on masculinity is that articulated by feminist paradigms in psychology (Addis and Cohane 2005). Feminist perspectives focus on power differences as critical to gender analysis. Material differences are not necessarily reflected in individual or subjective senses of power. "First, members of a privileged group are typically the least likely people to be aware of their privilege. . . . The second reason that many men may feel subjectively disempowered is that there are great emotional costs to the constant striving to erect and maintain positions of power. . . . Finally, power is not distributed evenly among all men" (642). Although feminist paradigms have been used primarily to treat and analyze women, there is no reason the feminist focus on power relations could not be used for men as well.

The difficulty of describing or agreeing on what masculinity is or should be is reflected in the work of scholars who have critiqued methods and measurements of masculinity (Hoffman 2001; Levant and Richmond 2007; Smiler 2004; Thompson and Pleck 1995; Whorley and Addis 2006). What seems especially stunning is the lack of integration in the field, reflecting a difficulty in translating recent theory into measures and a failure to link with other gender work. Masculinity was easier to measure when it was seen as a natural thing to attain or a socially constructed and acceptable thing to learn; when you problematize it, and multiply it, it becomes much more difficult to measure. The efforts to create measures seem to lead in the direction of stereotyping rather than investigating resistance or variation and toward reinforcing binary notions of gender and sex. It also exposes that the subjects of research have been predominantly white males.

The more complex and multiple the notions of masculinity, also the more difficult it has been to apply insights clinically, particularly the concept of hegemonic masculinity (Bankart 2005; Bennett and Jones 2006; Speer 2001). Speer complains that hegemonic masculinity does not explain how masculinity is reproduced, and she questions how useful is a dominant definition that no man ever achieves or that few do. At the same time, the notion that there are multiple masculinities is important in order not to essentialize men. Speer also frankly acknowledges the value of a less problematized masculinity: "Feminism has traditionally needed to have a stable object (patriarchy, men and so on) that is intrinsically negative, measurable, and linked with identity to work with, and against which we can collectively mobilize. There is no room for an 'always indexical' element to masculinity, as one would never be able to pin it down and capture it for long enough to make claims about the workings of social power. To some extent, then, selective reification of the object of our critique is unavoidable" (Speer 2001, 129). Bennett and Jones talk about the negative aspects of masculinity, the concept of the "male harness," meaning particularly the model of stoicism and success (2006, 333).

Bankart has the strongest critique of masculinities analysis not helping clinically, arguing that the concept of hegemony has the odd consequence of reinforcing a narrow notion of masculinity rather than the multiple masculinities that are also part of the model (2005, 435).

A significant portion of the research about boys has come from work of psychologists, especially from clinicians who treat boys and see patterns that they connect to the development and socialization of boys. The two substantive areas that have generated this examination in particular are boys in relation to education and to crime. Much of the focus of this research is on adolescents. What is especially striking is the pattern of emotional openness and expressiveness for young boys, and the gradual suppression of emotion and empathy, which leads to a lifetime pattern of both same- and opposite-sex relationships being stunted. The developmental pattern often targeted is the pattern of mother care and the demand that boys separate from their mothers. A second focus is schools and their view of boys. There is awareness, as there has been with girls, that our gender socialization carries serious consequences. But those consequences are different for boys and girls. It is especially apparent that education disserves both. There also is the clear concern regarding how young masculinity translates into juvenile justice issues.

Two authors who stand out as the articulators of the crisis about boys, and the lack of support for boys' development of empathy, are William Pollack and Dan Kindlon and his coauthors (Kindlon, Thomson, and Barker 1999; Pollack 1998, 2000). William Pollack, the author of *Real Boys* (1998) and *Real Boys' Voices* (2000), articulates a simple thesis to explain the yearning and emotional difficulties of boys: boys early on in their development are expected to separate from their mothers, and their fathers do not replace that relationship. This emotional price plays out in their differential patterns in school and in relationships, because of the "boy code" (1998, xxiii). Pollack discusses the myths and impact of the myths about boys. His main focus is the development of empathy. As discussed in the previous section, he also sees the emotional difficulties of boys as the foundation for the problems of adult men. Other scholars call the way masculinity is socialized "emotional miseducation" by teaching men "emotional stoicism" (Chu, Porche, and Tolman, 2005).

Boys have equivalent emotional expressiveness to girls until elementary school; increasingly from that point, their emotional lives are driven below the surface, particularly through a process of shaming. The education system reinforces this process and treats boys differentially, contributing or even causing their difficulties with school. Pollack catalogs myths about boys and argues that they are simply that, myths. They include "boys will be boys," or the myth of testosterone controlling boy behavior; that "boys should be boys," meaning boys should be "tough"; and that boys are by nature dangerous, even toxic. Pollack argues that boys are and can be empathetic and that they desire connection and relationship, but we fail to support this emotional development for boys. Pollack describes a very gender-specific role for mothers and fathers in developing the emotional skills of boys, a role that counters the separation model for mothers with connection and independence and that strengthens the emotional connection between fathers and sons. Pollack also describes the tension in the definition of masculinity that boys face, between egalitarian, caring manhood and traditional dominating masculinity (Pollack 1998).

Dan Kindlon shares Pollack's perspective that our socialization pushes boys into "lives of isolation, shame and anger" (Kindlon, Thomson, and Barker 1999, ix). He links this to the emotional suppression that we socialize in boys, so that they lack "emotional literacy" (5). Emotional literacy includes the ability to "identify and name our emotions, . . . [to recognize] the emotional content of voice and facial expression, . . . and [to understand] situations or reactions that produce emotional states" (5). Kindlon points out that as boys mature, they express less emotion, although there is evidence that they still feel plenty of emotion. Like Pollack, he disputes the role of testosterone and aggressiveness.

School is again a major institutional problem for boys' self-esteem. School is structured around a curriculum more closely linked to girls' developmental capabilities than those of boys (Kindlon, Thomson, and Barker 1999). In addition, boys' activity level also makes them more likely to "look ADHD" (ibid., 45). Kindlon notes that "history is full of great men who were notable misfits in the school environment," with Gandhi being an example (49).

Kindlon calls masculinity "The Big Impossible," a wonderful term borrowed from the Eastern Highlands of Papua, New Guinea, naming the standard that cannot be achieved (78). He sees boys as in a very stressful testing period in adolescence: "A boy lives in a narrowly defined world of developing masculinity in which everything he does or thinks is judged on the basis of the strength or weakness it represents: you are either strong and worthwhile, or weak and worthless" (78). This testing includes massive amounts of teasing and taunting about being "gay" or a "fag," all meant to limit male behavior. This leads to significant amounts of depression in boys, as well as a high rate of completed suicides—although more girls attempt suicide, more boys succeed. Annually of nearly two thousand suicides among fifteen- to nineteen-year-olds, 85 percent are boys. Essential to a different model of manhood, Kindlon argues, is a model that includes and values emotional attachment. Kindlon suggests seven key factors to transform boys (241–56):

1. Give boys permission to have an internal life, approval for the full range of human emotions, and help in developing an emotional vocabulary so that they may better understand themselves and communicate more effectively with others.

2. Recognize and accept the high activity level of boys and give them safe boy places to express it.

3. Talk to boys in their language—in a way that honors their pride and their masculinity. Be direct with them; use them as consultants and problem solvers.

4. Teach boys that emotional courage is courage, and that courage and empathy are the sources of real strength in life.

5. Use discipline to build character and conscience, not enemies.

6. Model a manhood of emotional attachment.

7. Teach boys that there are many ways to be a man.

Newberger, like Pollack and Kindlon, sees as a major problem boys' lack of emotional literacy (1999). "If the playing field is level at the beginning of life and infant boys and girls are pretty equally capable of friendliness, compassion, empathy and the like, and if emotional expressiveness can lead to a greater capacity for closeness and intimacy, then why should it be discouraged in boys? What is gained by the suppression of their emotional life?" (64). Newberger focuses on the creation of character. What he seeks to create is safe passage; what he wants to help boys avoid is the pattern that high-risk boys have for sexual activity, drugs, alcohol, violence, and crime. He argues that American institutions fail to support safe passage or intervene effectively to prevent high risk, leaving teenagers to a very individualistic model that especially disserves boys.

A second thread of research on boys focuses on the social context and meaning of adolescence. The pressure to conform to hegemonic masculinity, and the narrow range of acceptable alternative masculinities, makes puberty and adolescence a critical time in the development of masculinity. In addition, it is a time when the notion of gender difference is at its peak. School is a major site of gender construction, with peers as the most important influence at this stage.

James Messerschmidt has done fascinating work on adolescents and crime (1993, 2000a, 2000b, 2001). Messerschmidt exposes how little has been done about gender with respect to adolescents and crime. Even though crime is dominated by men as perpetrators and victims, gender as a factor is rarely studied. He sees gender not as imposed but as received and performed, what he calls structured action theory. Gender is never finished; it is always something both received and created (2000b). In his book *Nine Lives* he looks at the stories of nine boys involved in criminal sexual activity, and how they construct their masculinity by their actions, often creating power through sexual domination that they do not have in their lives as boys. Masculinity is achieved by the use of violence and, in the case of the boys he studied, the use of sexual violence. He identifies a culture of cruelty and peer abuse, producing cool guys and tough guys. Messerschmidt recommends several ways that this culture and these practices could be challenged and reoriented in a way that links parents and schools: managing the "culture of cruelty and the widespread peer abuse that it produces"; challenging dominant masculinities in schools; "making gender relations a core subject matter" in a way that is gender relevant and gender specific; shared parenting; good mothering and fathering; and "emphasis on empathy and pluralism in schools" (ibid., 143–46).

Boy culture is diverse. There are different voices, not solely those of white males. Yet a common thread is the concept of insecure masculinity—acting out to cover the sense of insecurity—and how boys are "bent" by gender at adolescence (Way and Chu 2004b). One study exposes how Hmong American boys have to create a sense of themselves amid racism and gender marginalization that constructs them as not "real men" or "real Americans" (Lee 2004). It is impossible for these boys to achieve the hegemonic ideal. Another study of immigrant boys notes that immigrant girls outperform immigrant boys and ties this to lack of social support and negative school experiences and expectations, which may be linked to stereotypes that are related to subordinated masculinities (Suárez-Orozco and Qin-Hilliard 2004).

The same sense of exacerbated or intensified struggle to become or be is expressed in a study about African American adolescent males, among whom hypervulnerability is translated into hypermasculinity (Stevenson 2004). "When Black adolescent males are using exaggerated macho identity stances, they are, in fact, coping. This coping is essential in social and ecological environments where danger to personal and familial safety is high" (60). Some of the coping styles are labeled as "cool pose" and "reactive coping." "Being missed, dissed, and pissed represents the struggle of constructing identity within a quicksand of false Black male images and is as vulnerable as one can get" (60). The study includes the familiar and devastating statistics on the presence of young black males in the criminal justice system and the evidence of racial profiling in all aspects of their daily lives. Society's perception of threat also carries over to schools, where young black children are expected to land in jail. Cornel West calls this the problem of nihilism (Stevenson 2004, 62; West 1993).

Hypervulnerability translates into showing off: "The more one experiences pressure to 'show oneself' and demonstrate masculine competency, the greater the hypervulnerability. The reason is that 'showing off' one's manhood is an emotionally immature process. This manhood is insecure and is based on what one does rather than who one is" (Stevenson 2004, 63). This is a masculine ideal that all men are subject to, but because minority men have less access to the tools needed to accomplish hegemonic masculinity, they make use of what they have, with the result being more violence and negative social interactions. What is striking about this analysis is that the ultimate perversion of the hegemonic ideal exposes the core danger for all men, which is heightened for disadvantaged men. The ideal limits their freedom. "True freedom can only come if they recreate their image and redefine the questions for themselves" (64).

Judy Chu describes how she found, contrary to the popular image of boys as relationally impaired and emotionally deficient, that boys were "clearly capable of thoughtful self-reflection and deep interpersonal understanding" (2004, 83). Self was negotiated with friends, family, and social expectations. Boys both resist and accept external pressures, but they are definitely aware. Parents are not totally irrelevant to adolescents. Instead, parents are a source of guidance and an ultimate place of support. Among certain boys for whom the cultural norm is one of family obligation (especially among Asian and Latin boys), that value is also recognized (Jeffries 2004). Hegemonic norms are enforced by peers, but boys have a private world of thoughts and feelings that often deviate from the norm (B. Walker 2004). Peers are clearly dominant, but there is a tension between individuals and this peer culture (O'Donnell and Sharpe 2000).

Psychological perspectives on adult men and boys contribute significantly to understanding masculinities and exposing the costs of current societal norms. The challenge for psychology is sustaining multiple norms. Even more so than in sociology, the push in psychology is toward a singular norm. The development of research on nonhegemonic, alternative masculinities is critical for inscribing antiessentialism at the core of masculinities theory.

Subversive/Alternative Masculinities

Although masculinities theorists consistently adopt the perspective that masculinities are plural and that race, class, and sexual orientation play a critical role in constructing those masculinities, the scholarship in these masculinities remains sparse. Thus the critique of masculinities scholarship as essentialist in practice, though not in articulation, remains true. In this respect it mirrors the challenges and shortcomings of implementing antiessentialism that persist in feminist theory as well.

These alternative masculinities, however, are critical to exposing the hierarchy within masculinity, the role of other identity factors, and the interaction of privilege and disadvantage. Most significantly, they suggest a less hierarchical, more egalitarian model of masculinity. This would argue for placing these marginalized models at the center.

Finally, the development of theory around sexual orientation, including the development of queer theory, is one of the progenitors of masculinities scholarship. The ongoing relationship between masculinities and queer theory is an important theoretical perspective to explore. Because queer theory resists sex/gender classification and "grand" theorizing as undermining the queer project, it is both a creative and yet sometimes unsatisfying force within masculinities theory.

Racial Minority Men

The literature on the masculinities of racial minority men primarily focuses on black men. There is a much smaller literature on Latino and Asian men. Minority men provide examples of resistance to hegemony but also sometimes demonstrate acceptance of gender inequality as entitlement, or of male equality as a priority, so resistance and support of hegemonic masculinity are tied together. An example of this is the sign carried by civil rights protestors in Birmingham, Alabama, in 1968 stating "I Am a Man" as a claim to equality (Berger, Wallis, and Watson 1995b). Carried by black men, this claim prioritized their equality in relation to the accepted standard of equality: white men. Implicitly, it might be viewed as asserting the primacy of race over gender, that the demand for racial equality should come first and perhaps that true equality would include exercising equivalent patriarchal power to white men. Forty years later in a commemorative march honoring the Birmingham protest and the death of Martin Luther King Jr., women as well as men carried the same posters, bringing black women's equality into the picture in an oddly gendered way.

The distinctive masculinity of African American men has been labeled "cool pose" by Richard Majors. "Black men often cope with their frustration, embitterment, alienation, and social impotence by channeling their creative energies into gesture, clothing, hairstyle, walk, stance, and handshake" (Majors 2001, 211). The pose, Majors argues, is both resistance and assertion against the race and gender subjugation of black men. At the same time, men of color sometimes follow the dominant script. Razack (2002) has asserted that when men of color are complicit in dehumanizing others, it is not compensatory humiliation but rather doing exactly what white men do, following the hegemonic script.

The masculinities of other men of color are just as distinctive, merging resistance and acceptance of hegemonic norms and cultural/racial traditions (Atkins 2005; Lazur and Majors 1995). Cheung (2002b) reminds us that in constructing a distinctive Chinese masculinity, the temptation is to draw from traditional models that subordinate women, such as the Chinese masculinist heroic tradition or the scholar warrior (see also Krishnaswamy 2002; Louie 2003). Hondagneu-Sotelo and Messner (1994) suggest that the Latino stereotype of macho masculinity may be a response to oppression, similar to findings of research on African American males. Equally or more significantly, they point out, immigration triggers a shift in gender relations, with a diminishment of patriarchal authority, more shared decision-making, and more power for women, who challenge patriarchal authority. Based on their study of the shifts in Latino masculinity, they strongly argue that the best way to undermine hegemonic masculinity is to study marginalized and subordinate masculinities.

Two other scholars that explore the possibility of models of change from subversive masculinities are Michael Awkward and Devon Carbado. Both focus on men as feminists and specifically on the place of black men in black women's feminism (Awkward 1999; Carbado 1999a; see also Adu-Poku 2001). Awkward suggests a potential model for masculinity grounded in the black feminist critique of feminism, a way of seeing the interaction between masculinities and feminist theory that is very atypical of white feminists or white male masculinities scholars. His view suggests that an outsider perspective can negotiate the difficult dance that is needed if masculinities are to be of value to feminist theory.

Awkward talks about the necessity of examining the benefits and disadvantages of feminist discourse: black men could be purely self-interested, or they could use this perspective to explore the privileges and position of men. One of the possibilities that black men have to offer relates to the structure of the black family and the strong role of mothers. Black men, he argues, using the work of Hortense Spillers, know the female within to a far greater degree than most men. "It is the heritage of the *mother* that the African-American male must regain as an aspect of his own personhood—the power of 'yes' to the 'female' within" (1999, 372, citing Spillers). Feminism, Awkward argues, might allow for reconceptualizing a black man in a nonoppressive way— in other words, masculinity that is not patriarchal and not linked to racial oppression.

Another positive characteristic of black masculinity is the value placed on responsibility. This is the key value noted in a review of the literature on African American men by Hammond and Mattis (2005) that exposes the value attached to responsibility and accountability, as well as showing a relational construction of manhood. This suggests a very affirmative model of manhood, contrary to the negative core of hegemonic masculinity.

Devon Carbado (1999b) also explores male feminism, arguing for the necessity of men coming to terms with male privilege, including heterosexual privilege. He claims male feminism must be male-centered (which masculinities is) but that it should focus on disconnecting from power. Carbado also critiques the dominance of men in racial discourse, as privileged victims in antiracist analysis (1999c, 2006).

Elijah Ward (2005) similarly raises concerns about black masculinity, particularly the links between black masculinity and homophobia. Ward argues that black masculinity is characterized by hypermasculinity, constructed in defense of the fear of black men and the denial of black men's personhood, and incorporates strong homophobia while denying a discussion of sexuality. One consequence of homophobia, he points out, is the deterrent effect on relationships of affection between black men. Neal (2005) similarly raises the concern that the need for strength and opposition in black masculinity can express itself in homophobic, misogynist ways.

The example of black masculinity also exposes how masculinity, particularly subordinated masculinity, includes an externally imposed model, and that model may conflict with masculinity constructed from within by men themselves. The denigration of black men has been strong and persistent. This is powerfully evident in the example of lynching. Manhood was at the core of lynching, a violent response to the perceived threat of black men being equal to white men. In addition, lynching was a way for white men to prove themselves to other white men. Lynching commonly included castration, and it was a public event. Acting like a white man was considered insubordination and an insult (Messerschmidt 1998). At the same time, during the Jim Crow era, black men asserted manhood despite its denial, to "man" the race (Ross 2004). The most common crime resulting in lynching was approaching, or being accused of assaulting, a white woman. Bound up with these gender and race messages against black men is also a denial, in a strange way, of the contemporaneous treatment of black women. "The institutionalized rape of black women has never been as powerful a symbol of black oppression as the spectacle of lynching" (Carby 1987, 39).

Frank Cooper (2006) suggests that the contemporary external construction of black masculinity differentiates between the "good" black man and the "bad" black man. Cooper examines how cultural representations function as a push to discipline black men to be "good" black men, emulating whites but still subordinate to white males. Gail Dines's study of pornography (2006) is perhaps an extreme example of these cultural representations. She finds the presence of black men to be widespread in porn, mostly animalistic, negative images linked with degrading images of white women.

Subordination remains typical, playing out structurally, in education, work, health, and criminal justice. Education exposes a pattern of lost opportunity and denial (J. Davis 2006; Ferguson 2000). Work has been epitomized by the denial of the breadwinner role by denial of economic opportunities (Pamela Smith 1999b). Health data expose significant differences in morbidity and mortality (Rich 2000). Finally, there is the highly disproportionate, epidemic representation of black men in all aspects of the criminal justice system (Brunson and Miller 2006; Provine 1998).

The created and imposed masculinities of racial minorities present the opportunity to expose hierarchy, see the dynamic of resistance, and suggest other models of masculinity. Race operates in complex ways that trump gender privilege. The development of greater study of race and of minority men holds great promise both to suggest models for change and to move gender analysis to take on race as an issue.

Queer Theory

Another influence on masculinities theory, and an alternative to hegemonic masculinity, is masculinities within the gay and lesbian communities and the insights of queer theory. As with racial masculinities, there are both external and internal masculinities. Homophobia is a powerful piece in the construction of masculinities. Men define themselves in relation to other men, often in homosocial environments (Kimmel 1997b). If "not being like women" is the negative definition of masculinity, that avoidance is also strongly linked to "not being gay." Indeed, men's strong homophobia is linked to their need to avoid being feminine in order to meet masculine norms (Wilkinson 2004; see also Hegarty and Massey 2006). This is expressed in avoiding men who are perceived as feminine, antigay harassment and violence, and men themselves avoiding characteristics and behaviors that would identify them as feminine or gay (Bartlett 2007; Kilianski 2003). These behaviors and attitudes begin in adolescence as "heteronormative masculinity" (Korobov 2005), which makes gay and lesbian youth particularly vulnerable (S. Martin 1996). Homophobic attitudes and behaviors are manifested strongly in the workplace with sexual harassment of gay men or men perceived as violating the norms of masculinity (Schroeder 1998).

Unlike other forms of discrimination, homophobia frequently is socially justified and defended, based on rationales that homosexuality is sinful, that it violates the rules of nature or is unnatural/deviant, that it violates social norms of sexuality, and that it is associated with other social evils such as prostitution and moral debauchery (B. Green 2005; Herek 2007). What one scholar calls "sexuality injustice" is distinctive because it is not expressed as disadvantage but rather as displacement: gays and lesbians are viewed as outside of civil society (Calhoun 1995). But as Sylvia Law pointed out in her classic work (1988), discrimination against gays and lesbians is powerfully linked to sexism: it represents a way of enforcing sex norms for both women and men. "Homosexuality is censured because it violates the prescriptions of gender role expectations" (196). The explicit regulation of homosexuality is one of the key ways in which law regulates masculinity and reinforces a particular male norm (Reinheimer 2006; Valdes 1995). This is done by the absence of legal protection, such as the absence of a federal cause of action for employment discrimination on the basis of sexual orientation, which permits discriminatory workplace culture that reinforces a narrow male norm of masculinity. Limiting marriage in most states only to opposite-sex couples and the criminalization of sexual practices associated most strongly with the intimacy of gays and lesbians also reinforce gender norms (Reinheimer 2006). The regulation is accomplished by linking sex, gender, and sexual orientation (Valdes 1995).

Asserting a legal theory to combat discrimination against gays and lesbians, as well as asserting a positive identity and culture of gays and lesbians, inevitably contributes to a more expansive notion of masculinity. Since being "not gay" is such a defining part of masculinity, undermining the negative perception and behavior toward being gay liberates all men. The focus of theory on gay and lesbian civil rights, and of queer theory, however, has not been on reconstructing masculinity but rather on sexuality, as it is sexuality that has been the defining characteristic of condemnation and regulation.

Queer theory pushes more radically, challenging the assumption of a gay/lesbian identity and more generally the notion of identity (Jagose 1996). One scholar identifies four major claims of queer theory: "(1) sexuality is central, not marginal, to the construction of meaning and political power; (2) identity is performative, not natural; (3) political struggle is better understood as ironic parody than as earnest liberation; and (4) popular culture provides a unique insight into the everyday operation of political power that may under certain circumstances transform, rather than simply mirror, status quo power relations" (Burgess 2006, 401). Queer theory in particular attacks the notion of categories, particularly the binary notion of sex and gender (Hostetler and Herdt 1998). Instead of arguing that gays and lesbians are an identifiable category or class with a culture and interests that fit within a civil rights concept of rights, queer theory contests categories themselves as reproducing hierarchy by accepting the notion of categories (Kepros 1999–2000). Queer theory rejects identity politics and finds categories repressive instead of liberating (ibid.). The focus of queer theory includes exploring how sexual identities are socialized and limited, how heterosexuality becomes the dominant position and sustains itself, arguing that sexuality is based on unstable, changing categories and not limiting itself to a "queer position" on sexuality (Schlichter 2004). Thus, "queering" an area of study or analysis is not limited to gay and lesbian issues; rather, it is a way of critiquing categories, seeing how categories limit, and refusing to use categories to achieve liberation and equality. The approach of queer theory, then, as applied to the study of masculinities would challenge the category itself. Moreover it would challenge the promotion of heterosexism by raising arguments grounded in concepts of privacy and antidiscrimination (G. Smith 1998).

Queer theory both challenges the categories of sexual orientation and disrupts heteronormativity (A. Green 2007). "Queer theory seeks to demonstrate that all sexual behavior is socially constructed and that sexuality is not determined by biology" (Brooks and Parkes 2004, 89). "The *principle* of 'queer' . . . is the disassembling of common beliefs about gender and sexuality. . . . The *activity* of 'queer' is the 'queering' of culture. . . . As *theory*, [it] leads to the rejection of all categorizations as limiting and labeled by dominant power structures" (Kirsch 2000, 33). In this respect queer theory is very distinctive from mainstream gay and lesbian politics, which have emphasized a category and argued for the recognition of equal rights and justice for the category (Currah 2001).

A chief criticism of queer theory has been whether it can translate into pragmatic political strategy. "[If] the insights of queer theory were to be seriously integrated into the reasoning of the rights advocates of sexual minorities, those advocates would find themselves facing something of a quandary: how to articulate a rights claim on behalf of an identity that is, in fact, radically contingent—an illusion, a fiction, or at best, an only occasionally coherent narrative" (Currah 2001, 180; see also Ball 2001). A second critique is seeing queer theory and feminism as being at odds, because feminists would reject discarding the category of women and because of a fear that "queer" has a dominantly male orientation (Halley 2004; McLaughlin, Casey, and Richardson 2006; Zeidan 2006). Another critique of queer theory is the need for greater diversity or antiessentialism (Hutchinson 1997; Mingo 1998; Valdes 1998).

Several insights from queer theory are particularly useful for masculinities. One is Kenji Yoshino's concept of covering, his exploration of the ways gays and lesbians hide their true selves in order to avoid discrimination and harm (2002; see also Hanna 2005). Something akin to covering, I would argue, is more broadly part of masculinities, since so much negativism is part of the definition and it is so harmful to deviate from the norm. Also, the pressure to conform affects all men. A second insight is that if the concept of affirmative action is used to remedy the treatment of gay men and lesbians in the workplace, then inevitably it would to expand the culture of permissible masculinity, but it could do so in such a marginalized way that it would reinforce hegemonic norms (Byrne 1993).

Queer theory has enormous potential for masculinity because it rejects the category and exposes it as clearly socially constructed and malleable. It argues for change not by recognizing the category but by rejecting it. It disrupts the sense of inevitable, natural binary sexual opposites. One example of this disruptive potential is Judith Halberstam's work on female masculinities (1998). Because masculinity is socially constructed, it is a performance that does not require a male body. If masculinity is performed by a nondominant body, do we get a glimpse of a nondominant masculinity? Halberstam emphasizes that female masculinity is not simply women aping men. Her work on tomboys reveals how much greater the concern is for male effeminacy than female masculinity. Halberstam also emphasizes that female masculinities are multiple, and not all are progressive. Simply crossing a boundary does not mean oppositional masculinities (173).

Surprisingly, within queer theory there is not a lot of specific focus on masculinities. Because categories are challenged, no alternative masculinity is explored since that would accept categorization or identity as real. On the other hand, it is very clear that homophobia is powerfully used to construct and limit masculinity. This is especially well demonstrated in Pascoe's book *Dude You're a Fag: Masculinity and Sexuality in High School* (2007). Pascoe describes the culture of masculinity in high school and how "fag" is used most often not as a label for homosexuality but rather as a label for behavior considered unmasculine. Pascoe's work rests on Butler's insight that gender is performative and interactive; we follow the scripts, but we also change and modify them. What he observed with adolescent boys in a California high school were repeated acts of "sexual mastery and the denial of girls' subjectivity" (14), as well as relationships of rivalry and limits between boys. The insight that homophobia is a key piece of dominant masculinity is well established. What Pascoe observed is how it is used to discipline all boys and men. "Fag is not only an identity linked to homosexual boys but an identity that can temporarily adhere to heterosexual boys as well. The fag trope is also a racialized disciplinary mechanism" (53). The term is used less to accuse someone of his sexual orientation and more to limit what he can do: "*Fag* may be used as a weapon with which to temporarily assert one's masculinity by denying it to others. Thus the fag becomes a symbol around which contests of masculinity take place" (82). So the epithet means "You're not a man" (82).

A formal policy of defining manhood as not being homosexual is within the organizational mission of the Boy Scouts, which is to make boys into men (Poirier 2003). The defense of the policy of exclusion of gay scoutmasters became a defense of an explicit model of masculinity: "compliance with the Scout Oath ('morally straight') and Law ('clean'), and unacceptability of an 'avowed homosexual' as a role model" (279). The preferred heterosexual model is identified as "normal" and "natural," not as socially or culturally chosen and constructed. The antigay exclusion is linked "to the issue of constructing a normatively heterosexual masculinity and at the same time maintaining that that masculinity is natural and normal" (303).

One of the potentials of same-sex relationships is another form of masculinity or masculinities. There is some evidence of more reciprocity in same-sex relationships (Connell 1992). Scholars who have considered gender conflict theory in the context of same-sex relationships have found not that same-sex male relationships generated double the conflict but rather that conflict was lessened, suggesting a different relational model (Wester, Pionke, and Vogel 2005). If there is the potential for a different model of masculinity from gay men, it might come from a detailed understanding of gay men as individuals and in relationship, and how they construct alternative masculinities.

Critique and Concerns

As this broad overview of the field suggests, the field of masculinities scholarship has expanded enormously. Within the field exists the kind of healthy disagreements characteristic of most gender scholarship. Two areas of debate that merit attention when considering the role of masculinities scholarship in feminist analysis are criticism of the concept of hegemonic masculinity and concerns about the goals of masculinities as a field. First, the concept of hegemonic masculinity, although widespread in the field, has drawn considerable critique. Stephen Whitehead, among others, finds the use of the term to be reductionist (2002). According to Whitehead, the benefit of the concept of hegemonic masculinity is the attempt to connect male power to institutions and structures and to expose the power of some men. But it has the tendency to be read as if gender relations are predictable and preordained. He suggests as an alternative the term *masculinism*: "the ideology that justifies and naturalizes male domination [comparable to patriarchy]" (97; see also Brittan 1989). Richard Collier similarly critiques the concept as oversimplified. Collier (1998) argues that it lacks a nuanced study of the relationship between sex and gender. He is wary of the idea that there is such a thing as essential masculinity, and he also argues that the concept tends to refuse to recognize anything positive in masculinities. Others critique the tendency toward a static view of masculinities, as opposed to a view that emphasizes how masculinity remakes itself and changes constantly (Demetriou 2001). Although the theory embraces multiple masculinities, the tendency also is to focus on the dominant form, thus reducing masculinity to a single essence (Petersen 2003; see also Halberstam 1998; Spector-Mersel 2006).

Other scholars critique hegemonic masculinity as simply vague and ambiguous. John MacInnes (1998) points out the lack of a definition of masculinity in the literature and argues, as some others have, for focusing instead on material inequality, using a human-rights approach to move away from a false gender-difference position. He argues persuasively that "in contrast to the politics of identity . . . pursuing a politics of justice and equal rights to its logical conclusion is a more radical option, once we have solved the problems caused by the confusion of sexual genesis and sexual difference" (59). Jeff Hearn also raises the problem of imprecision in definition and makes four proposals: to use the term more precisely, to focus analysis on men instead of masculinity/-ies, to focus on the discourse, and to explore the differential experiences of women and men regarding men (1996, 214).

The critique has not gone unanswered. Connell and Messerschmidt, in a joint 2005 article, summarized five critiques of the concept: (1) that the underlying concept is flawed because it deemphasizes power and dominance; (2) that the concept suffers from ambiguity and overlap; (3) the problem of reification, portraying men as simply violent and toxic, explaining lots of bad things; (4) the lack of good theory of the subject; and (5) the lack of clarity about how hegemony is sustained (837–44). They reiterate, however, that the core of the concept is hierarchy and the plurality of masculinities. They justify the concept as still sound, although they suggest the need for reformulation in four areas: analyzing the nature of gender hierarchy, developing a greater geography of masculinities, examining the role of bodies, and exploring the dynamics of masculinities. They also point out the asymmetric positions of men and women and the importance of a vision of democratizing gender relations.

The second significant area of critique in the field involves concerns about the implicit goals of masculinities theory. Harry Brod is critical of masculinities theory becoming separatist and argues that it is essential that it retain the perspective of viewing men in relation to women. "Too much of what was written on masculinities did not sufficiently emphasize, if it noted at all, that masculinities are also patriarchies" (1994, 86). Roussel and Downs (2007) also critique the concept of masculinities as insufficiently focused on femininity. The focus on masculinities, they suggest, is "a strategy to end the displacement operated by feminist [analysis]. . . . We should resist the whole apparatus of masculinity and stop defining ourselves as masculine at all" (180, citing Seth Mirsky).

Nye (2005) questions whether the theory of hegemonic masculinity is about erasing masculinity or reforming it. In an interesting interchange, several theorists considered whether men can (and should) be proud to be men. Harry Brod (2001) argues for the need for a "male affirmative foundation" for men to work with one another. What Brod means by male affirmative is men standing together for justice. He also makes the observation that the movement rarely speaks in the language of "brotherhood," reserving the term for men of color and not using it for the white men who predominate in the men's movement. Schmitt focuses on the conflict between being profeminist and still seeing value in being a man; he sees having pride in being a man as confusing. Yet he argues that it is necessary both to fight against oppression and still to be proud. For him, "pride means not hating ourselves" (2001, 397).

A follow-up piece to this dialogue by Bob Pease (2002) identifies three ways men might relate to feminism: first, because they benefit from women's oppression, they might reject feminism or a different masculinity; second, because men are oppressed by masculinities, out of self-interest they might join in the feminist project; and finally, if they are devoted to ethical and moral stands, they might be drawn to feminism in order to imagine a relationship with women that is ethical and moral (as opposed to built on oppression). Pease argues that significant change requires changing material and structural conditions, and two ways he suggests are important are encouraging empathy in men and reconceptualizing their pain as need.

Feminist analysts have also been critical of the goals of masculinities scholarship. Hanmer (1990) argues that the lack of parity between analysis of men and women is apparent when you ask the core questions of feminist analysis about men. According to Hanmer, women's questions about oppression and overcoming oppression relate to powerlessness. For men, the issues are totally different: "The study of men involves the recognition of the use and misuse of social power that accrues to the male gender, of recognizing benefits even when none are personally desired" (29). This recognition would lead to examining, for example, men's relationships to women and children in the family or violence against women and children, analysis that could be done from both a male and female perspective. She also emphasizes that feminists have had to call attention to the lack of focus on women. Men, however, have not lacked from being studied and have been assumed to represent all people. What has not been present is studying them as gendered beings, in gendered institutions, engaging in gendered practices, as part of their history, sociology, and so on. Sally Robinson (2002) makes the point that masculinity and feminism are not complementary inquiries and that men must be distanced from masculinity without being distanced from feminism.

Judith Kegan Gardiner (2002a) expresses similar concerns in an overview of masculinity scholarship. She notes the asymmetrical relationship with feminism (3); the presence of a victimization model in masculinities, despite men's retention of power (5); the common rhetoric of men or boys in crisis (7); a sense of ambivalence toward feminism (9); and that it is a "coded" field that actually focuses on heterosexual masculinity and crisis (10). Meg Luxton (1993) reminds us of the profound differences between the gender issues of women and men, making masculinities very tricky for men and for feminism. She sees the issue for men as taking responsibility for their privilege, while "feminism is an emancipatory project" (351).

The concerns regarding the goals of masculinities analysis as well as the debates within the field regarding theoretical concepts should not be a deterrent to benefiting from what masculinities scholarship can bring to feminist analysis. It counsels caution but not rejection. The critiques simply remind us to use this perspective with care and subject it to rigorous questioning. This analytical approach, recognizing that insights are frequently partial and subject to change, useful in some but not all situations, has been the hallmark of much feminist analysis as well as other bodies of scholarship.

In the next chapter I summarize masculinities theory and then explore how it can enrich feminist analysis by further amplifying and solidifying feminist critique. It can further expose gender issues that have remained largely invisible. The mutual gain of these two bodies of scholarship from dialogue, critique, and critical absorption most importantly might lead to greater gender justice.

4

Toward a New Theory of
Feminist Jurisprudence

What does masculinities theory add to feminist theory? How is feminist theory advanced, enriched, solidified by adding the insights of this scholarship? There is no doubt that masculinities theory and applications enrich gender understanding, analysis, and strategizing. At the same time, there is the potential to obfuscate and hide a justified continued primary focus on women's inequality with false notions of symmetry. The greatest promise may lie in the more nuanced understanding of the replication of power amid an ideology of equality.

Insights from the Theoretical Work of Masculinities Scholars

Masculinities scholarship suggests a series of insights about men that are critical for gender analysis. I list them here as a distillation from the scholarship explored in chapter 3.

1. Men are not universal or undifferentiated. This is a very important insight, although it seems particularly simple and unremarkable. Much of feminist theory presumes universality, or that the benefit of manhood is universal enough to justify treating men as a class. It is important to see men as residing within another hierarchy, a hierarchy of men, as well as sometimes losing the "benefit" of being a man entirely. In order to dismantle male privilege it is critical to recognize that not all men are similarly situated and that gender privilege may even be trumped by another characteristic or by nonconformity to gender norms. It is also a core insight of masculinities theory that manhood is experienced by men as something constantly to be achieved, not something simply attained and lived. This instability is critically linked to hierarchy among men. It also is apparent from the research on boys that the transition in adolescence to manhood is particularly challenging and pushes toward the most traditional, conservative, inegalitarian definition of manhood, yet at the same time young or younger men may generate new lived patterns of masculinity as they try to attain it. Differentiation, hierarchy, and even the negation of privilege may also suggest that gender is only a rough indicator of inequality, not an absolute.

Do differences among men open up opportunities for collaboration by revealing the hierarchy and destabilizing its power? Or will men close ranks in defense of gender privilege, even if they might not be the ones to enjoy it? Differences among men at a minimum suggest the need to calibrate policy and pay attention to men who might be differently situated so that they are not ignored or disproportionately burdened.

2. *Men pay a price for privilege.* Even the most privileged men exercise privilege at a cost. This insight means that we have simply ignored certain issues because clearing away privilege comes first. Yet uncovering the price paid might be a way to undermine privilege or to understand the appeal of seeking or having it. One example of the price paid for privilege is military service. Military service, in the form of registration for a potential draft and, more generally, the predominant sacrifice of men's bodies in war as epitomized by their exclusive role in ground combat and other forms of direct combat, reflects both the association of men with military service and the role of warrior/soldier/military leader, as well as more generally associating men and masculinity with violence, in this case, with the focused violence and destructiveness of war. Men's association with military service and war confers privilege, most notably, the notion of full citizenship because of the literal sacrifice of their bodies. Military service is prized as a qualification for political leadership and generates entitlement to benefits including educational and health benefits. The price paid, however, is significant. Most importantly, it is men that we sacrifice in times of war. Although women increasingly play an important role in the military, it is men that we expect to carry the burden. Women have not embraced this burden or responsibility as part of equality; it remains culturally normative to support equality but resist military service as necessary to achieve equality. The military remains "male" in culture and training, disadvantaging women but also limiting men and reinforcing a traditional male definition of masculinity by its continued discrimination against women and on the basis of sexual orientation. It thereby manifests very directly the traditional masculine command not to be like a girl or to be gay. It can represent hypermasculinity in what is rewarded and

taught. The example of the military also raises the question of what changes would constitute equality if we presume the military as essential but no longer want the military or the obligation of service to be gendered.

A second example of the price for privilege is the position of men in wage work. While men as a class benefit from a favored position in wage work, the price of that privilege is the unrelenting pressure to be a breadwinner, which as currently constructed exacts a price in the burdens of particular work, the burdens imposed on men who do not meet the masculinity standard, and the undermining of men's role as caregivers. Breadwinner expectations have translated into male work privilege but also into the structuring of work around a norm that separates the worker from his family and assumes that work comes first. Patterns of gender segregation at work are often linked to wage differentials that push strongly toward a pattern of men being the dominant or sole breadwinner. Men's absence from caregiving work, their secondary role, or their struggle to be an equal partner or the primary caregiver reflects the burden attached to the reinforcement given to perform wage work. The sacrifices men make are often viewed as heroic and necessary rather than tragic. A reimagination of men's work/family role would require massive structural and cultural changes in the wage workplace.

There are consequences associated with the demands of masculinity that are apparent in the demographics of men and boys. Men's health is clearly affected by the stresses and demands of masculinity and the refusal to seek out care, physical or mental, when care is needed. Boys' rate of injury as well as their higher rate of completed suicide, and their rate of victimization from crime as well as commission of crime, are all data that reflect the demands and burdens of masculinity norms. Perhaps the saddest example of the burdens of privilege is the consensus among researchers of men and boys that social and cultural masculinity norms reinforce emotional limitations that play out lifelong in a lack of empathy and difficulties with intimate relationships including both friendships and partnerships, whether heterosexual or homosexual. The emotional life of men is stunted and limited, as a group. This is a price that affects every aspect of their well-being. It also, I suggest, has an impact on their leadership and perspective.

That privilege would be embraced with such a price exposes the strength and attraction of male privilege. The price paid becomes justification and entitlement. Would exposing the price change the dynamic? Certainly, it is indefensible to ignore the disadvantages and burdens of men; to do so would undermine the powerful equality claim of feminist theory. But it is equally indefensible to argue that men's priorities should come second because they are combined with privilege. In part this is because the price of masculinity is often intertwined with women's inequalities and the benefits conferred to the subordinate. This complex inequality dynamic is critical for feminists to explore, understand, and address. Simplistic either/or approaches (either women or men) or prioritizing inequalities (women are more unequal) move us away from comprehending that we need to understand the interactive nature of men's and women's inequalities and privileges.

3. Intersections of manhood particularly with race, class, and sexual orientation are critical to the interplay of privilege and disadvantage, to hierarchies among men, and to factors that may entirely trump male gender privilege. There are scholars who have urged us to pay attention to what happens at the intersections of critical characteristics, both when privilege is reinforced and when it is undermined (e.g., Ehrenreich 2002). Dismantling male privilege means understanding how it is constructed. Intersectionality suggests how men remain committed to and supportive of male privilege even when they do not benefit from the most favored male position. Hegemony importantly includes the concept that those who are subordinated may be complicit in the structure of hierarchy. Among men that pattern seems apparent at the intersections that create hierarchy among men. One of the most interesting patterns from men of color is the potential they open up for a different model or models of masculinity, while at the same time displaying a hypermasculinity in response to the denial of privilege. This might translate into a goal to achieve the power/privilege of a white man and only then turn to issues of gender equality with women. In the civil rights struggle, the sign claiming personhood reads "I Am a Man." It should not be read to suggest "give me the privileges of hegemonic masculinity, and then we can begin to talk about gender equality."

Just as significantly, the primacy of race in the masculinities hierarchy reinforces how patriarchy is racialized and how that plays out for men and women. The linkage across gender lines suggests that feminists should give greater attention to the place of race in the construction of gender and more generally embrace race as a feminist issue.

4. Masculinity is a social construction, not a biological given. This conclusion is widely held among masculinities scholars; it directly contradicts social mythology that reinforces gender essentialism and gender difference.

Masculinity is a set of practices that one constantly engages in or must perform; it is fluid, not fixed. This opens the hope that masculinity can change and that it is plural, not unitary. Historical analysis confirms that the concepts of masculinity have changed over time and thus can change again. But just as women experience their gender as powerful and fixed, so too do men experience their masculinity.

5. *Hegemonic masculinity recognizes that one masculinity norm dominates multiple masculinities.* Unlike the feminist norm of equality, albeit with much debate about what constitutes equality for women, hegemonic masculinity is a negative norm in relation to equality. The focus is on the negative mold rather than an alternative, egalitarian one. This may provide feminists with more ammunition to describe how this norm infuses cultural, social, and structural norms. It also suggests that there are alternative or subversive masculinities that might provide an alternative model or that would suggest opportunities for collaboration. As many masculinities scholars have pointed out, it is the rare man who meets the hegemonic masculinity standard. Indeed, it is part of the standard that the norm is one you must constantly demonstrate. This demanding, unstable position may open up opportunities even as it is depressingly strong, without as strong an egalitarian alternative. The dominance of this negative standard bears some similarity to the critique of the dominance of American or Western norms in feminist theory. To the extent that feminists have reflected on their own position and issues, there is a similar critique of the focus of masculinities on the concerns of the most privileged of men. So in identifying "problems," masculinities and feminist theory both err in viewing problems from the vantage of the most favored and from a globally insular perspective. But in identifying egalitarian goals or models, masculinities scholarship has much to learn from feminist scholarship to imagine egalitarian masculinities.

6. *The patriarchal dividend is the benefit that all men have from the dominance of men in the overall gender order.* Identifying and naming this dividend, and showing how it operates, has been a key goal of feminist theory, particularly as facial discrimination has largely disappeared and deeper structural and cultural discrimination continues to perpetuate patriarchy. The patriarchal dividend is so pervasive that it goes largely unnoticed; it is taken-for-granted oppression. Patriarchy has not collapsed; only the idea or acceptance of it has; men's predominance remains. While it is not equally enjoyed by all men, it is power that men as a group draw on. Even men who

reject this unearned benefit still have this advantage. Indeed, it is a challenge to articulate ways that the dividend can be rejected, as opposed to eliminating the dividend. One way of exploring the patriarchal dividend is to identify the daily examples of privilege.

7. *The two most common pieces defining masculinity are, at all costs, not to be like a woman and not to be gay.* A critical piece of masculinity is this negative definition, which is linked to issues of power and hierarchy (in addition to race and class). The rejection of things female, things associated with mothers, is lifelong. To admit weakness, to admit frailty or fragility, is to be seen as a wimp, a sissy, not a real man. The ultimate fear is to come up short in front of other men. There is much here connected to fear, shame, and emotional isolation. If these two pieces remain core to the definition of masculinity, then the ability to attack the hierarchy of men over women and of heterosexuals over homosexuals is fundamentally stalled. Subordination will be reworked but not destroyed. It seems critical to imagine or create a positive definition of what it means to be a man, but this simple goal seems strangely difficult and is largely ignored.

One of the most important potential places to look for alternatives is to explore in greater depth the masculinities of minority men and gay men. Minority men may provide a model, but it is a complicated one, since subversive masculinities are both resistant and complicit. That very complexity, however, may teach us much more than looking at hegemonic males. Focusing on males who are more at the margin of masculinities may be more revealing.

8. *Masculinity is as much about relation to other men as it is about relation to women.* The importance of this insight cannot be sufficiently underscored. Much of feminist theory has focused on women's relationship or comparison to men. Some feminists have pointed out that not all women are oppressed, or not all are oppressed equally, and also have identified examples of when women have oppressed other women. For example, the structure of work and family operates differently for women depending on where they work and their income; also women employ women to do domestic and care work and frequently overwork and underpay other women, as well as pay them insufficient benefits or neglect to ensure that they are able to balance work and family for their own families. Similarly, the relationship between white women and women of color has been a vexed one, less based on solidarity

than on distrust, which poses a challenge to collaborating to identify priorities and leads to the absence of race consciousness in the women's movement and feminist scholarship.

Masculinities scholarship points out similar dynamics, but there is also an underlying dynamic in masculinity that pits every man against every man. In addition to being challenged to meet a standard of masculinity that must continuously be performed, masculinity also is a process of comparison, of measuring, that puts each man against all others. This isolation and hierarchy is not, in general, a part of women's identity or collective action. To identify equality issues as solely focusing on male/female issues, then, misses this important piece of the equality puzzle. This is an important component of what makes men "male," especially in dominantly homosocial settings.

9. *Men, although powerful, feel powerless.* This insight of masculinities scholarship seems very strange and counterintuitive. Is this sense of powerlessness linked to denial of men's power? Or does it represent a form of backlash to women's gains? Or is it a central component to men's masculinity, linked to their constant measuring against other men and against the standard of masculinity, "The Big Impossible"? Whether false consciousness or real consciousness, this sense of powerlessness might explain the failure of men to be drawn by feminism or the difficulty of recruiting men to feminism, because feminism's core claim of male power does not ring true for men. It is a perception that is helpful for strategizing, although ultimately the data tend to undermine the reality of this view of things. But we have long recognized that irrationality sustains much of the unconscious as well as conscious thinking about inequalities of gender, as well as those of race, class, and sexual orientation. What may be most important is to understand that this conviction is real and stands in the way of changing consciousness of men about men and of women about men so that movement forward toward equality is possible.

10. *Masculinities study exposes how structures and cultures are gendered male.* Some of the most important work of masculinities scholarship is the strong support it provides for the feminist claim that structures, such as work, are gendered male. As Ann McGinley has suggested in the context of employment discrimination law (2004), the data and expertise of this scholarship may provide the expert testimony necessary to expose gendered cultures and structures of the workplace. In this area masculinities study has

the potential to supplement and support feminist theory in significant ways. Where this might lead is a richer debate over the vision of a truly egalitarian workplace, given that masculinities scholarship exposes not only the male imprint on work culture and structures but also the hierarchy among men within that male culture.

11. *The spaces and places that men and women daily inhabit and work within are remarkably different.* Related to the gendering of cultures and structures is the gendering of actual physical spaces. Masculinities scholars have explored a number of spaces that are male dominant, such as sports arenas and pubs. If you imagine the daily spaces where men and women function, they include a different range of spaces that we identify as male or female, as well as different spaces within locations that are gendered. Pediatrician's offices are female spaces, as are elementary school classrooms; sports fields and especially football stadiums are male spaces. Particular educational course areas and the work spaces for those areas, such as engineering and agriculture, are gendered male, while teaching and nursing are gendered female. If we followed the geography of daily life, and how spaces function, they are quite different for men and women as a whole. This different geography of life and places is important to explore, to determine how the environment (and thus areas such as zoning and planning) supports gender integration as well as gender separation and to determine the implications for equality. There are many places that are sex segregated, and we should identify them, as well as how segregation is carried out even within the appearance of integration. It would be a fascinating exercise to determine not only where men function and where women function but also how men and women interact within same-sex and mixed-sex environments.

12. *The role of men in achieving feminist goals is uncertain and unclear.* Can a man be a feminist? And if so, what would his goals be—to support feminism or to articulate goals for men that are distinctive as well as supportive of the equality project of feminism? This is a wonderful question to ask: why should men want to change? Judged from masculinities scholarship, men have little incentive to change because the pull of privilege is too great, while the pull of equality is solely moral and emotional. Changing men is far more difficult than changing women. One is opening up opportunities; the other is giving up power. The implication is that change will have to be pushed or taken; it is unlikely to be given or shared. As with the asymmetric position of masculinities to feminist theory, so too there is a difference in the relation-

ship of men and women to feminism. The most essential change for men is to imagine a different manhood, which has direct implications for the success of the feminist project. Men's most direct contribution to feminism is to focus on what masculinities scholarship exposes, while at the same time recognizing and supporting women's equality goals. There are parallels here to the relationship of whites to antiracism: their position should be one of support of the equality of people of color, while challenging the unearned skin privilege of whites. So too men can support, in the strongest possible way, women achieving equality while actively engaging in dismantling male privilege and exposing the harms of the gender hierarchy for men as well.

13. *The asymmetry of masculinities scholarship and feminist theory reflects the differences in the general position of men and women.* Masculinities scholarship is not, predominantly, about understanding and dismantling male power and privilege; instead, it is about understanding how male identity is constructed and sustained. Although this is not true of all scholars who study men, it does describe a great many, and dominant theory is much more descriptive than it is analytical or critical. At least one critic says this is not the right focus; instead of masculinity, scholars should refocus on men and men's dominance, not on the dominant form of masculinity. There are not many voices, however, talking about gender transformation or about how power is sustained. So what masculinities has to offer feminist theory, in general, is the enrichment, contextualization, and refinement of theory, as well as making men simply visible. What feminism has to offer masculinities theory, on the other hand, is a set of tools to address much more strongly inequality, subordination, and how to shift from power-over to power-with.

Implications for Feminist Theory

With these insights of masculinities scholarship in mind, the implications for feminist theory are a further refinement in analysis and methodology. I suggest how masculinities scholarship might be incorporated into feminist theory in the following series of questions and steps.

1. *Ask the "man question" in gender analysis.* Probably the most significant change in feminist theory suggested by masculinities scholarship is to include men in gender analysis by thinking about men differently. This would require asking the "man question" in gender analysis, just as the overarching question of feminist theory has been to ask questions about, and question on

behalf of, women. Asking the man question would include a number of more nuanced approaches to equality issues to benefit women, as well as making visible men's relationship to women's equality and men's unique issues of subordination, whether in relation to women or to one another.

Mari Matsuda is responsible in feminist theory and critical race theory for encouraging us to "ask the other question" (1993, 1189). When we tend to classify a particular situation or scenario as "a gender issue" or "a race issue," Matsuda encourages us to look for other forms of subordination that we might be missing, noting both how various inequalities reinforce each other and also that there is the opportunity in approaching things this way to open up opportunities for collaboration and a more robust strategy for equality. Angela Harris in a classic piece on race and gender (2000) used this same approach to ask how the Abner Louima case represented an issue not only of race subordination but also of gender subordination: how the means by which the police officers, all men, acted represented classic male subordination of another man, carried out in the hypermasculine world of police work as reinforced by a hypermasculine model of policing.

So, borrowing from Matsuda and Harris and building on their example, I suggest that asking the man question means asking the other (gender) question, the question about men, in any situation where we identify women's equality as the primary issue. We should ask, what about men or boys—are they also disadvantaged in this situation? For example, suppose that we focus on the issue of domestic violence, where women are the disproportionate victims and gender constructs play a role in the thinking of batterers. What happens when we ask the man question is that we expose situations in which men are victims but rarely report their victimization, the places where boys are direct victims or witness the victimization of others, and how boys frequently model as adults the very behavior that terrified them as children.

In addition, we might further refine the man question by asking whether all men or boys are similarly situated. We know from masculinities scholarship that frequently there are hierarchies among men and boys. So, in the domestic violence example, we might learn that men of color would be even more strongly dissuaded from using the available criminal justice remedies than would other men, and that gay men and gay youth are also likely to find the system unresponsive to their unique concerns.

A second way in which the man question should be asked is not asking the other question about potential victimization but rather asking the question of how male privilege actually functions in this situation. That is, rather than asking how men also might be subordinated, focus more closely on the process of privilege and subordination. Would masculinities scholarship help to unravel the dynamic, and does it suggest that the dynamic is differentiated among the range of masculinities? Again, using the example of domestic violence, masculinities scholarship links it to the role of violence in constructing masculinity, the suppression of emotional learning among boys and men and its link to relationship problems, the combination of greater egalitarianism and hypermasculinity among minority men, and the core construction of masculinity as being *not* female and *not* gay. Masculinities scholarship may help construct more effective interventions with batterers, and even more effective strategies of prevention as opposed to reaction.

Finally, asking the man question also should include exploring what price men pay, both when men are privileged and when they are disadvantaged. It is clear that those who are privileged may nevertheless frequently pay a price and that privilege reinforces the price paid and ongoing subordination of others. Even when men are disadvantaged, it often plays itself out as privilege. All of this helps us to understand how dominance works, to keep the dominant tied to gender hierarchy even when it is unconscious and taken for granted. In the arena of domestic violence, men's gender privilege is directly connected to the use of violence. The price of privilege is the destruction of relationships, of families, and of self. The link between this form of violence and others is direct and significant. The gendered nature of violence has a massive impact on boys and men who are victimized along with women. We lose sight of the patterns of gender-specific violence by naming it in a way that identifies women victims, making them visible, but continuing to render invisible male-on-male violence.

2. Including the man question does not mean shifting focus away from women; the reality is gender asymmetry. Including men means situating women within a more realistic picture of gender subordination, while acknowledging men's subordination in that picture. It is critical to resist the notion of either/or, of choosing either women or men, of equating the position of women and men and thereby feeding into the backlash characteristic of a significant portion of the men's movement. This is the danger of "we're all harmed" feeding into "we need now to shift the focus to men/boys," when the reality is asymmetry. There is not enough focus in masculinities theory on inequality; the danger is very real because women often disappear when we look at men. For example, critics of the educational system focus on how schools fail to serve boys and how schools undermine and even damage boys' emotional and intellectual development. The familiar claim of "boys are different" can reinforce traditional notions of gender difference and inequality. In addition, a justified focus on boys can too easily lead to a blaming of girls and to a belief that addressing the gender issues of girls is the culprit in failing to serve boys.

There is a very real difference in most gender areas in the position of women as a group and the position of men. Making men visible does not mean hiding women or claiming equal harm. This is simply a false dichotomy that must be resisted in favor of a comprehensive gender picture. Returning to the example of education, such a comprehensive picture would mean that both boys' issues and girls' issues should be considered, and imagining an educational system of gender equality would not necessarily be wedded to a singular model of success or assume that all boys and all girls learn in a particularly gendered way. It would also recognize how strongly schools are gendered, both formally and informally, and begin to address how that could be used positively to achieve gender equality.

3. Gender specificity is critical in order to achieve gender equality. If the man question in all its complexity is asked, and if the broader view of gender inequality is sustained rather than succumbing to simplistic gender prioritizing or balancing, then the next important piece is to incorporate the teaching of masculinities scholarship in strategies to achieve equality. Most importantly, there is considerable asymmetry in gender-specific goals. Although gender neutrality might be a useful goal in some situations, even neutrality might require specific strategies in order to achieve truly equal results. But to presume a single standard or a single and balanced strategy ignores the asymmetry revealed by adding masculinities scholarship to feminist theory. At the same time, and consistent with the argument that bringing men into gender analysis should not render women less important or visible, adopting gender-specific strategies requires connection between the gender-specific perspectives, rather than insularity.

An example of the importance of gender-specific strategies is balancing work and family, or our models of motherhood and fatherhood. For fathers, the dominance of the breadwinner role overshadows support for and the economic practicability of care. For mothers, social expectations and work expectations of family primacy undermine their role as workers and challenge the ability to parent in partnership or as a single caregiver and also to stay economically afloat. The stresses of work and family affect all parents, but typically they do so differently for mothers and fathers. A linking of mothers and fathers is essential to prevent the replication of a fixed role of parenthood defined by gender and to create a vision of equality based on multiple models of parenting without reinforcing traditional gender roles.

4. Masculinities theory reinforces central feminist positions, especially how patriarchy constructs and infuses institutions. Masculinities theory helps to make concrete the claim that structures and culture are "male." For example, an exploration of the juvenile justice system makes it clear that the system has assumed boys as the objects of the system and has assumed particular masculinities in understanding the predominance of boys in this system. This assumption affects boys to the extent that those constructions are inaccurate or grounded in hegemonic masculinities or stereotypes of the masculinities particularly of minority males. It also affects girls, because the system has not adjusted to the distinctive needs of girls.

Identifying how ideas of masculinity gender institutions or cultures may expose gender in the structure, but it does not necessarily provide a vision of an egalitarian structure or culture. Early feminist goals were geared toward allowing women to compete with men under the same rules. If those rules are biased toward socialization or skills identified as "male," then only those women able to perform those masculinities and to be accepted in their performance as equal to men can achieve equality. If "female" rules are simply added to the mix, then a dual system emerges that effectively perpetuates male power by identifying it with the preferred male track. It is not easy to identify a liberatory structure that does not constrain either men or women as we try to move toward equality while being attentive to our unequal context. Nevertheless, making the case more explicitly of the "male" structures is a contribution that masculinities scholarship can make and that feminists should embrace.

5. Masculinities scholarship reinforces the key principle of antiessentialism. The naming of the field as plural, "masculinities," is the simplest acknowledgment of antiessentialism. The critique of hegemonic masculinity as essentializing similarly reinforces the multiple natures of masculinities. At the same time, however, some work in the field is arguably even more essentialist than feminist theory. The struggle within both feminism and masculinities scholarship to incorporate antiessentialism may be a way to reinforce the importance of antiessentialism to gender analysis. Antiessentialism makes attention to perspective and who is included critical. Antiessentialism also points to those at the margin as having the potential for alternative models, as well as exposing the interplay of systems of subordination and privilege. The perspective of minority men reinforces once more why race should be a core feminist issue linking men and women. By that I mean, feminist theory should embrace antiracism as a core goal, just as feminists ask men to embrace being a feminist as a core goal.

More than adding race in methodologically or considering race in the construction of priorities, as the critique of antiessentialism demands, *the insights of masculinities scholarship reinforce the need to confront and challenge racial inequality and imagine a world of racial justice at the core of the feminist agenda.* Feminists should take on race unmodified. Racial equality should be integral to sexual equality because of the interconnectedness of race and sex identities and the use of race to police gender.

Taking on race presents an opportunity for coalition with men. Doing so requires seeing connections between men and women rather than opposition, and seeing how racial patriarchy operates. It challenges strategies, whether chosen from within or imposed from without, that separate equalities instead of combining them. Equalities would be reinforced, rather than pitted against each other.

6. Masculinities scholarship presents surprises or revelations about men that may have strategic or substantive implications. First, privilege comes with a price. But exposing that price does not create a movement toward change in the same way that exposing women's inequalities begs solutions and strategies. Men are willing to pay the price, and women have no sympathy because male privilege remains so visible and rectifying women's inequality seems so daunting by comparison. Second, many men have a sense of powerlessness, despite their privilege, which suggests we need to refine our understanding of power and subordination, particularly how this sense of powerlessness reinforces and perpetuates male power when manhood is defined in terms of power and hierarchy.

Third, the research on boys suggests that intervening early is essential to gender change. Men's lack of empathy, and lack of emotional literacy, has been linked to childrearing patterns that are reinforced particularly by educational structures. This lack of empathy poses a significant barrier to men's relational engagement and collaboration. This seems to be so not only at an individual level but also in the drive to create stronger social commitments to equality. Changing our patterns of socialization and nurture is an extremely challenging task, yet the strong commitment of many fathers to involvement with their children presents an incredible opportunity to benefit children, fathers, and mothers.

7. The need to create a new model of masculinity seems obvious, yet it is incredibly difficult to achieve. The chance for collaboration between women and men, and the value of collaboration, seems obvious, and yet it also still seems unlikely. This conundrum demands more investigation and thought. It also demands good strategic thinking about what issues and strategies might generate the best possibility for collaboration.

With these insights in mind, how might a masculinities analysis actually work? In the following chapters, I consider how masculinities analysis might be applied to concrete issues. I look at boys and men in several contexts, though I do not mean to limit masculinities analysis to male subjects, just as feminist analysis has never been inherently limited to engaging only in the inequalities of women. My focus on boys and men instead is meant to suggest what we may have missed and how in each of these areas boys' and men's inequalities inevitably link back to girls and women. It exposes what masculinities scholarship can bring to feminist theory and, more importantly, to the pursuit of justice.

Part II

Boys

Boys and men are gendered beings, functioning within culture, structures, and institutions that are infused with masculinities norms. As feminists have long argued and explored, as a group men have disproportionate power and privilege over women. Masculinities analysis, as suggested in part 1, adds to that analysis by further unraveling how male power and dominance, as a group, is sustained. Masculinities analysis also suggests how boys and men can nevertheless be unequal and/or subordinated as part of dominance, how they can be rendered invisible and hidden even as they define dominant norms. In parts 2 and 3, focusing first on boys and then on men, I take the insights of feminist analysis infused with masculinities scholarship and apply that enriched feminist approach to areas where boys and men are negatively affected by gender. In this part, I examine boys in the contexts of education and juvenile justice. Education is an area where there has been considerable attention to the "crisis" of boys, who are doing poorly compared to girls on many measures. At the same time, much of this debate is essentialist and hierarchical. Although focused on boys, it has not focused on gender as a factor in boys' performance or the structure and culture of education. Examining the position of boys in education also exposes the danger of treating gender analysis as a zero-sum game, where attention to boys means relegating girls to a secondary position. The "either/or" tendency in this area must be combated with "both/and" strategies.

Juvenile justice presents a different context. Here boys are not coequal in the system; rather, boys are the primary focus of the system. Boys predominate at every stage, and the system was created with them in mind. Although explicit in its inception, in its contemporary form the gender of the system has been largely unexamined. Oddly enough, although the system is presumed by all to be about boys, gender is rarely discussed. There are parallels to this strange absence of gender talk in systems disproportionately filled by women—most notably, in discourse about the welfare system. This results in a kind of "doublespeak" where welfare "recipients" are always coded female (and usually, as black females). Similarly, juvenile "offenders" or simply "juveniles" are coded male (and usually, as black males). Unexamined gender policies, strongly raced, are characteristic of both. Policy reinforces, in the case of juvenile justice, a hypermasculine norm, to the detriment of boys who intersect with the juvenile justice system. This male-specific norm also harms, in a different way, the increasing number of girls who come into the juvenile justice system.

These two examples suggest how feminist analysis, infused with masculinities analysis, might expose the more complex workings of gender in structures and cultures and suggest solutions that support gender equality for both boys and girls. The analysis here is suggestive and preliminary rather than comprehensive. At the same time, it clearly shows how masculinities analysis can serve the goal of exposing gender subordination while still clarifying the gender-specific ways that subordination plays out. Finally, it ensures that boys can be the focus, and should be the focus, of gender equality efforts in addition to girls, rather than as rivals for an equality constructed as being a choice between one or the other.

5

Boys and Education

Masculinities affect boys as they move through the educational process in a number of ways. The evidence that boys as a group are doing poorly in comparison to girls as a group includes lower grades, being held back more, a higher dropout rate, lower test scores, more behavior problems, more suspensions, more failure, and a lower likelihood of attending college. Boys are also disproportionately diagnosed with learning disorders, particularly ADD and ADHD, and show up more frequently in special education classes.

The dialogue about why this is so frequently is antifeminist and antigirl. It is said that girls and women have been overly assisted as a result of the feminist critique of education and that efforts to correct girls' disadvantage have tilted the system against boys. The concern about boys and education dovetails with a more general concern about the "crisis" of boys and men as a result of feminist progress.

A more sophisticated analysis, according to the critics, reveals several things. Most significantly, the differences *among* girls and boys are far more striking and significant than the differences *between* them. The disadvantages of boys are disadvantages only for some boys, not for all boys. A more balanced view of gender and education is that girls are advantaged or do better in some areas, boys in others. What has changed in the past few decades is the removal of barriers that held girls back, so that their achievement is now more related to their actual effort.

As the data on boys and education is unpacked, what emerges is a complex picture, because external factors play such a huge role in gender and education, including familial socialization and gender norms. It is here that masculinities scholarship has much to offer from a developmental perspective, as well as in exposing the social and structural dynamics of school. Boys' underachievement seems particularly linked to pervasive social norms that dictate that doing well in school is *not* a desired part of masculinity.

Education is one of those areas where the benefit of incorporating masculinities scholarship into feminist analysis is very clear but also very challenging. It demonstrates the potential for masculinities work, while also illustrating the dangers. Most importantly, masculinities analysis reveals the complexity of the gendered nature of education and the need to approach education issues from a carefully nuanced analysis that does not buy into "either/or" analysis but rather expands gender analysis to include boys and men.

History

Concerns about gender and education historically have focused exclusively on boys. John Locke, for example, worried about boys' lack of achievement in the 1600s (Frank et al. 2003; Locke 1692). In colonial New England, only boys were educated, and there was significant resistance to educating girls (Lesko 2000). If boys failed to achieve, the system was viewed as failing them (M. Cohen 1998). Boys were assumed to have sufficient ability, so if they failed, blame was placed on external factors. Girls, on the other hand, historically were assumed incapable of being educated because they were not intellectually the equal of boys (Frank et al. 2003). If they failed, it was due to their inherent, essential nature.

Contemporary concern about girls and education emerged with the feminist movement in the 1970s and 1980s, peaking in the mid-1990s with studies documenting how girls were cheated of classroom time and respect as compared to boys (Lesko 2000). Title IX was enacted to remedy gender inequality in education in 1972 (20 U.S.C. 1681 [2000]). Following on the heels of this focus on girls, a focus on boys emerged in the mid- to late 1990s (Weaver-Hightower 2003; see also Connell 2000b). This "boy turn" was highlighted in several best-selling works that claimed a "crisis" in boys' education (Weaver-Hightower 2003).

The sense of crisis for boys is tied to a sobering set of statistics that indicates how education fails boys. The data include lower grades, a higher rate of being held back a grade, a higher dropout rate, lower test scores, more frequent behavior problems, a disproportionate representation in the pool of students labeled learning disabled and emotionally disturbed, a higher rate of suspension, a higher rate of suicide, a greater likelihood of inflicting or being victimized by physical violence, and being less likely to attend college (Kimmel and Traver 2005). The boy crisis is also linked to concerns about violence, including bullying, harassment, homophobia, and the most dramatic instances of violence at schools, school shootings (Frank et al. 2003).

One of the strongest persisting concerns is about achievement differences. There is an international gender gap that favors girls (Francis and Skelton 2005; U.S. Department of Education 2004). But this simplistic statement hides more than it reveals. First, the differentiation overall is strongly linked to girls' better performance in language and literacy (Francis and Skelton 2005). Boys do better at math, while the genders are about equal in science. Second, researchers have noted that this is not generalized, that is, certain boys are disadvantaged, and that disadvantage is linked to class and race (ibid.). Third, the achievement data are questioned as a real measure of educational outcomes. Testing is a very narrow view of "achievement." Moreover, school tests and grades do not correlate to real-world outcomes: boys and men still do better in the workplace than girls and women do (ibid.). In this sense the gap can be questioned as to its significance: is it a difference that does not make a difference, because boys' underachievement has no market consequence? Clearly there are arguments that outcomes other than market outcomes are important; most significantly, the literacy gap may have an impact on relationship capabilities and the quality of life (ibid.). Achievement data demonstrate that both girls and boys are disadvantaged at school but that the disadvantages are different (Jenkins 2006). Thus attending to one group while ignoring the other is a poor strategy. In addition, selecting a strategy without attending to these differences can lead to unintended results.

There is no consensus on the cause for the achievement patterns. Explanations that have been offered include natural differences, learning style differences, the feminization of schools, biased assessment, and the impact of student behavior, including the construction of masculinity, on achievement (Francis and Skelton 2005). Several high-profile critics in popular works have articulated the view that boys are in crisis and blame girls and feminists, or they have reinscribed an essentialist portrait of boys. Christina Hoff Sommers's scathing critique (2000) targets both feminists and masculinities scholars. According to Sommers, nothing is wrong with boys; they are simply different from girls and need "discipline, respect, and moral guidance. . . . They do not need to be pathologized" (14–15). William Pollack, on the other hand, claims that boys have been harmed by a "boy code" that suppresses their emotional growth, and that code is reinforced strongly by schools (2006). Michael Gurian, based on brain research, argues that boys and girls are different and that schools need to be structured in ways that take those differences into account, so that education would be gender based (Gurian and Henley 2001; Gurian and Stevens 2005). For example, he presents research data on boys' vulnerability, based on neural fragility, and links that to a higher rate of learning and behavioral disabilities (Gurian and Stevens 2005). Gurian advocates strategies based on male learning styles in order to help boys (Gurian and Henley 2001; Gurian and Stevens 2005). These include both whole-school and within-classroom strategies in coed and single-sex schools. Gurian views the educational system as needing a corrective phase to help boys, following on an era that has focused on girls.

Constructing the issues of boys and education as a "crisis" is itself problematic. One pair of scholars characterizes the discourse about boys as one that distinguishes between "problem boys" and "at risk boys" (Francis and Skelton 2005). "'Problem boys' are a threat *to* society; 'at risk' boys are made vulnerable *by* society when [society] fails to tackle (traditional) forms of masculinity" (52). Another group of researchers characterizes the "crisis" discourse as the "poor boys" discourse versus the "boys will be boys" discourse (Epstein et al. 1998b). "The first is a backlash to feminism; failing schools fail boys; and the biological model often is taken as boys are showing their superior intellect by failing at schools" (6). The ultimate irony, according to these researchers, is that boys and girls are more alike than different: that is, while there are differences in specific subjects and levels, if you looked for overlap or similarities, those are present to an equal or greater degree.

"Boys will be boys" is a particularly common expression that translates into policy that fails to assess boys critically, or to assess the impact of boys on girls—the impact of a limited, negative masculinity—by "biologizing" boys as simply incapable of change (Dalley-Trim 2006). Masculinities scholars argue that we should recognize that boys in fact construct their masculinity: "Boys, in constructing themselves as identifiable masculine subjects, use a sophisticated repertoire of performance practices and draw upon a range of complex discourses of gender and, more specifically masculinity" (ibid., 32). Not only does boys' masculinity operate in opposition to academic achievement, but it also includes practices of harassment of girls.

Masculinities research has exposed how the structure, culture, and norms of education are gendered, as well as how boys negotiate this gendered environment in the context of social expectations of what it means to be a boy. Scholars have exposed how education is an institution and culture where masculinity is reproduced in a multitude of ways (Martino 2003; Thorne 1993; Weaver-Hightower 2003). These include "systems of management, instruments of discipline, institutional values and rituals, tracking and failure, patterns of authority, academic curriculum, definitions of knowledge, 'style,' normative concepts of reason, rationality and rigor; distinctive control/release of bodies and emotions; race and ethnicity; definitions of good teaching; patterns of talk; public performances of teaching, bullying and harassment; compulsory heterosexuality and homophobia; sports and other extracurriculars; and distinctive uses of space and time" (Lesko 2000, xxi; see also Frank et al. 2003).

The barriers to learning are multiple and complex (Murphy and Elwood 1998; G. Wilson 2006). Teachers are often complicit in constructing a culture that supports traditional, hegemonic masculinities, and male teachers in particular often feel compelled to construct themselves within that model to establish their legitimacy amid a culture that devalues learning as feminine (King 2000; Martino and Frank 2006). Teaching is thus feminized by men, rather than vice versa (Martino and Frank 2006). The express curriculum is infused with traditional masculine norms (Kuzmic 2000). Masculinities scholarship can have a significant impact on literacy strategies (Martino 2003) and may challenge the need to devise creative strategies such as using technologies or expanding the scope of what is read to include more of what appeals to boys (Newkirk 2002; Swann 1998; Young 2001). The hidden curriculum is not simply a matter of unrepresented female figures as opposed to male figures, but it is also the characterization of males and females with traditional, gender-stereotypic traits (Evans and Davies 2000). Space is another fascinating facet of this issue: masculinities are expressed by the physical space occupied by boys in classrooms and on playgrounds, as well as by the domination of space in the sense of discussion and dialogues (Nespor 2000).

One of the most critical pieces to the construction of masculinity that has an impact on boys' achievement is that achieving the most valued hegemonic masculine role dictates the importance of *not* working hard in order to be "cool" (Epstein 1998; Phoenix 2003). To be viewed as sufficiently masculine, boys must not be seen as working too hard at schoolwork, so boys are not "free" simply to achieve at school without great social cost. This valued norm is strongly reinforced in a number of ways, and it is even more strongly enforced by race. First, boys are more strongly gender policed than are girls (Mac an Ghaill 1994, Pascoe 2007; Stoudt 2006). The policing comes dominantly from peers, although not exclusively so (Dalley-Trim 2007; Young and Sweeting 2004). Much policing is done by labeling deviance as being "gay" or a "fag" (Jackson 1998; Mandel and Shakeshaft 2000; Pascoe 2007). "The form of heterosexism we are seeing is misogynistic, where boys exert (exploit) their masculinity in ways that are antifemale and homophobic and where girls both exploit and down-play their femininity largely to attract attention from boys" (Mandel and Shakeshaft 2000, 75). In adolescence in particular, gender identity is constructed in relation to gender roles and stereotypes that are highly traditional (ibid.). Homophobia is especially virulent and is an everyday part of life at school (Crozier 2001; Frank et al. 2003). Calling someone gay or a fag is not simply used to identify sexual identity or orientation; rather, more commonly it is used by boys against other boys as a policing mechanism. It reinforces a heterosexual norm as well as an anti-achievement norm as part of conforming to the preferred masculinity.

A second way the dominant masculinity is reinforced is by the social hierarchy within school. The top of the social hierarchy remains the jocks. Sport is so important that even those boys who are not jocks construct their identity by some relationship to this preferred masculinity norm (Pascoe 2003). Another key to conforming to the norm is violence. The connection between masculinity and violence is strong, and this connection is frequently part of the hidden curriculum of school (Mills 2001). Bullying, punking, and harassment are everyday practices in boys lives, intended to marginalize the victim, whether another boy or a girl (Katz 2000; Phillips 2007; Weaver-Hightower 2003). Power over others is critical, and that power can be exercised by explicit violence or even just the threat of violence (Mills 2001). Power over women is seldom exercised by hitting, but rather by other forms of coercion. This includes the dominance of space and creating fear by harassment and the implied threat of sexual violence (ibid.).

Masculinities scholars have been particularly concerned about how focusing on boys can serve to reinforce privilege rather than to achieve equality. This is a key facet of analysis because it exposes how easily legitimate subordination concerns can be hijacked to serve only to reinscribe privilege and limit boys. For example, Kimmel and Traver (2005) expose how mentoring as a strategy (and the closely linked idea of role models, leading to a push for more male teachers) frequently reinstates traditional masculinity. That is, mentoring programs such as Big Brothers aim to provide a male mentor who is typically characterized as having the characteristics, and providing the education, training, or model, of traditional, dominant, or hegemonic masculinity. Although mentoring in theory could present an alternative masculinity model, in reality most mentoring programs are centered around a very traditional masculine model.

Even more significantly, a focus on boys can displace a focus on race and class. Not all boys are disadvantaged. Many scholars argue passionately that class and race are far more significant in the differentiation of outcomes in school (Jackson 1998; Kimmel and Traver 2005; Martino 2003; J. Smith 2007; Tsolidis and Dobson 2006; Warrington and Younger 2006; Weaver-

Hightower 2003). Every educational indicator for black boys is more strongly negative than that for boys as a whole, and race, whether for boys or girls, is a far more powerful indicator of educational disadvantage and bias than is gender (Kozol 2005; Orfield 2004). Thus a gender focus can unintentionally but very powerfully move attention away from race. Interestingly, one strategy of resistance to *Brown v. Board of Education* was a call for single-sex education—instead of Jim Crow, Jane Crow (Mayeri 2006). Single-sex education was proposed to prevent black boys and white girls from being educated together. "Sex segregation struck many observers as the perfect answer to fears that racial integration would lead inexorably to social intimacy and, ultimately, to interracial marriage and the horrors of 'amalgamation' or 'mongrelization'" (ibid., 189). The goal was epitomized by a Florida newspaper headline announcing enactment of the state's sex-segregation bill: "Segregation by Sex: Florida School Bill Seeks to Bar Racial Intermarriage" (ibid., 199–200). Ironically, sex segregation as a response to integration was also perceived as necessary to help boys.

One of the race/gender intersections that one scholar has noted is that it is predominantly white women who teach most children in pubic schools (P. Smith 1999a). This potential source of bias has largely been unaddressed. "Black boys face systemic discrimination in every interaction that they have with the school system. The silence surrounding the possibility or the reality that white women could be the primary or contributing victimizers of these children has gone unrecognized" (ibid., 118). The interaction of these teachers with white girls and black boys is very different: recognition and mirroring for white girls, difference and dissonance for black boys (ibid.). And as several masculinities scholars have emphasized, it is critically important that black masculinities not be essentialized into a single masculinity in understanding race and education, and the same is true for other racial or ethnic minorities (Martino and Pallotta-Chiarolli 2003; Sewell 1998).

Framing equity as attending to boys *and* girls, rather than taking an either/or approach grounded in a simplistic binary view of gender, is part of an analysis that links the construction of masculinity to the overall gender order and the impossibility of attending to gender by focusing only on boys or on girls (Jackson 1998; Mahoney 1998). "Policy formation and curriculum development in schools must avoid the populance tendency to assert a binary oppositional and 'competing victims' perspective on the factors impacting on the social and educational experiences of boys and girls" (Martino and Meyenn 2001a, xii). Otherwise, not only will issues be overlooked, but they may also be viewed from a limited perspective, such as limiting violence issues to those experienced between boys rather than linking those issues to violence toward girls as well (Mahoney 1998).

The tricky path that needs to be taken in the area of education may perhaps be exemplified by the debate over single-sex schools and the underutilized potential of Title IX. These two areas also suggest, however, how the consideration of gender and education could be reoriented and enriched by infusing feminist or gender analysis with masculinities scholarship.

The debate over single-sex education is typically framed as advocating for the availability of single-sex classrooms or schools as a means to counter educational bias against girls, versus the argument that sex segregation, like race segregation, inherently stigmatizes (Levit 2005; Pinzler 2004–5; Salomone 2004). Thus despite its gender-neutral name, single-sex education is widely understood as a strategy for girls. In 2001, when Congress passed the No Child Left Behind Act (20 U.S.C. 6301), part of the legislation made it clear that under Title IX, single-sex education was permissible and would not violate the prohibition of sex discrimination in educational programs receiving federal funding (Chalk Talk 2003). The legitimacy and advisability of single-sex strategies has been revived with the focus on boys' educational difficulties (Heise 2004; Kisthardt 2007). The tendency of some advocates is to see girls and boys as being in equivalent, though different, positions, and thus separation might best serve their different needs. Others, however, point out that the differences in the challenges and the gender dynamic are significant and would counsel against the idea of equivalency. "At its best, single-sex education can be an effective tool of empowerment and self-realization for some girls and boys. . . . At its worst, and as history has proven, single-sex schooling can unwittingly become a tool of gender polarization and oppression, perpetuating stereotypical images that produce feelings of inadequacy among girls while reinforcing exclusionary and sexist attitudes among boys" (Salomone 2004, 93–94). Many critics argue that the available data do not strongly support the efficacy of this structure for girls, the chief intended beneficiary, and even less would it benefit boys, although there appears to be some benefit for minority boys. "While some researchers have found that single-sex education may have some advantages for minority-race boys, the general consensus is that males do not flourish in single-sex environments. Providing separate classes for boys is either a neutral or negative along dimensions of socialization and academic quality. For both sexes, but particularly for boys, placement in sex-segregated classes is associated with the development of attitudes that favor traditional, even stereotypic, views of gender roles" (Levit 2005, 486). Within the debate on single-sex education is an implicit recognition of the impact of culture on learning and of gender norms as a significant factor for students and teachers. The further infusion of masculinities scholarship exposes both how that affects girls and also how it affects and limits boys.

Title IX is a critical part of the debate about single-sex education, and more generally it is the logical statutory framework for analysis and reform to achieve gender equality for both girls and boys. Title IX is framed broadly to prohibit sex discrimination in programs or activities receiving federal funding, and because of its broad interpretation, it affects education at all levels. Yet the bulk of the focus of Title IX, and the areas in which it has had the most impact, are athletics and sexual harassment (Brake 2007; Conn 2005; Pieronek 2005; Ryan 2008). The statute has not been used to focus on academics or pedagogy, or even more broadly school culture (beyond harassment) (Davies and Bohon 2007; Pieronek 2005). "What Title IX has achieved on the playing field remains undone in the classroom" (Pieronek 2005, 303). According to one scholar, the lack of attention to these issues may in part be linked to "a lack of awareness that Title IX covers academics" (ibid., 332).

The irony of this powerful statute being so incredibly limited means it fails to address some of the most intractable and difficult, and well-documented, examples of persisting gender bias for both girls and boys. Feminist analysis, infused with masculinities analysis, focusing on the subordination of both boys and girls, might provide a means for a redefinition and reinvigoration of the statute. It is important to remember that such an approach does not mean seeing gender-specific problems as equal but rather seeing them as connected and intersectional, and this approach must guard against, as in all areas involving gender analysis, reinscribing privilege. Translating the insights of masculinities and feminist analysis into concrete change is by no means easy, since it requires strategies to address both the explicit and hidden curriculums, as well as other cultural and structural components of gender bias. The statute, however, provides an existing framework capable of being used to implement far more radical change than that for which it has thus far been used.

In addition, gender analysis in education must be race conscious. Masculinities analysis should lead us to embrace race as a feminist issue because boys' failings in education are so strongly classed and raced. Masculinities scholars have consistently pointed out that the inequalities faced by boys are far surpassed by racial inequalities. The danger of gender analysis can be to deflect attention from race. Instead, it should shine further light on this issue. Educational equality remains a glaring problem fifty years after *Brown v. Board of Education* (1954). Race inequality profoundly affects the ability to achieve economic equality. Making race central to educational issues requires focusing on racial needs.

To the extent that affirmative action has succeeded, it would appear that it has succeeded more fully on the basis of gender than on the basis of race. There is the fearful prospect, then, that progress along gender lines is at the expense of racial progress or that racial progress is along gender lines, for example, benefiting women of color more than men of color. It is incumbent on those who have benefited from gender progress to make this point and to commit to racial equality as central.

The Supreme Court's recent endorsement of affirmative action with diversity as a compelling state interest opens up the content of diversity and challenges feminists to put race first, at the center, of educational equity. Race would be prioritized in this strategy, but in a way that addresses the issues of women of color and men of color differently to the extent that gender differences must be taken into account to achieve race equality. Putting race at the center, and meaningfully addressing race inequality, would inevitably have a positive impact on gender equality. In addition, constructing an egalitarian curriculum and educational structure suggests a model of collaboration among all those groups that have sought equality, but with the recognition that racial inequality threatens all other equality goals and that therefore racial equality is the core of educational equality.

Implications of Masculinities Scholarship

Masculinities scholarship on the psychology of boys, and on boys and education, provides powerful insights into the privileges and disadvantages of boys in education. The dialogue about boys and education exposes the potential pitfalls and dangers, but also the promise, of incorporating masculinities work into gender analysis. Boys have been deemed in crisis, the object of a gender war in which girls and women have dominated, and thus in need of protection and resistance to the feminization of education. But the reality is that there are both advantages and disadvantages in education for girls and boys. A more refined look at the data indicates this more complex pattern and how the two interrelate.

Feminists have understandably fought and continue to fight for equality for girls in education (American Association of University Women 1992; Pipher 1994; Sadker and Sadker 1994). Internationally, "girls' education [is] the single development intervention with the greatest individual and social returns" (Wible 2005, 513). Feminists have succeeded in removing formal barriers and attending to specific areas of need, such as math and science. Implicit in this model is comparing girls to boys and assuring that girls are not held back from learning due to structure or cultural norms. But ironically, some of that emphasis on achievement, especially measuring by test scores, has come back to haunt advocates as others argue that boys now are disadvantaged, using those very tests as their measure. In addition, measuring by simply comparing all girls and all boys hides significant variations among girls and boys that cross gender, especially by class and race. Finally, comparison to one group often leaves norms and structures unchallenged.

Masculinities research can be used to expose the complexity and, most significantly, to expose the masculinities present in boys' construction of identity, in teachers, in curriculum, in school culture, and in our standards of what the goals of education are. This uncovering of masculinities is critical for both girls and boys. Approaching this analysis not as a zero-sum game but as a comprehensive strategy to benefit both girls and boys is also important. Education might then be a place where gender-specific strategies are developed as gender-connected, a necessary and critical model for change. This is clearly the lesson of pulling apart the "boy turn" and "crisis" focus of the popular and scholarly discourse on boys and education. Adding men should not mean displacing women, and it requires a willingness to consider the position of the dominant gender group while demanding that the dominant group acknowledge and commit to the achievement of liberation and justice for women while raising men's and boys' issues. Masculinities research also points to class and race as equal, if not more significant, questions to be asked. In other words, asking the man question leads to asking the other questions of class and race. In this way, feminist analysis, infused by masculinities scholarship, might lead or contribute to making race and class feminist issues.

6

Boys and Juvenile Justice

Unlike the contemporary education system, which is expressly gender neutral, the juvenile justice system is a gender-specific system designed to manage, control, and respond to boys. Although girls are in the system, boys are the overwhelming subjects. In this, the juvenile justice system mirrors the gender composition of the adult prison population. The juvenile justice system reflects and operates on assumptions about masculinities and reflects masculinities norms. Yet we rarely think about or discuss this system as a gendered system. Rather, we simply assume it.

Where the sexes are asymmetrically represented, it is critical to consider gender analysis, of both the over- and underrepresented group. The evaluation of the juvenile justice system from a masculinities perspective exposes its gendered core and the implications of that for boys and girls. There has been some concern, as girls have become an increasing proportion of offenders, that they are disserved by the system because it was not designed for them. Oddly, however, this insight has not led to an examination of how the system *is* gendered for boys, why boys are its primary subjects, and the impact of this gendered structure and culture on boys.

Overview of the Juvenile Justice System

The juvenile justice system deals overwhelmingly with boys. Most of juvenile crime involves boys (Barnickol 2000). In 2006, boys constituted 70 percent of all arrests; in 2004, they were 75 percent of those prosecuted; in 2003, they were 85 percent of those in residential placement, and they stayed almost twice as long in those placements as compared to girls (U.S. Department of Health and Human Services 2008). Between 1994 and 2004 there was a 21 percent increase in the number of youth held in adult jails; almost all of that increase represented male offenders (ibid.). But those within the system represent only a fraction of the offenses committed by juveniles: many juveniles break the law as they are growing up, but only a fraction are arrested and adjudicated, and they often are not held accountable for all of their lawbreaking. Self-reporting indicates that lawbreaking behavior is common but dissipates through adolescence (Snyder and Sickmund 2006).

Girls are not absent from the system: they represent one in four arrests. But their offense pattern is different, with offenses focused on sexuality and disobedience to parents, and therefore they are disproportionately charged with status offenses (MacDonald and Chesney-Lind 2001). When they are convicted of status offenses, they are more harshly treated that boys. In addition, if girls move deeper into the system, they are more harshly sanctioned than boys (ibid.; see also American Bar Association and National Bar Association 2001).

Although the media often focuses on violent crimes when committed by juveniles, the bulk of criminal cases are crimes against property (larceny, vandalism, and motor-vehicle theft) (Snyder 1999). Overall, the juvenile crime rate is falling, especially the violent crime rate. Juveniles were involved in one-quarter of all violent victimizations not including murder over the past twenty-five years (PBS Frontline website 2009a). Children are both victims and perpetrators in crimes. On a daily basis, 9 children are homicide victims; 20 die from firearms; 4,000 are arrested, 180 for violent crimes and 367 for drug offenses, and 17,000 are suspended from school (Dowd 2006). Children are more at risk for victimization than any other group. Children ages twelve to nineteen are victims in three out of ten crimes, one in four thefts. Gun-related deaths are the leading cause of death of African American and Hispanic youth under eighteen (ibid.).

Juvenile courts were created roughly a century ago. Their creation reflected a core understanding: children are different from adults, and their cases should be handled differently (Coupet 2000; Feld 1999, 2007; S. Fox 1996). Female reformers argued for a system infused with maternalism, a system that would fulfill mothers' role of guiding children toward adulthood (Clapp 1998). Male judges and court personnel often saw the courts as replacing fathers, with a goal of instilling character and traditional masculine values (Clapp 1998; Rose 2002). But the object of the system for both women and men involved in the creation of juvenile courts was boys, particularly urban, working-class boys (Meis-Knupfer 2001; Myers 2005). This initial focus on class, an explicit effort to change "other" boys, over time became a thinly veiled focus on race. "At its inception, [reformers] attempted to assimilate and 'Americanize' the children of southern and eastern European immigrants pouring into industrial cities of the East and Midwest. A century later, one of juvenile courts' primary missions is to control young black males"

(Feld 2007, 189). Gender, ethnicity, and race therefore have deep history in the juvenile justice system, although explicitly contemporary courts are gender, race, and class neutral.

The juvenile justice system has sustained its distinctiveness from adult criminal justice in theory and practice. Despite procedural due process rights similar to, although not identical to, those of adult criminal defendants (*In re Gault* 1967; *In re Winship* 1970; *Kent v. United States* 1966; *McKeiver v. Pennsylvania* 1971; see generally Fondacaro, Slobogin, and Cross 2006), the process and administration of cases is quite different from the adult criminal justice system, with a high degree of discretionary, subjective judgments at each phase of the system. In addition, even the mandated due process requirements are often not present (Bookser 2004). The process begins with referrals, primarily from law enforcement agencies but also including social service agencies, schools, parents, probation officers, and victims. After arrest, roughly one-third of the juveniles are diverted (that is, they agree to enter a program to address their underlying problem, such as drug education); of the remaining juveniles, half become the subject of a petition to the court, and the other half are dismissed, diverted, or handled informally through voluntary agreement or informal probation. Thus, at this early stage, subjective factors come into play regarding the direction or resolution of a case. Nearly 60 percent of the juveniles who enter the juvenile justice system never return a second time, but of those who do, each reappearance increases the rate of recidivism (Snyder 1996). Once the juvenile is the subject of a petition, or even if he or she is diverted, the system in theory should treat the juvenile in an individualized and rehabilitative manner. These goals reflect the recognized differences between children and adults, particularly the differences in culpability and the potential for rehabilitation.

The goal of the juvenile justice system, however, has shifted away from rehabilitation since the 1990s. Concerns and fears about juvenile crime, juvenile violence, and "superpredators" led to various "reforms" to shift cases from the perceived "lenient" juvenile justice system to adult court (Feld 2007; Mallett 2007). The trend is encapsulated in the phrase "adult time for adult crime." States enacted legislation making it easier for prosecutors to try children as adults in adult criminal court. Since 1992, all but one state has enacted laws making it easier to permit transfers, which now account for roughly two hundred thousand transfers annually (Mallett 2007). Critics have pointed out that transfer has not achieved any increase in public safety or youth accountability (Fagan 2002, 2008; Fagan and Zimring 2000; Shepherd 2008). Data show an increase in recidivism, and adult prisons focus on punishment rather than rehabilitation. They also lack treatment for mental health, substance abuse, or special education issues and put youth at risk for being assaulted, especially sexually, while in prison. Because of the lack of empirical support for the practice of transferring youth from the juvenile to adult system, and because this practice is contrary to a wealth of developmental data, some critics argue that this practice should be deemed unconstitutional (Fagan 2002; Mallett 2007).

The punitive trend in juvenile justice at its extreme has led to sentencing teenagers to life in prison, or as critics call it, "death in prison," since these sentences are without the possibility of parole. The Equal Justice Initiative issued a report in 2007 documenting seventy-three cases of thirteen- and fourteen-year-olds with sentences of life in prison without parole. As this book goes to press, the U.S. Supreme Court has granted review of two Florida cases involving these sentences. The rate of such sentences has increased three times over the past fifteen years. The United States is the only country in the world known to punish youth with such a sentence (ibid.).

At the same time that transfer to adult court increased, the "get tough" mentality also resulted in an increase of arrests and more serious consequences within the juvenile justice system. As the Annie E. Casey Foundation reported in 2008, the system became transformed into one characterized by bias, disparities, and harshness. Of the kids who entered the system, 40 percent were status offenders, and more kids were arrested in school settings based on "zero tolerance" school policies adopted in the 1990s. Punitive policies became dominant, with no better, and arguably worse, outcomes. "Tragically, virtually all of these 'get tough' practices violate what we know about youth development and behavior, and all are producing worse, rather than better, outcomes for youth, communities and taxpayers" (Annie E. Casey Foundation 2008, 4). The Casey report identifies six deficiencies in the system: blurring or ignoring differences between adults and juveniles; increasing incarceration, which is costly and ineffective; ignoring the role of families as positive agents for change; prosecuting with increasing propensity minor cases rather than diverting them or resolving them informally; failing to serve kids who need different kinds of help, such as assistance with mental health or learning disabilities; and continuing severe patterns of disproportionate minority involvement in the juvenile justice system. Other critics of the system have suggested a range of reform models, including restorative or therapeutic justice, unified family court, or eliminating the separation between delinquency and adult criminal justice (Coupet 2000; Danziger 2003; Feld 1999; Krisberg 2005).

The racial disparity noted in the Casey report is a critical piece of the juvenile system (and the adult system as well). "By virtually every means of measurement, African American, Latino, and Native American children receive much harsher treatment than do European American children. They are more likely to be arrested, charged, to receive more severe sentences, and to stand trial as adults" (Nunn 2002, 683). Black males are disproportionately represented at every phase of the system, and countless studies indicate that no factor other than race explains the disparity (Feld 1999; Glennon 2002; Miles 2003; Nunn 2002). One in three black males is in the juvenile system; they are 25 percent of those arrested, half of those tried as adults, and half of those housed in prisons (Dowd 2006). "Because the system operates cumulatively the risk is compounded and the end result is that black juveniles are three times as likely as white juveniles to end up in residential placement" (Feld 2007, 251). The disproportion exists at every stage of the juvenile justice system other than prevention, diversion, or rehabilitation. It brings more black males in and gets them deeper in the system and more likely to become adult criminals. As one critic argues, the reason is tied to deep racial stereotypes that construct black children as "other," and most significantly for juvenile justice, "the other is to be feared and controlled" (Nunn 2002, 698). Constructing black children as other comes both from their status as children and from their race, according to Kenneth Nunn (ibid., 700). I would argue that a third factor also makes them "other": that they are boys.

Masculinities Analysis and Juvenile Justice

What are the implications of masculinities scholarship for boys and juvenile justice? We can begin by looking for three possible patterns, in this area and in other areas as well. First, there are places that we assume a female norm or preference. For example, we might assume that girls and women are law abiding. This renders men invisible. It also perpetuates a gendered norm by failing to consider the relative positions and reasons for the differential average circumstances of men and women. Gender preference itself may be a double-edged sword, as it imposes assumptions and supports for women, but at a cost, and only to some extent; it may give men greater freedom, but at a cost of failing to support them. It also may trigger resistance.

Conversely, there are areas where we assume men as the objects of the system but do not recognize them as gendered subjects, and they are invisible in a different way; we simply assume they are the subjects, and do not ask about gender. This is the case with the juvenile justice system: we assume it is predominantly populated by boys, so girls surprise us. When we think about gender in the system, some recognize that the structure assumes boys and that it may not be a good system for girls, but this recognition has not led to an inquiry about the gendered construction of the system and its effects on boys. Certainly boys have been the focus of study, but not as gendered subjects.

Finally, the tendency has been to see gender as *either/or* rather than as *both/and*. We tend to approach gender analysis as requiring the identification of one subordinated group rather than seeing subordination among both boys and girls, both men and women. The approach has been as if gender is a zero-sum game, and that means one or the other. It also leads toward adopting "gender neutral" solutions that assume the situation of boys and girls is the same and the goal is to make them the same, when the gender issues may be different and require gender-specific responses in order to get to equity or equality.

The juvenile justice system is a good example of these patterns. We have generally not focused on gender at all, rendering gender invisible. For example, one of the most critical perspectives for evaluating the juvenile justice system has been a developmental perspective. One of the core premises of the juvenile justice system is that juveniles are different from adults and therefore should be dealt with differently. Because they are not yet fully developed, their behavior should be understood differently, and it is possible to rehabilitate them. This core developmental perspective has been ratified by voluminous social science data on the distinct developmental aspects of adolescence (Margaret Beyer 1998; Marty Beyer 1999, 2000; Feld 2007; Scott and Grisso 1997; Scott and Steinberg 2008). Teenagers are less competent decision makers, and their involvement in actions that create criminal liability is therefore somewhat predictable. They are "less capable . . . of using their capacities in making choices. . . . [Their] emotional and psychosocial development is behind their cognitive maturation; they are more susceptible to peer influence, more likely to take risks, less skilled in balancing risks and rewards, and immature in their judgments" (Scott and Steinberg 2008, 14; see also Marty Beyer 1999, 2000). The height of poor risk evaluation and bad judgments is age seventeen, and data bear out that the crime rate for teenagers drops dramatically after that age (Scott and Steinberg 2008). So a significant proportion of juvenile crime is linked to adolescent development; only a very small number of juveniles persist in crime as adults (Scott and Grisso 1997). Relevant factors that intersect with the developmental issue are peers, family, and community, as well as individual differences (Coughlin and Vuchinich 1996; Howell 2003; Scott and Grisso 1997).

The developmental data potentially would significantly affect and reform many parts of the juvenile justice system. For example, juveniles frequently do not understand their Miranda rights and therefore are disadvantaged in interrogation (Feld 2006). They often appear without benefit of counsel or ineffectively interact with counsel (Berkheiser 2002). Residential programs or confinement are developmentally unsound: "'It seems unlikely that institutional treatment, retraining or punishment is effective in decreasing delinquency. It is even possible that there is a harmful effect because of the alienation, stigmatization and 'contamination' suffered by those who are incarcerated together with other offenders" (Arredondo 2003, 20). The inconsistency of developmental data with imposition of the death penalty was the basis for the U.S. Supreme Court's decision that punishing juveniles with death was cruel and unusual punishment and therefore unconstitutional (*Roper v. Simmons* 2005). One notable aspect about the arguments surrounding developmental data and juvenile justice, however, is that the data are presented in a gender-neutral way, with few gender-specific points raised. What generally is not a part of this perspective is the interaction of the developmental data with the social construction of gender. Gender therefore is rendered largely invisible.

To the extent gender has been focused on with respect to juvenile justice, it has been a focus on girls. The increase in the presence of girls has raised gender concerns, but oddly, it has not triggered an examination of how the system is gendered for boys. This literature does suggest, however, how gender functions in the juvenile justice system for the underrepresented group.

What does the literature on girls suggest about gender and juvenile justice? The number and proportion of girls in the system has risen dramatically, increasing 59 percent between 1990 and 1999 (Goodkind 2005). Girls commit different crimes than boys do, suggesting a powerful interaction between conduct and offending but also raising the question of whether the system responds more strongly when girls do the same things that boys do. This has been the observation with respect to status offenses, with which girls are charged more often than boys and for which they often receive harsher penalties (Datesman and Scarpitti 1980; Humphrey 2003; MacDonald and Chesney-Lind 2001; Pope and Feyerherm 1983). In cases not involving status offenses, however, boys may be treated more harshly. At the same time, the gap between girls and boys has been narrowing (Bishop and Frazier 1992). Congress addressed the lack of programs oriented for girls (and thus implicitly recognized the structuring of the system for boys) in 1992 by requiring states receiving money under the Juvenile Justice Delinquency and Prevention Act to provide gender-specific services, with that neutral phrase being understood to mean services for girls (Biden 2003; Goodkind 2005, 56; Kempf-Leonard and Sample 2000; MacDonald and Chesney-Lind 2001). The attention to girls, according to some observers, exposes the gendered nature of the system: "Research on girls' problems and experiences in the juvenile justice system suggests that gender has long played a role in juvenile justice, whether officially recognized or not. The challenge . . . is to take what is known about girls' development, the influence of culture, and the ways in which girls' problems evolve into delinquent behavior to craft appropriate policies that address gender equity in processing and programming" (MacDonald and Chesney-Lind 2001, 191; see also Poulin 1996). Some particular issues for girls are patterns of family dysfunction, physical and sexual abuse, higher mental health disorders, and differentials in how they are perceived by the juvenile justice system (Jackson and Perlaky 2008). The focus on girls can, however, have the ironic consequence that programs may simply reify gender difference. "[We must consider] how delinquency and the juvenile justice system itself are constructions, whose interests such constructions serve, and how to look beyond the juvenile justice system in meeting the needs of the young people who are currently engaged in it" (Goodkind 2005, 68). The American Bar Association and the National Bar Association commissioned a report on girls in the juvenile justice system in 2001 that concluded that the increase of girls in the system reflected changes in responses and categorization of their behavior rather than any increase in offending by girls, that the root causes of girls' offending was significantly different from that of boys, that many girls have been traumatized by abuse, that girls of color are disproportionate in the system, and that the system does not reflect an understanding or commitment to girls' differences. The report called for gender-specific approaches and thorough reform. Interestingly, the call was limited to girls, which is typical of much of the attention to girls: the gaze has not been turned around to think about whether the system serves boys.

What the literature on girls suggests is that gender is pervasive in the system, which would suggest that it is as pervasive and saturated for boys. Because the system sanctions deviation from the norm, the norm is one that models societal expectations and gender roles. Just as the literature on girls suggests that social norms and expectations significantly affect the definition of deviance or criminality, the same is true for boys. Girls do not fit the mold of offending, which sometimes leads to more lenient treatment ("girls are not as 'bad'") but also sometimes leads to harsher treatment ("this is really dangerous and socially off the norm because it is so far from our model of girl-hood/womanhood"). In addition, the rehabilitative focus of juvenile justice is infused with a model of socially accepted and ratified norms. Just as for girls this may reify a traditional, inegalitarian norm, so too the same may be true for boys. Given that the norms at adolescence tend to be narrower and more traditional, this may then reinforce a strongly inegalitarian model in order for a juvenile to demonstrate that he or she has been rehabilitated. For girls, this may mean acceptance of parental authority, even domination, and passivity, along with a limitation of sexual activity. For boys, this may mean adhering to a hegemonic model that is not a rejection of criminal conduct but rather pulling back to an acceptable place on the continuum that puts conduct within social norms.

The few scholars who have explored the intersection of boys, masculinities, and juvenile justice conclude that the system serves to reflect and inculcate hegemonic masculinity. These studies suggest that the acts that boys commit are expressions of hegemonic masculinity, and the system deals with them in a way that reinforces that masculinity, rather than challenging it. If this is so, then the system reinforces inequality, and the mere existence of the system is not a deterrent but rather a support, for those who offend and those who do not, of a picture of boys (and men) as violent and dangerous (and therefore to be feared and respected).

Of the few studies to examine masculinities in juvenile justice, not all focus on the U.S. system, but the parallels are strong. Annie Hudson, focusing on the UK juvenile justice system, notes that not only the offenders but also much of the court personnel are male (1987). Hudson suggests three ways in which gender has an impact on the juvenile justice system: the definition of normalcy, and thus what is deemed deviant and subject to arrest; distinctive patterns of social control of young men and young women; and normalization of conduct as permissible or predictable (such as "boys will be boys"), contributing to delinquency and perpetuating male power. "What society expects of its white young men and views as 'normal' behavior is different more in degree than in kind from behavior condemned as delinquent: these expectations contrast significantly with the agenda for young women who are expected to learn for a life of passivity, servitude and domesticity" (37). Ironically, then, for boys, the juvenile justice system is consistent with the social expectations of them as men, while for girls involvement with the system signals deviance from social norms. Hudson also notes that for young black men, being "in trouble" proves masculinity but is perceived as dangerousness and results in harsher punishment.

A second study by Chris Cunneen and Rob White (1996), based on Australian data, exposes three examples of juvenile offending that mirror the norms of hegemonic masculinity: attacks on gay men, offenses related to motor vehicles, and aggressive masculinity directed toward women. Each of these offending patterns is consistent with the policing and dominance norm of hegemonic masculinity.

An American study of two California residential treatment programs (Abrams, Anderson-Nathe, and Aguilar 2008) points out the lack of gender analysis in evaluating residential programs, despite the disproportionate population of boys in such programs. In the study, three themes emerged from the two programs: "the overarching hegemonic masculine milieu, explicit validation of dominant and competitive masculine ideals and behaviors by staff, and inconsistent encouragement of residents to experiment with alternative forms of gender expression" (9). These programs reify hegemonic masculinity; they do not challenge or reorient the boys, but to the contrary, they reinforce the very masculinity that is linked to offending but is also linked to a rehabilitated self.

Recent work on the fate of LBGT youth in the juvenile justice system suggests how different masculinities are treated within the system. LGBT youth are a classic illustration of how deviance from masculinity means that they are ignored or harassed. LBGT youth are overrepresented in the child welfare and juvenile justice systems, which is linked to a pattern of rejection by their families, although they are often unknown in the system because of the danger of consequences from declaring their gender identity, and they are concerned for their safety (Estrada and Marksamer 2008).

Beyond these bits and pieces of gender analysis, if we look at the history, structure, and operation of the juvenile justice system as briefly described in this chapter from a masculinity perspective, what else do we see? The harsh punishment characteristic of the current system reflects the view of boys as dangerous and inherently violent. Boys of color are particularly dangerous, as are gay boys and lower-class boys. So the hierarchy of masculinities is evident in those who come into the system and how they are treated.

The strong shift to more punitive outcomes, the shift to treating boys as if they were adult men through transfer policies, the view of boys as super-offenders particularly identified by race, and seeing offenders as hyper-masculine—all these trends reflect assumed masculinities and stereotypes of boys that fly in the face of developmental data to the contrary (Arredondo 2003; Scott and Grisso 1997). The strength of the cultural norm of masculinity overcomes empirical data. Moreover, the justification of harsh punishment as necessary in order to control boys silently sanctions the worst offenses as part of confinement, most notably prison rape, leaving them unchallenged and permitted as a part of punishment (Giller 2004; Robertson 2003).

What masculinities analysis most strongly exposes is how we have constructed the juvenile justice system to essentialize and biologize boys' presence and propensity, denying that masculinities are socially constructed and therefore denying our social responsibility for the pattern. This essentialism also reinforces difference and hegemony. This construction of masculinity is the ultimate power, the power to transcend the rules. It reinforces at the personal level the danger men pose to one another and to women. It reinforces the hierarchy among men and of men over women. The juvenile justice system therefore reveals how hegemony works. Its reinforcement of hegemony benefits boys and men who are not criminals.

The system demonstrates the power of social construction: the pattern of boys in the system feels and acts like a biological, hard-wired norm. It is no mistake that boys commit crimes or that they engage in acts of violence, because their task at this stage in their development requires that they do so in order to take their place among men. The system also perfectly reflects the hierarchy among boys and men by its racial configuration: black boys are disproportionately represented in the system, and the identity of juvenile defendants is strongly racialized. Those who have noticed and critiqued this pattern are absolutely right that this represents the continuing harsh price of racism. I argue in addition that this price is easier to exact because it is taken from a male body: race makes black bodies the most dangerous and stigmatized, but this is overlaid on assumptions about boys that makes males the object of punishment.

The punishment or rehabilitation of boys, moreover, is not with the goal of making them better or different men with a different sense of masculinity. Rather, the system reinforces traditional notions of masculinity rather than challenging them, at the very time when those traditional notions are the focus of adolescent masculinities and contribute to the actions of boys. Admittedly, effective means of confronting boys may have to operate within masculinities if they are to be successful. That creates a tricky gender context for rehabilitation. Ultimately, the lens of masculinities exposes the biases in a gendered system not of juvenile justice but of boys' justice. Most significantly, it raises the question not only of when and how we sanction boys (and which ones more than others) but also what our model is that we rehabilitate them to be (or fail at that goal).

Conclusion: The Story of Lionel Tate

When we enter the courtrooms of the juvenile justice system, we are not surprised that mostly it is boys that are there, and more of them are black than would be proportionate to the population. We expect this to be a place where we will find boys; it is part of our cultural norms of masculinity. If juvenile justice is to do justice, however, this strongly gendered, racialized system should trigger analysis and careful consideration. If feminism is to do gender justice, then with the infusion of masculinities analysis, the juvenile justice system is a place where race becomes and should be a feminist issue.

Lionel Tate's story can be our talisman. Lionel Tate has the distinction of being the youngest American ever sentenced to life in prison without parole, in 1999 for a crime committed when he was twelve years old. Lionel was at home with his mother and his six-year-old cousin. After his mother, a police officer, went upstairs and fell asleep, Lionel showed off some wrestling moves that he had seen on television. Lionel was big for his age, 166 pounds; his cousin was 46 pounds. Tragically, as a result of his actions, his cousin was accidentally killed. Lionel was criminally charged under the child abuse statutes. His mother was offered a plea bargain whereby he would have served a three-year term for second degree murder, but she turned it down, believing he would be acquitted. Instead, he was convicted, and the trial judge imposed the harshest possible sentence. Lionel was then age fourteen. One other significant fact in Lionel's story is that he is African American (Woodhouse 2008).

Lionel came from a family where there had been significant family disruption, and he had exhibited misbehavior and disruptive behavior in school. These mental health issues were unaddressed. He was shuffled back and forth between his divorced parents, who were living in different states. He had only recently come back to live with his mother when the incident occurred that caused the death of his cousin.

Lionel's case drew national and international attention because of his age at the time of the crime. Nearly three years after the trial, an appeals court overturned the conviction on the grounds that his mental competency to stand trial had not been evaluated. The prosecutor then offered the original plea bargain again, and it was accepted. With time served, he was to serve one year of house arrest and ten years probation.

The story does not end there, however, because Lionel had a difficult time staying out of trouble. Less than a year after his original sentence was overturned, Lionel was discovered out of his house with a knife, violating the terms of his probation. He was placed on zero-tolerance probation for an additional five years. He violated that probation less than a year later, in an incident involving a pizza delivery. Allegedly Lionel called and ordered pizza, and when the delivery person arrived, Lionel had a gun in his hand. The pizza man dropped the pizzas, ran, and called the police. Lionel was charged with armed robbery. He eventually admitted that he possessed a gun (remember that his mother was a police officer), which was enough to constitute a violation of his probation, and he was sentenced to thirty years in prison for the gun-possession charge. He subsequently pled no contest to the pizza robbery and was sentenced to ten years, to run concurrently with his thirty-year sentence for gun possession. By the time he leaves prison, if he is not eligible for parole, he will be nearly fifty.

Throughout this case, Lionel was not offered any mental health treatment, counseling, or other services to enable him to succeed on his original sentence, nor was his family engaged in any program to help improve the family dynamics that affected his ability to change his behavior.

Lionel's case, and others like it, is an extreme example of how the juvenile justice system treats boys. But the extreme cases are simply part of a continuum; they are not exceptional. In addition, Lionel's case is an example of the particularized treatment of black boys in the juvenile justice system. Again, this is pervasive, not exceptional.

Through the lens of masculinities analysis, the story of Lionel Tate becomes a predictable tale of harsh outcome and ultimate failure because he was a black boy. The system is designed not to save him but to send him deeper in. Before his fateful night with his young cousin, his needs were ignored because he was written off as a boy; once his cousin was killed, he easily fit into a familiar stereotype of danger that is exacerbated for black boys. The trial judge dehumanized him in a way consistent with the long tendency of treating black boys not as "our" children but as "other." Although he was formally given a second chance when his harsh lifetime sentence was appealed, his reprieve was undermined by the failure to give him the help to remove him from the presumption of dangerousness. By the time he began to serve his long prison sentence, he had grown from a tearful twelve-year-old into a fearsome nineteen-year-old, the epitome of dangerousness without redemption.

We expect Lionel's case to end this way. In a less dramatic way, when we enter the courtrooms of the juvenile justice system, we are not surprised that mostly it is boys that are there, and more of them are black than would be proportionate to the population. We expect this to be a place where we will find boys; it is part of our cultural norms of masculinity. If juvenile justice is to do justice, however, this strongly gendered system should trigger analysis and careful consideration. We must examine and reform the gendered norm and operation of the system so that this system is not the price paid for being a boy or the punishment for being a girl.

Part III ——

Men

Just as the two chapters in part 2 apply masculinities analysis to boys, the two chapters in this part are examples of the application of masculinities analysis to men, in the context of fatherhood and men as victims of sexual abuse. In the discussion of fatherhood in chapter 7, we have an explicitly all-male category that has drawn some gender analysis but not much of an explicit look at masculinities. Masculinities analysis would be particularly helpful, I argue, in understanding the economic and cultural barriers to involved, egalitarian fatherhood. It exposes how the construction of gender identity gets in the way of social change, comparable with the understanding that women experience work/family conflict to a far greater degree than men, because their work role conflicts with the traditional and even ongoing reconstruction of motherhood.

Masculinities can help us uncover the structures of work and the cultures of work that not only benefit men but also barricade them at work instead of balancing work and family. So men simultaneously experience the positive and the negative. But most significantly, masculinities analysis might be useful toward further understanding and uncovering the relationship of men to care and how masculinity affects that relationship. If we are to change the way men behave (and if we really mean and support that change), then it means changing masculinity, in the sense of relation to self or identity and to others. It means incorporating a central commitment to care. If care is associated with women and masculinity is defined quintessentially as not being female, then men doing care is a liberatory act, but also one fraught with potential conflict (played out in custody battles, among other places). Masculinities analysis can help, then, to identify barriers and offer the hope of reconstruction, as indeed, reconstruction of fatherhood is ongoing toward a greater embrace of care.

The dialogue about fatherhood has some parallels to boys and education. It is an area where we do engage in gender analysis to some extent. But akin to the dialogue about boys and education, very often we do so in an essentialist way, which leads to treating fathers differently in a way that reinforces

| 101

hegemonic masculinity. And masculinity is not the only piece that limits fathers: a huge piece is economic, which is strongly but not exclusively linked to masculinity.

In chapter 8 I explore, along with Ted Shaw, men and sexual abuse. We focus on men as victims of sexual assault as children. When we think about gender and sex in relation to sexual abuse, we think about girls and women as victims; men are invisible. Using masculinities analysis we examine our treatment of child sexual abuse and our consideration of the impact of these experiences on men as adults. When we study the data, we find a high rate of sexual assault for boys. If we ignore that, we fail to see those victims. In addition, this area is a place where we might benefit from a gender-specific approach. Similar to the analysis of education and boys, this does not mean that we ignore girls and women but rather that we look at boys and men in addition, and by doing so, we benefit both.

Chapter 8 explores the invisibility of men as sexual victims and the implications of this invisibility. On the one hand, the issue links backs to boys, because it is critical to expose the extent to which boys are victims of child sexual abuse. The critical link to men is that the victimized boys become men and must construct their identity and self as men with this victimization as part of who they are. What happens to these boys as men? Because of the link for some men between childhood victimization and adult sexual offending, most often we understand and deal with adults as offenders. But the empirical data tell us that not all victims become victimizers. Our focus on helping adult victims requires a much broader scope, to support and assist those who may still be living with the scars of childhood harm. Our failure to identify and treat men when they are sexual victims is not limited to this scenario, since we also know that male rape is largely ignored, particularly when it occurs within prisons. Masculinities analysis can potentially be helpful to uncover and notice what we have hidden about men and sexuality.

Feminists have long been justifiably concerned about and have focused on men's abuse of their sexuality by victimizing women. Some feminists have also confronted women's victimization of their children. But rarely have feminists considered the gender-specific nature of child sexual abuse when the victim is a male or considered whether we have identified and worked with adults who were victimized as children. What I mean to challenge in chapter 8 is the unidimensional treatment of men as sexual beings.

The purpose of these two chapters is to suggest the ways in which masculinities analysis, as a part of feminist analysis, can enrich gender analysis to expose how subordination functions and to suggest how we might achieve equality. It is to ensure that in focusing on the inequalities of women we do not essentialize or ignore men. Although these chapters focus on areas of men's disadvantage, this is not to suggest that we shift our focus from women's inequalities but rather that the expansion of the lens ultimately is to the advantage of all. Looking at the reorientation of fatherhood toward the commitment of men to care has enormous implications for women's equality; and the proactive engagement with men's sexual victimhood will contribute to a similar reorientation of men's adult sexuality, to the benefit of men and women.

7

Men and Fatherhood

Fatherhood is inherently male identified. When we talk about fathers we talk about men. Yet fathers remain strangely invisible as gendered subjects. We do not talk about masculinity; rather, the tendency is to essentialize fathers. This is done *to* men as well as *by* (some) men. At the core of fatherhood, however, is a tension that resonates in the contemporary practice of fatherhood. Fatherhood is one of the critical life roles for men, but care of children is significantly at odds with the concept of masculinity. One of the core principles of masculinity is "Don't be a girl." Care is associated with women and girls. Hegemonic masculinity drives fatherhood away from care.

In this chapter I explore the patterns of contemporary fatherhood that embody this core tension. Our model of fatherhood has shifted to the involved, nurturing, caregiving father, and that pattern has grown among a proportion of fathers. For those fathers, the challenge of policy and practice is to refashion masculinity to include care, to provide support (cultural and institutional) for men's care, and to connect men's care to collaborative parenting with women. On the other hand, an opposing dynamic is the phenomenon of disconnection between fathers and children. The dissonance between new fatherhood norms and this strong pattern of disconnection is remarkable and troubling. From this perspective, cultural norms and hegemonic models block nurturing relationships with children and collaborative parenting with partners.

Fatherhood exposes how masculinities confer privilege with a price. Power is defined in a way that ultimately separates men from their children and makes it difficult for them to embrace opportunities for care and relationship. This not only harms children; it harms men. In this chapter I set out the patterns of fatherhood, the characteristics of involved fatherhood, and variations of fatherhood policy. I suggest how masculinities analysis within a feminist structure might help to frame how law and policy could achieve more care, for the benefit of children, mothers, and fathers. I include differences among fathers, in particular the challenges for low-income fathers.

Multiple masculinities are critical to ensuring that policy is not class defined. Our naming of low-income families as "fragile families," for example, may be explicitly sympathetic but implicitly can become coded language for race and class.

The danger in reconstructing fatherhood without analyzing its relationship to masculinity is to "masculinize" care in a way that sustains hegemony. This danger is clear from new claims of hierarchy cloaked in the language of equality (Collier 2009; Fineman 1994, 2005). What is really needed is the reconstruction of fatherhood and masculinity away from power *over* women. Reformed or reconstructed masculinities might suggest a path to recognize and channel men's emotional connection to their children into more meaningful and nurturing connections that would benefit children, men, and men's partners.

Fathers: Patterns

"In recent decades . . . fewer men enter fatherhood and more leave it" (Hobson and Morgan 2002, 1). The disengagement is both economic and emotional. "New census data on family living arrangements suggest that fewer fathers may be participating in their children's lives than in any period since the United States began keeping reliable statistics" (Tamis-LeMonda and Cabrera 2002, 525). This demographic reality means sharp differences in the patterns of fatherhood and motherhood. "Parenthood has become a much less central and stable element in men's lives, not only compared with the past, but particularly as compared with its role in the lives of women" (Oláh, Bernhardt and Goldscheider 2002, 25). Men are less likely to live with their biological children and more likely to live with the children of their partner (ibid.).

Measured biologically, most men are fathers at some point during their lifetime. Measured socially, by nurture, the pattern is just the opposite: most men do not nurture children to a significant extent. As fathers, men can be divided into several groups: nurturing fathers, who care for their children as primary parents or as coparents with a partner; breadwinner fathers, who provide economic support as their primary care for their children; and disengaged fathers who have little or no connection to their children. Along this continuum, primary or coequal nurturing fathers are a small albeit growing group. Those who nurture to some extent, as secondary or backup nurturers to mothers, are a more sizable group. Breadwinner fathers may or may not overlap with nurturers. Typically they focus on providing instead of care, and they range from those who provide minimal care to those who make only financial contributions to the care of their children. Disengaged fathers are those who have minimal economic or social connection or none at all (Dowd 2000).

Fathers are not limited to husbands, nor are they limited to those biologically connected to children, or coresident with children (Dowd 2000). But each of these factors continues to play a strong role in fathering patterns. One pair of scholars focusing on the demographic data has examined fathers on the basis of whether they share a household with children (Tamis-LeMonda and Cabrera 2002). This focus moves away from biology or legal fatherhood to social fatherhood, epitomized by coresidency. Evaluating data from the 1990s, the researchers found that most men did not have a child coresiding with them; only four of ten men did. Significantly, nine out of ten fathers with coresident dependent children were married. This is important because one in four children is born into a nonmarital family (Ventura 2009). Work is nearly universal among fathers, although it is not always full-time. Limited education and consequent limited work opportunities particularly affect black and Hispanic fathers. In the researchers' study, an overwhelming percentage of fathers, 87 percent, lived with biological children only; only one in seven fathers cared for step-, adopted, or foster children.

The number of children who live in mother-only households is an estimated one-fourth of all dependent children (Tamis-LeMonda and Cabrera 2002). The commitment of fathers at birth to their children is quite strong: of nonmarital births, nearly 40 percent occur to cohabiting couples (Ventura 2009). But in families with the least resources, fathers have difficulty remaining involved over time (Carlson, McLanahan, and England 2004; Fragile Families Research Team 2005). Thus, a significant and growing number of fathers live apart from their children. Although some continue to maintain a nurturing relationship, that number is small. "Forty percent of children in father-absent homes have not seen their fathers at all during the previous year. Only one in six sees his or her father at least once a week. Only one-quarter of nonmarital fathers visit their children consistently beyond age four" (Dowd 2000, 23).

Fatherhood patterns are linked to the high rate of relationship breakdown, whether divorce, the end of cohabitation, or the failure ever to share a household. Because children do not live in equivalent numbers with their biological or social fathers as compared with their mothers, this means that fathers are more likely to parent according to a serial pattern, rather than a linear pattern. Their fathering is mediated by their relationships with their partner as well as by whether they live with their partner. Mothers, by contrast, parent in a linear way, continuing to nurture and cohabit with their biological children and sometimes also parenting the stepchildren of their partner. Fathers in general nurture the children they live with. They parent by household. In each relationship, they fit somewhere on the continuum from nurturing to breadwinning to disengaged father. Although some sustain multiple nurturing relationships, including biological and social relationships once established, irrespective of what happens to their partner or coresidency, such patterns are relatively rare (Dowd 2000).

When fathers are involved in nurturing children, whether they are coresident or not, they engage in considerably less nurture than that of mothers. Based on 1980s and 1990s data, father time with children is two-fifths of mother time (Tamis-LeMonda and Cabrera 2002). Patterns of attachment are different as compared to mothers, as are patterns of care. Michael Lamb (1997) links less involvement both to men's attitudes and women's gatekeeping and to power issues between men and women.

Interestingly, fathers' patterns remain largely consistent whether or not women work. When mothers work, fathers are involved to a greater extent, but when the pattern is examined more closely, it turns out that "fathers are *proportionally* more involved, . . . [but] the extent of their involvement in absolute terms does not change to any meaningful extent" (Lamb 1997, 5). In other words, the pattern of care when mothers work is that mothers are doing less, increasing the proportion of what fathers do. Also, fathers do different things with their children than mothers do, but they still do not do more than mothers. It has long been reported, for example, that fathers engage in play as a major part of their involvement with children. But it turns out that mothers play more; play is just more of what fathers do.

Biology appears to have a significant role in father involvement. Although stepfathers are involved with stepchildren in their household, stepfathers are deemed lower in parental warmth than are biological fathers. Involvement with children is significantly correlated with whether the child is a biological child and with the strength of the man's relationship with the mother. This data is consistent with the demographic data on coresidence that is linked so strongly to biological children and marriage to the mother. Multiple fatherhood is not uncommon, but what appears to be uncommon is multiple nurturing fathers. For example, among some low-income parents there is a distinction between the father and the "daddy," with the father recognized as the biological father, while the daddy is the social father (Tamis-LeMonda and Cabrera 2002).

Another way to look at father involvement is to consider the impact of men's nurture on child development. According to Michael Lamb (1997), the developmental impact of fathers is tied to their relationship with their partner rather than their direct care of children. Lamb concludes that it is the value of coparenting and parental satisfaction, not the essential or unique parenting of fathers, that benefits children. Many early developmental studies explored men's importance as role models but found that irrespective of how "masculine" fathers are, sons learn masculinity from cultural norms. They found instead that the benefit to boys of their fathers is not the presence of a role model but rather the existence of a loving, warm relationship. "The characteristics of the father as a parent rather than the characteristics of the father as a man appear to be most significant" (ibid., 10). Mothers and fathers influence children by their nurture, not by their gender (ibid.; Dowd 2000). Father absence effects reflect not the absence of a critical gender piece but rather the loss of economic support and coparenting support (Lamb 1997).

Rob Palkovitz has been one of the leading scholars on reconceptualizing father involvement. He argues for a broad definition of involvement that includes the contributions of nonresident fathers (Hawkins and Palkovitz 1999; Day and Lamb 2004). Palkovitz rejects the categorization of "good" and "bad" fathers, which ignores the complexity of men's involvement with their children as well as the barriers that prevent greater involvement (Marks and Palkovitz 2004). For example, the findings of the most exhaustive research to date on low-income nonmarital fathers belie our stereotypes of these fathers. Overwhelmingly these fathers are present and desire to be involved in the lives of their children, but they have great difficulty doing so (Fragile Families Project 2005). Palkovitz also affirms the importance of fatherhood for men's development (Palkovitz 2002; Maurer and Pleck 2006).

What affects fathers' involvement in care? Lamb (1997) notes that while some men say they would like more time with their children, almost an equal number do not. Men worry about their competence, and the level of support from mothers continues to be crucial—and women frequently do not want men to be more involved, which Lamb attributes to their reluctance to give up power in the one sphere in which they have it. Structural supports, or the lack of them, also have an impact on men's ability to be involved.

Coexistent with men's pattern of childcare is a similar asymmetry about housework. Scott Coltrane, who has focused on household work patterns, notes that the study of household labor has tended to divide childcare and household work, which obscures a dynamic of persistent inequality with respect to both (2000). As with the patterns on actual father involvement versus the cultural norm of greater father involvement, in household labor the equality norm exists in theory but not in reality. "Although men's relative contributions [to housework] have increased, women still do at least twice as much routine housework as men. Consistent predictors of sharing include both women's and men's employment, earnings, gender ideology, and life-course issues" (208). Despite agreement in theory about sharing, men simply do not take on household work: women do two or three times more. Surprisingly, *both* men and women see this as "fair." It is viewed as fair because men do more wage work or earn more money. "The person with less power and fewer resources does more of it" (218). Change in this pattern is more likely in the working class, for whom reallocation of tasks is an unavoidable issue, than it is for upper-income/elite professionals, who buy services (often hiring working-class and immigrant women) rather than displace or challenge the assumed privileges of husbands and fathers.

Less domestic work is an expression of power, and power is tied to work and income (Coltrane 2004). It reflects what Nicholas Townsend (2002) calls the "package deal" of masculinity: fatherhood, employment, marriage, and home ownership. Implicit in the deal is that employment translates into a limited role in caregiving and an even more limited role in household work. The breadwinner ideal sets up men to identify work as the source of power, whether that is implicitly or explicitly acknowledged (Townsend 2002). Moreover, structurally both the state and the workplace reinforce this equation. The workplace identifies men with families as good workers, seeing no conflict between their work and family roles (a huge contrast with how the workplace views women, who are often marginalized because their family ties are assumed to be predominant). Similarly, the state is complicit by identifying economic providing as the primary responsibility of fathers, pursuing them for child support, while weakly supporting their care relationships with their children (Coltrane 2004).

Definitions and Differences

The definition of fatherhood persists as an economic role rather than as a nurturing role (Dowd 2000). But even with respect to breadwinning, many fathers do not, or cannot, fulfill that traditional role. Men are most likely to support children when they are married and when the children are their biological children (Dowd 2005). If men are not or have never been married, or are divorced, the level of child support that can be legally demanded of them is insufficient to support most children, yet it is an obligation resisted by many fathers (Grall 2007). A huge amount of child support goes unpaid, most often because fathers cannot pay but, in a significant number of cases, because they will not pay even though they are able (Grall 2007; Sorenson and Zebman 2001). Low-income fathers are particularly disproportionately burdened, with little benefit to their children (Lockie 2009). The child poverty rate remains unacceptably high, linked to an unwillingness to make children's support and family support a social, instead of an individual, responsibility. Nearly 40 percent of children live in poor or low-income families, based on 2008 figures (National Center for Children in Poverty 2008). *Two of every five children are in low-income families.* Roughly half of those children live in families that earn below the federal poverty level of $22,050 for a family of four; the other half of those children live in low-income families with income below twice the poverty level, or $44,100, an amount necessary to meet basic needs according to most scholars (ibid.). The brunt of the public policy of private support, a horrifically inadequate policy, falls on men, but its ultimate impact is on children.

What is most important in poverty patterns is that economic providing is gender defined as primarily male (even if women's wage work has been the only thing keeping families afloat economically or minimizing loss). This has huge implications for men's ability to give care and nurture. Within a policy framework of private responsibility, fatherhood is locked in conflict with care. Yet like other patterns, there is a dissonance between social ideal and reality. It locks in a hierarchy of masculinities, with only some men able to perform the breadwinning role, and then only at a cost.

Class differences among fathers are a reminder that other differences exist that should be recognized as part of the context of fatherhood. For example, men of color, especially black men, have been challenged in their ability to be fathers by the unique characteristics of black masculinity that both support nurture and resist it. As Michael Awkward has argued (1999, 2002), black men are more connected and in touch with nurture because of the strong position of black women in black families. At the same time, black masculinity has been identified by cool pose and hypermasculinity, characteristics that may be inconsistent with nurture (Majors 2001). In addition, the difficulty associated with achieving breadwinner status that is faced by all men in changing economic times is exacerbated for black men (Maldonado 2006; Pamela Smith 1999b). Finally, the labeling and perception of black men as dangerous creates the stark barrier of incarceration or connection to the criminal justice system for far too many black men (D. Roberts 2004).

Another distinctive group of fathers are gay men, who are assumed to be feminine, to practice a masculinity that would open the door to an embrace of nurture (Law 1988; Poirier 2003). At the same time, our stereotypes and homophobia have typically resisted the notion of gay men as partners and parents. This is evident in the resistance to gay marriage and gay adoption (Eskridge and Spedale 2006; Gher 2008; Novkov 2008). The idea of multiple fathers as we socially imagine it connects to patterns of paternity and non-marital and divorced fatherhood; it has not typically been associated with having two dads as the dual parents of children (Dowd 2007; Jacobs 2007). The resistance to gay men as fathers taps into stereotypes of sexual danger and risk that actually link to heterosexual men but instead are tied in the public to gay men. The barriers for gay fathers are explicit in the dominant resistance to gay marriage and continued resistance to gay couples, as well as in the high level of resistance to gay adoption even where it is not formally proscribed.

These differences, along with others, among fathers are important to keep in mind when considering how law and policy currently construct and might differently support men as fathers. Fatherhood policy must attend to differences among men. Masculinities analysis, explicitly multiple and resisting the imposition of a dominant norm that reinscribes hierarchies among men, can be a valuable tool in constructing law and policy.

Fatherhood as Care: Father Involvement

If the goal of law and policy is greater father involvement in care, and if masculinity norms are in conflict with care, then examining the patterns of nurturing fathers is important for policy. Is involved fatherhood as we currently know it a real shift or a reconstruction of hegemonic masculinity? (Plantin, Mansson, and Kearney 2003).

From studies of involved fathers, it appears that a dominant trend is to masculinize care. "The changing nature of fatherhood is . . . complicated by two issues. First, . . . many fathers need to cognitively redefine those tasks that are nontraditional for men as still somehow being masculine to reduce the threat to their own masculinity. . . . Second, . . . providing caregiving is still more discretionary for fathers than it is for mothers" (Maurer and Pleck 2006, 101). Social modeling and expectations are key to changed behavior by fathers. Interestingly, involved fathers are more likely to model their behavior on their peers than on their fathers or their partners (Masciadrelli, Pleck, and Stueve 2006). In relation to their own fathers, they may reject their fathers' low involvement or affirm their high involvement (ibid.).

One small study of Norwegian fathers describes how fathers constructed care to make it "masculine" (Brandth and Kvande 1998). "Masculine care" for the men in this study included being a friend to the child, being and doing things together, and teaching independence. Men were constructed as "active" parents. Also, parenting did not include housework. Men felt they controlled their time and what they did and did not do. They continued to be strongly tied to work in the labor market. Socially their care was respected, and they were viewed as "cool" for staying home and being the primary parent.

The behavior of involved fathers was examined by another set of researchers to determine whether their behavior and functioning as an involved father reflected the traditional assumptions of sociologists such as Parsons that men and women divided parenting functions by gender, with fathers as "instrumental" and mothers as "expressive" (Finley and Schwartz 2006). In examining what involved fathers do, these researchers found a remarkable reflection of this stereotyped norm. Highly involved fathers scored higher on instrumental functions (discipline, protecting, responsibility, career development, and developing independence) than on expressive functions (caregiving, companionship, sharing activities, emotional development, social development, spiritual development, physical development, and leisure) (51). Of the instrumental functions, the highest levels of involvement were in the most traditional functions of fathers—income, protection, discipline, moral/ethical development, and encouraging responsibility (52). This would suggest that even with greater involvement, the actions/functions are skewed toward traditional male ones within the family.

One of the most fascinating and nuanced studies of fathers is Andrea Doucet's study of primary care fathers, *Do Men Mother?* (2006). In an earlier article based on this work (2004), Doucet notes the challenge of leaving wage work for full-time care of children. As one father noted, "As a man you have no status at all if you don't work" (278). In this new role these fathers were moving against that work-oriented norm, embracing care. In order to take on this role, they needed to make it distinctive. These fathers strongly characterized their caring as masculine and manly. Intertwined with the change in these fathers' role, therefore, was an attachment to masculinizing care.

Doucet concludes that while men *can* do many of the things that mothers do, they experience parenting as distinctive and different, and this difference is important to them (2006). That is, they emphatically state that they are *not* mothering. "They want to distance their fathering from mothering and indeed from any feminine association attached to it" (122). Doucet also found that there is a strong connection of fathering to mothers, that it is mother led, and that fathers continue to recognize something unique about mothers. Ultimately, she would answer the question posed in the title of her book ("Do men mother?") as both no and yes, and I think if pressed, she would say no. She characterizes the fathering of these primary-care men as emphasizing difference while engaging in "borderwork," that is, crossing the borders into doing what is identified as the feminine work of care (219). In the process, she sees the revisioning of masculinity taking place, not simply the masculinizing of care. So in the process of reinventing and redefining fatherhood, by this difference in practice, masculinity itself, she argues, has been redefined.

Research on Swedish fathers, who operate within probably the strongest cultural and institutional framework supportive of nurturing fathering, also exposes the challenges of reorienting fatherhood (Plantin, Manssen, and Kearney 2003). "Developing a more nurturing, caring, and equal form of fathering depends on a coherent discourse and supportive family policy. However, this is not a guarantee that individual men's behaviors will change" (24). Scholars have debated whether the reformed Swedish concept of fatherhood is still patriarchal or whether it is egalitarian. Can you create "child-centered masculinity" (Almqvist 2008)? This requires a work reorientation as well as change in the family (ibid.; Bouchard et al. 2007). One scholar suggests that the evidence indicates that changes at the household level precede changes in wage work: "Households [are] more dynamic than jobs. . . . Instead of work changing gender, we often found women's new work roles as part of changing homes and homes changing men, with a beginning dynamic effect back into working life" (Holter 2007, 453). So it may be changes at the personal level that bring change at work (even though it is cultural and structural change that appears to facilitate personal and familial change).

One pair of researchers characterizes fathers not as abandoning traditional roles but rather as refashioning them (Catlett and McKenry 2004). The new fatherhood combines traditional characteristics, especially breadwinning, with greater involvement. Traditional roles are not displaced; new characteristics are simply added on. But is it possible to sustain these inconsistent models of fatherhood? And is the effort to do so linked to the influence of traditional masculinity norms? Clearly there is a significant challenge to this modified hegemonic role at divorce, when the power dynamic that supports the traditional breadwinner model changes dramatically. This might explain the disconnect between the expressed desire of divorced fathers to have more time with their children and the pattern of disconnection so prevalent at divorce (ibid., 166). "Men perceive divorce as prompting a re-organization of their families' gender relations. . . . It redistribute[s] power and may well lead to a post-divorce family structure in which men's perceived relative position is dramatically altered. . . . Divorce also can be conceptualized as a central influence on men's constructions of masculinity as they respond to changing relations of gender power and entitlements within their families" (180). Because of this impact, gender analysis of divorce is critical.

Class differences have an impact on fathers' ability to succeed at this redefined traditional breadwinner/involved role. Low-income fathers have difficulty with the provider role, while high-income fathers can use resources to assist with the caregiving role. Middle-income fathers experience great stress between the two roles (Catlett and McKenry 2004). Working-class men have a difficult time because the economic barriers make it difficult for them to be involved parents (Plantin, Mansson, and Kearney 2003).

The patterns of more involved fathers thus expose how masculinities are a critical piece of the shape of law and policy. It is clear that redefined fatherhood means redefined masculinity. Law and policy create both institutional and cultural supports that presume a model. Masculinities analysis reminds us to be attentive to the context and the actual practice, as well as being explicit about the norms or models we support. The issue is whether redefinition will revive hegemonic norms or support a model of nurturing, collaborative, nonhierarchical fatherhood for all fathers.

Fatherhood Policy: Structural Change

Public policy relating to fathers is a factor contributing to father involvement, and that policy is premised on a model and set of cultural assumptions about men, masculinities, and fatherhood. A recent collection of work comparing fatherhood policy in North America and Europe unravels how policy constructs and supports an understanding of fatherhood and masculinity. Much public policy about fathers has come from a concern about the state supporting children rather than fathers, and in response to the growing number of single-parent, mother-headed families. Child support has been a major focus of policy and reinforces a norm of fathers as breadwinners, even as exclusive breadwinners (Lewis 2002; J. Roberts 2005).

A significant issue in fatherhood policy is the broader issue of private versus public support of families. A private model, gender linked, reinforces a core construction of traditional hegemonic masculinity. In countries where there is strong state support for families, there is a higher proportion of household or coresidential fathers as compared to in the United States (Oláh, Bernhardt, and Goldscheider 2002). U.S. fathers must provide support from employment alone, as opposed to being able to draw on the kind of social support available in other advanced capitalist countries (Orloff and Monson 2002). The suggestion from some scholars is that it is essential to look at men as gendered beings in gendered social policy regimes. In that view, U.S. policy is characterized as treating men as economic providers and particularly targeting poor men (ibid.).

If the private economic model is retained, then policy is focused on making low-income men fit or achieve this model. Anna Gavanas has written extensively on the U.S. "fatherhood responsibility movement" (2002, 2004). The movement is split between promarriage and fragile families' advocates, and both these policy wings frame fathers very traditionally. The promarriage wing of the movement identifies feminists and changing gender roles as the culprit causing men's inability to provide economic support; it focuses on men's *difference* as essential and important to children and identifies heterosexual marriage as the solution. The fragile families wing, on the other hand, blames racism and classism for the barriers facing low-income men and does not see differences between mothers and fathers as important but identifies differences *among men* as disadvantaging low-income fathers (Gavanas 2002). Gavanas argues that both groups construct masculinity as "'naturally' constituted by a gender-specific sexuality that has to be harnessed or else men will run berserk" (ibid., 237). One group seeks to control this essential masculinity through marriage, while the other seeks to empower a weakened masculinity (ibid.). She characterizes the fatherhood responsibility movement as trying to "masculinize" fatherhood while "domesticating" masculinity (2004).

If men continue to be constructed as breadwinners, then their obligation is primarily economic, and the issues become whether the support obligation should be biologically or socially based and whether child support is singular (the responsibility of one man) or plural (biological and social fathers or only social fathers). If the state steps in to provide support, and men are allowed to step away from the breadwinner role, does this facilitate nurture or undermine it? What obligations are thereby imposed on or assumed for mothers?

Another way of looking at models of economic policy is to determine what kinds of families they support. If payments substitute for women's wages (like a family allowance irrespective of wage work), then the traditional division of labor is perpetuated. The American tax system is an example of this set of assumptions (McCaffery 1997). Alternatively, policy might be linked to wage work, with a presumptive dual-earner family and additional supports for a single parent, which is an implicit "worker-carer" parenting model (Oláh, Bernhardt, and Goldscheider 2002).

Beyond child support, a second thrust of fatherhood policy has focused on caregiving, within a conception of family and parenthood as a gender-neutral, egalitarian partnership. In response to women's greater engagement with paid work, and consistent with a commitment to gender equality, policy has responded to a perceived care deficit for children, rather than an economic deficit (Hobson and Morgan 2002). For many observers this is a gender-specific deficit, a need for father *presence* (although not always care). Concerns about fathers are clearly linked to masculinities: "The social politics of fatherhood cannot be divorced from masculinity politics. Men's authority in the family and male breadwinning are at the core of masculinity politics" (ibid., 5). If policy orients to households as opposed to marriage, then it accepts and works within patterns of coresidence and cohabitation; to the extent policy promotes ongoing relationships with biological children, it promotes a concept of parenthood that transcends residence and even, to some extent, relationships among adult partners. A major policy choice also is whether to support biological or social fatherhood, to support care rights based on status or on actual caregiving conduct.

Public policy aimed at supporting men's caregiving has particularly focused on parental leave at the inception of the parent-child relationship. The strongest policies include those of Sweden and the Netherlands, and all European Union fathers are entitled to at least fourteen weeks of parental leave. But these rights have largely gone unused: except in the Scandinavian countries, only a very small proportion of fathers use their entitlement to any leave (Hobson and Morgan 2002).

The impact of structural and cultural norms is clearly evident in patterns of fathers taking (or not taking) parental leave. Greater use of leave and greater father involvement with children is linked to "egalitarian beliefs, the amount and source of income, education, and hours worked" (Seward et al. 2006, 405). The negotiations of couples around leave and care of children take place within a "gender contract": This is a context is which negotiations "tend to be subtly male dominated and to take place against a background in which women's greater family orientation and men's greater employment orientation are taken for granted" (Haas, Hwang, and Russell 2000, 146). Men may take sick leave or vacation time rather than parental leave, particularly as half of American employers are not required to provide leave. Moreover, many men are deterred from taking leave because of negative employer or coworker attitudes (Seward et al. 2006). Leave does not correlate with greater father involvement, perhaps because most fathers' leaves are relatively short and thus do not support significant participation in child care or a long-term pattern of care (ibid.). In fact, in one study, the longest leave taken was thirty days, and the mean was two to five days—hardly enough time to establish a changed pattern of care (ibid.; Ranson 2001).

One set of researchers found that the response of couples to becoming parents rested on three factors: "the financial situation of the couple, the relative structural position of the spouses, and their expressed parenting role ideology" (Singley and Hynes 2005, 386). Work/family policies interact with these factors. Women's leave from work tends to be viewed as necessary, as linked to disability related to childbirth, while men often view leave as akin to taking vacation time from work (ibid.). For some couples, their decisions reflect a commitment to traditional parenting roles; for others, decisions are driven by "the logic of gendered choices" (Risman 1998, 29), meaning their decisions are driven by what is most practicable according to existing institutional arrangements and cultural norms (Singley and Hynes 2005).

Another area of policy regarding men's caregiving is whether the state supports men's ongoing connection with children after divorce, or if the men are no longer cohabiting with or never married the mother. A significant proportion of fathers gradually disassociate with their children, but a growing number maintain contact and relationship in a very significant way, aided by rules that promote those relationships (Dowd 2000). A vociferous fathers' rights movement has vigorously argued for greater access and care support, at the same time that the pattern of lack of involvement is so strong (Collier 2009).

The Swedish model is probably the strongest existing model of supporting men's care role. It is characterized by what two scholars have called "compulsory fatherhood," because of the strong support for joint custody (Bergman and Hobson 2002). The twin core components are compulsory paternity (every child has a registered father) and obligatory joint custody. The meaning of joint custody is quite flexible, from shared, fifty-fifty custody to occasional contact only. This model is based on the primacy of biological fatherhood and assumed custodial entitlement. It is also based on a model of gender equality that presumes combining work and family, thus a dual-earner model. "Men-friendly in the Swedish context implies a father-friendly state in a dual-earner family mode, which presupposes gender equality" (122). But this model still operates within a work context that penalizes men if they fully exercise or live this model, and the division of family labor still tracks traditional gender divisions. "Making men into fathers has meant celebrating participatory fathering, while at the same time not disturbing the division of labor within the family or the gendered inequalities in the labor market" (124). The Swedish model might be read in a number of ways, but at the least it clearly exposes the resistance to changed masculinities.

Sweden is fascinating also for the proactive government effort to urge men to use the benefits to which they are entitled. One fascinating study looked at the shift in focus and conception of fatherhood in the Swedish campaigns focused on fathers (Klinth 2008). The core vision of Swedish policy is equality, to be achieved by men and women entering each other's spheres. To encourage men to take advantage of parenting leave, early campaigns emphasized men's difference and manliness. The epitome of this was the famous Swedish wrestler Lennart Dahlgren posing with a baby, delivering the message that real (hypermasculine) men are involved fathers (ibid.). The critique of this early campaign was its focus on difference and constructing leave as a choice rather than as a responsibility. In 2002, the campaign shifted perspective to the catch phrase "half each," denoting leave as a responsibility and presenting parenting as a joint, coequal responsibility. It remains to be seen whether this reconstruction of masculinity and fatherhood will be reflected in coequal use of leave and involved, coequal parenting.

An alternative to the Swedish model is to support social parenting rather than biological parenting. The Dutch model for promoting caring fatherhood is a voluntary model and does not privilege biological fathers. Instead the model supports actual care. It also includes supporting fathers who are not living with mothers so that they can sustain their relationships with their children (Knijn and Selten 2002). Various U.S. legal doctrines support social fathers, such as de facto parenthood, psychological parenthood, and the ability of social fathers to acknowledge paternity, but these legal principles still defer to a primary biological parenthood norm.

The policy and legal dilemmas for constructing fatherhood suggest the value of masculinities analysis as part of essential gender analysis to ensure egalitarian families. In the final section of this chapter I summarize some of the threads suggested in this chapter as to how masculinities analysis could be helpful in reminding us of our context and challenging our models to achieve fatherhood that does not rest on traditional hegemonic norms.

Masculinities Impact on Fatherhood and Fathering

The patterns and challenges of fathers, and the value of nurture to children and to women and men, expose how masculinities affect fathers in several ways. Men are blocked from embracing nurture by the command of masculinity that they not be like girls or women and that identifies care as feminine (Dowd 2000). As characteristic and as action, nurture is unmanly. Just as significantly, men embrace the role of breadwinner as the defining characteristic of partnership with women and of being a parent (Dowd 2005; J. Roberts 2005). This role also is conceived as one that either defines parenting economically or that cannot be done in conjunction with care because of the way wage work is constructed (Dowd 2000; Selmi 2000, 2001, 2005, 2007; Selmi and Cahn 2006). Thus fatherhood as a social construction, as a cultural norm, presents challenges for men unless masculine norms take over or reconstruct what has been seen as quintessentially female. In addition, social norms support limited or secondary parenthood based on the breadwinner role. We remain far from an actual experience of shared care or of seeing men as competent nurturers (Dowd 2000; Silbaugh 2007). On the other hand, we have moved, at least ideologically and to some extent practically, to a role model of more involved fatherhood, demonstrating the malleability and ability to change norms that masculinities scholarship has exposed.

Typically, feminist evaluation of work/family issues and fatherhood has come from the perspective of women (Kaminer 2007; Kessler 2007; Silbaugh 2007; Williams and Westfall 2006). Women's interest has been to increase the involvement of men in family care, both childcare and housework, as well as having the value of family care and family work recognized in a way that does not leave mothers economically subordinated. Women have sought greater economic security and the ability to combine family work with wage work. Women have sought not only to work in comparable occupations and fields with men but also to restructure the way work is done and the culture of work so that work not only does not function in a way that devalues and subordinates them because they are not men but also permits combining work and family (Albiston 2005; Jacobs and Gerson 1998; Kessler 2005; Murray 2008; Schultz 2000). Some advocates have argued for a comprehensive family-support structure including childcare, health care, paid leave and reduced work schedules, and family-support payments (Dowd 1989, 1990; Silbaugh 2007). Many others have argued that these changes need to occur in a way that does not simply support women but that encourages men to engage in family care (Selmi and Cahn 2003, 2006; J. Williams 2001).

Feminists also have argued that mother care and its relation to wage work must be recognized in family law in structuring parental obligations in nonmarital and divorced families, as well as in marital families (Ellman 1989; Fineman 2005; Perry 2003; Scott and Scott 1998; Silbaugh 2001). Feminist efforts in family law have been focused on making the law responsive to the actual provision of care and its consequences, rather than an abstract notion of equality that fails to reflect the realities of most families (Fineman 1994, 1995, 2005). Feminists have focused on the increase in nontraditional families as essential to devising fair rules of support for partners and children (Carbone 2000; Garrison 2005; L. Glennon 2008; Polikoff 2004). Some of this advocacy has been reflected in greater obligations and rights for fathers with respect to paternity, but still with an economic model of fatherhood (Dowd 2005). Family law has been one of the areas where men have given voice to a claim of bias against male care and have been successful in raising the issue of systemic refusal to shift the norms and practices of judges (Dowd 2000, 2005; Taylor 2008). But this critique has come primarily from an antifeminist, backlash perspective rather than one supportive of women's nurture and care. Yet family law remains largely unrealistic about the incompatibility of nurture and wage work. At the same time, it reflects powerful assumptions about the superiority of mother care, as long as mothers act like nurture comes first over wage work. Mothers remain the dominant caregivers after divorce, but within an ideal that mothers put family first and career second; there is evidence of judicial bias against working professional mothers (Runner 2000; Weisberg 1995).

What masculinities analysis adds to this perspective, if we now ask the man question, is to consider the barriers for men with respect to fatherhood as both social/cultural and economic (Dowd 2000). To the extent that feminists seek the involvement of fathers along with the support and recognition of mothers' care, strategies and analysis can benefit from the insights gained from masculinities scholarship. It is very clear from masculinities work that the negative definition of masculinity and the inconsistency of care with masculinity norms, especially hegemonic norms, create a significant barrier. On the other hand, the fact that masculinity is socially constructed and the changes in fatherhood norms and legal support for fathers indicate that the situation can change and has changed. The responsiveness of some men to fatherhood suggests a model for further programs that would help both fathers and mothers. For example, there is an opportunity to support a reorientation of fatherhood by supporting men at the birth of their children, including both marital and nonmarital fathers. In addition, feminists' perspective on the barriers to collaboration between mothers and fathers could lead toward addressing the essential issue of violence (Dowd 2000). Masculinities scholarship can be enormously helpful in further exposing the place of violence in masculinity norms and therefore the necessity for proactive policies; feminist scholarship can be helpful in pushing masculinities scholars to analyze how power is replicated and how it might be undermined.

Richard Collier and Sally Sheldon describe fatherhood as "fragmented" (2008). The model of fatherhood that has disintegrated connected marriage, parenthood, and the heterosexual family. This characterization of the model is remarkably similar to Townsend's (2002) description of the "package deal," the informal cultural norm that includes fatherhood, work, marriage, and home ownership. Fragmentation, then, is connected to the decline in that model; the reality for many men that their experience of fatherhood is not linear or singular; the fact that fathers may share parenting with another man who may even be legally recognized as another father, thus fragmenting rights and responsibilities; and the recognition that there are both patterns of disconnection and patterns of greater involvement. Most significantly, Collier and Sheldon point to confusion, difference, and fragmentation in the concept of fatherhood itself. One other theme in their analysis is the concept of "crisis," the intertwining of a sense of crisis in both fatherhood and masculinity. If there is a crisis, then that presumes a norm, so it is important to question what it is that "should" be or what seems missing. In this dialogue, men are sometimes characterized as perpetrators, as a source of danger or harm, and sometimes as victims, as disadvantaged by the "system" (2008, 217). Fathers are also cast as the solution to a range of problems, which implicitly assumes mothers cannot fulfill the same role. "'Active' fathering is thus necessary to ensure the presence of qualities deemed less likely to be present in the mother" (221–22). Thus calls for greater father involvement carry an implicit critique of and intervention in women's lives. "Greater paternal involvement may be a twin-edged sword for mothers, challenging their own authority with regard to their children and forcing them into a continued relationship where one is no longer desired, for example in the post-separation context or following a brief sexual relationship" (230). In the same way, ideals of fatherhood can also implicitly contain ideas about "social class, race, ethnicity and (hetero) sexuality" (231).

What Collier and Sheldon particularly point out so well is the contradictory pieces in current concepts of fatherhood and the potential for either a more liberatory, fluid concept of fatherhood or the reinforcement of patriarchal power. They point out a series of current tensions: the disruption of the concept of the sexual family; the range of roles now encompassed in the term "father"; the relationship between motherhood and fatherhood; whether fathers are victims of institutions and cultural norms or selfish actors who have created their difficulties; and related confusion about the role of men in families. This characterization of the current situation connects to the role of law in embracing a model for fatherhood and families, what it supports and/or sanctions. The caution is against law taking a unitary position in this complex and contradictory context, as the danger is clear that doing so can so easily turn toward reinforcing male power.

Indeed, Jeff Hearn (2002) reminds us how much fatherhood research and policy debates have *not* been about gender and power. Fatherhood, in his view, should be viewed as "a form of certain men's power" (245). The goal of masculinities study should be, he argues, to deconstruct that power and reconstruct masculinity. The state is a critical party in achieving that goal. "The state, through civil, family and property law, population registration and numerous other policies, . . . devised, sanctioned, constructed, constrained and determined what fathers are and what a father is. Men's and father's actual, potential or absent citizenship has been developed and maintained in relation to women. Above all there has been a pervasive assumption . . . of the enfranchised, autonomous, adult, heterosexual, married, fathering, family-heading, individual, male subject" (251). State power and family power are connected through fathers, so reconstruction of the model of fatherhood is challenging and difficult. Hearn argues that three particularly important aspects of the model of fatherhood are "violence, rights and responsibilities, [and] birth and sexuality" (256).

Feminist analysis as enriched by masculinities scholarship could move fatherhood issues into a gender-specific but gender-linked direction. The position of fathers and mothers with respect to the care of children is asymmetrical but interlinked. One of the core common areas is the economic support of families and the resistance of the culture and structure of work to combining wage work and family care. All of these concerns are linked to what our vision is of fathers and mothers, particularly whether we assume a model of shared care or primary care and whether we mean that model to be infused with gender equality.

8

Men and Sexual Abuse

with Ted Shaw, PhD

Sexual abuse is the antithesis of any vision of fatherhood, whether traditional or redefined fatherhood. We do not imagine fathers as perpetrators or as victims when they were children. Men are typically linked with sexual abuse in our minds as perpetrators of sexual offenses against girls and women. The paradigmatic sex offender is the sexual predator male who ruthlessly attacks and violates multiple victims, classically the rapist or the child molester. This offender is always a male, and often a stranger; the attack is random; and the gender of the victim is always female.

We miss several things in this paradigm. Offenders just as often are family members, not strangers, and include fathers, brothers, and even mothers. In this chapter, however, the focus is on another missing piece of our picture of child sexual abuse. What we have left out about victims is the reality that boys are victimized as well. Indeed, the genesis of this chapter lies in a real story of one offender and his victims.

In the 1980s Ted Shaw, a psychologist who specializes in work with sex offenders, was a therapist for a young adult man in a secure residential treatment program in north central Florida who had been convicted of molesting a child. In the course of therapy his client admitted to molesting four hundred boys, a total of many thousands of times, over the course of seventeen years. The sexual history could be used to treat and evaluate him but could not be used to prosecute him for additional offenses as it was presented without specifics or details which could in any way determine the victims' identities. The man's first arrest for a sex offense occurred when he was twelve, and although he was caught and sanctioned, the therapeutic intervention was minimal and ineffective. He admitted during treatment as an adult that at the time of his first arrest he had already molested at least six boys and that he began molesting again almost immediately after being arrested. He continued molesting boys throughout his teens and had abused hundreds of boys (and several girls) by the time he was arrested again in his late twenties. In the course of his prison term he volunteered for and entered treatment, which was then a well-funded comprehensive program aimed at rehabilitating sex offenders. In therapy he was ready to confront his problem and worked effectively in therapy over the course of several years. His offense was committed prior to registration requirements, so upon successful completion of therapy in the mid-1980s, he returned to the community, successfully completed ten years of probation and community-based treatment, and did not reoffend during his supervision period. He is still followed informally and has asserted that he remains in recovery and has not reoffended, using the strategies he learned throughout his treatment. But what of his victims? Shaw, now a forensic psychologist nationally known for his expertise regarding sex offenders, frequently passes through the same area where the offenses occurred, and more than once he has wondered what happened to those four hundred boys, now men in their forties and fifties, only one of whom officially reported his abuse.

Shaw's knowledge and work with offenders and victims suggest the possible paths and outcomes for these victims. His expertise is brought to bear in this chapter linking masculinities analysis and adult male victims of child sexual abuse. It is these men, and others who have experienced sexual abuse as children, who are the focus of this chapter. Their victimization has largely been hidden and ignored, legally and socially. This is the case not only because we assume girls are the victims of sexual abuse but also because we assume that perpetrators are exclusively male.

In this chapter, we focus on the adult male survivors of child sexual abuse and how masculinities analysis, informing and infusing feminist analysis, might expose their experience and contribute to a more complete and effective approach to child sexual abuse. In the first section, we set out the context, including both what we know and what we do not know about child sexual abuse. We next consider the legal framework for dealing with child sexual abuse, which is remarkably recent in origin and owes much of its genesis to feminist activism. What emerge in this account are both the remarkable contribution of feminist theory to constructing criminal and civil remedies and also the limits of theory when all the manifestations of gender are not included. We then look at the available psychological data on male victims of child sexual abuse and what the data suggests about the role of gender in victim injury and response to abuse. Finally, we consider how masculinities analysis exposes or suggests how we might understand injury or harm for male victims and how we might construct an effective support structure as well as more proactive intervention aimed at reducing the rate of child sexual abuse, and more generally child abuse, for all children.

Context: Data about Child Sexual Abuse

Sexual abuse of children is remarkably prevalent, within a broader context of child neglect and abuse. The exact statistics for child abuse generally and any subset of abuse are highly disputed. Because of the disincentives for reporting, because the victims are children (often very young children), and because much offending occurs within families, the context is particularly difficult to establish with certainty (London et al. 2005). It is widely assumed that data based on reports or arrests hide a significant amount of abuse that goes unreported (Todd 2004).

There are general patterns, however, in the range of data. In the broad category of child abuse and neglect, boys and girls are equally victimized. The most common perpetrators are female (nearly 60 percent of all perpetrators), and the most common female offenders are mothers. In data from 2001, based on reports to the National Child Abuse and Neglect Data System, the dominant form of maltreatment was neglect (nearly 60 percent of victims), followed by physical abuse (nearly 20 percent of victims) and sexual abuse (10 percent of victims). Slightly over 25 percent of victims suffered from multiple forms of maltreatment. At the most extreme end, abuse results in death, most often from neglect, and most fatalities are children under age six. The fatality rate from abuse and neglect is *higher than any other cause of death by injury* for children under age four (Todd 2004). The highest rate of victimization is for the youngest children, birth to age three, and rates decline as children get older (Children's Bureau 2007).

Two factors strongly linked to the prevalence of child abuse and neglect are substance abuse and domestic violence. Parental alcohol or drug abuse is a factor in nearly half of substantiated cases (Todd 2004, citing a 1998 report from the Child Welfare League of America). A second risk factor is the presence of domestic violence, which links to batterer abuse of children in addition to partners but also to a higher likelihood of abuse of children by female victims of batterers (Todd 2004).

The patterns within child sexual abuse are distinctive in several ways from those of overall child abuse. First, the rate of child sexual abuse appears to be dropping, with speculation that public education, longer incarcerations for identified offenders, and greater public awareness may be factors in this decline (Finkelhor and Jones 2006). As noted, most available data estimate sexual offenses as roughly 10 percent of child abuse and neglect (Todd 2004). Centers for Disease Control data from 2008 estimate a rate of 8 to 9 percent (Centers for Disease Control 2008), and the latest report of the Children's Bureau in 2007 reports a rate of 7.6 percent (Children's Bureau 2007). Second, the age pattern is different. The most common victims of sexual abuse are older, as compared to the generally high rates of all forms of abuse among younger children. For sexual abuse, 35.2 percent of victims were children twelve to fifteen years old; 23.8 percent were eight to eleven years old, and 23.3 percent were four to seven years old (Children's Bureau 2007).

Most significantly, the gender pattern varies among forms of abuse. "While boys are at a greater risk of serious injury and of emotional neglect than girls, girls are sexually abused three times more often than boys" (Todd 2004, 497). As with other child abuse statistics, experts vary in the estimation of child sexual abuse by gender, although there is consensus that girls are more frequently victimized. Some experts estimate the rate at which child sexual abuse occurs as one in three women and one in four men (Leibowitz 2003). Another compilation suggests one in three women and one in ten men (E. Wilson 2003). An international survey of twenty-one countries by the World Health Organization (WHO) estimates that worldwide, between 5 and 10 percent of men have a history of childhood sexual abuse, with a range of prevalence of 3 to 29 percent of males, compared to 7 to 36 percent of females (Stemple 2009). One national survey of U.S. adult men and women found that 16 percent of men and 27 percent of women reported experiencing sexual abuse as children (Finkelhor et al. 1990). In the specific context of sexual abuse committed by members of the Catholic Church and reported to the Church, the gender pattern is strongly reversed. According to a survey covering the years 1950 to 2002, 81 percent of the victims were male and 19 percent were female (Stemple 2009). The Ryan Report issued by Irish authorities in May 2009 by the Commission to Inquire into Child Abuse detailed physical, emotional, and sexual abuse in church-run residential schools and orphanages and singled out sexual abuse in boys' schools as "endemic" (Ryan Report 2009).

The bulk of child sexual abuse is committed by family members or persons known to the child, not strangers. According to a study of child victims, 80 percent of abused girls and 60 percent of abused boys were victimized by adults known to them; half of the offenders were parents or other family members (Lieb, Quinsey, and Berliner 1998). A study of assaults occurring between 1989 and 1992 found assaults by teachers, coaches, or others to be double (44 percent) the rate of offenses by parents (22 percent), but there was also a category of other family members (15 percent) (Gitlin 2008). A 1986 study found that 29 percent of offenders were related to the victim, 60 percent were known but unrelated, and only 11 percent were strangers (E. Wilson 2003). The younger the child, the more likely the offender is a family member (and younger children are disproportionate victims of abuse) (Gitlin 2008).

Child sexual abusers are quite varied. They include preferential child molesters, usually pedophiles, who prefer sex with children to their age-appropriate peers; pedophilic child molesters who are sexually attracted to children but may also be attracted to age-appropriate peers; situational child molesters who may have a normal sexual history but have turned to sexual molestation of a child during some type of situational stress, incident, or event; intrafamilial child molesters, usually referred to as incest offenders, who are generally fathers, stepfathers, or brothers but can include more distant relatives such as uncles and older cousins or steprelatives; stranger molesters, a rare but high-risk group (Hanson and Bussiere 1998); and acquaintance molesters such as family friends, older adolescents, babysitters, teachers, priests, or scout masters (Freeman-Longo and Blanchard 1998). The motivation for molesting ranges from sexual attraction to children to curiosity and includes, for at least some offenders, the unhealthy resolution of the trauma from their own childhood sexual abuse through identification with the abuser, emotional identification with the victims, and a myriad of other reasons, both logical and irrational (Barnard et al. 1990). Although most individuals who molest children, including boys, are men, adolescent males constitute a significant group of molesters and offend for many of the reasons just mentioned. Adult and adolescent females, though underrepresented, constitute a small percentage of overall offenders. Research on the connection between being a victim and an offender has found that while some offenders have histories of being sexually abused (about 30 percent for adult males, about 40 percent for adolescent males), there does not appear to be a direct connection. Mediating variables associated with the connection appear to be a history of exposure to family violence and disruption (Salter et al. 2003).

Most sexual abusers are men, but more recently it has been recognized that women are abusers as well. The data on that subject as elsewhere are conflicting as to exactly what proportion of the offender population is female. Based on arrest data from 2000, females were 8 percent of those arrested for sex offenses (other than rape and prostitution). Victim reports suggest higher rates: according to a 1981 study, females were the offender for 13 percent of female abuse victims and 24 percent of the male victims; a second study showed a rate of women as the offender for 6 percent of female victims and 14 percent of male victims (Levine 2006). More recent studies have reported even higher rates. Some suggest that offenses by women are even less reported than offenses by men. This is linked to several reasons, including the view by some experts for decades that women could not commit sexual abuse. One commentator stated in the early 1970s, "What harm can be done without a penis?" (Mathis 1972, 54), and in the 1990s one researcher summarized the view of several experts on this issue as "No penis, no problem" (Kirsta 1994, 344–77).

In sum, the statistical context of child sexual abuse lacks precision because of difficulties connected to reporting, but broad outlines are apparent that indicate some key elements for boys and men. First, boys do not appear to be victimized at the same rate as girls, but boys nevertheless constitute a significant number of victims. Second, the predominant abusers of boys are men. The most common pattern for boys is same-sex abuse, while for girls it is heterosexual abuse. The meaning of that for adult males within the context of dominant masculinity may be significant. It may affect the likelihood of reporting and the nature of the harm experienced as an adult in ways distinctive from women's harms. If the legal system does not imagine male victims, then those victims are even less likely to be heard. In addition, when the abuser is a woman, the dynamics of a female offender and a male victim also are framed within heterosexual, masculine-dominant sexuality norms. Ignoring the possibility of female offenders was long a part of the system and rendered those instances of victimization for boys particularly invisible. This also hid female abuse of girls and any distinctive gender implications of that pattern. Third, abuse happens usually with someone that the boy knows, as is the case with girls, so it functions within a family or close community gender dynamic. This does not mean, however, that the gender dynamic of family operates the same for boys as it does for girls. Fourth, sexual abuse of boys occurs within a broader context of child abuse in which boys are equally victimized as compared to girls and a context in which physical abuse of boys is a subset of abuse where boys are the most likely and most serious victims. Given that sexual abuse as with other forms of abuse is often connected to other maltreatment, it is important to keep this broader perspective of child abuse in mind. While we mean to focus here on sexual abuse of boys and its implications for adult men, we should not let this focus lead us to ignore the broader range of child abuse and neglect.

The Legal Response to Child Sexual Abuse

Given the scope and traumatic nature of child abuse, and the particularly strong and widespread contemporary social abhorrence of child sexual abuse, one of the most startling and jarring realities is that this victimization was so long ignored by the legal system. Not until the 1970s and 1980s did the legal system take child sexual abuse seriously. Feminist activists and scholars were responsible for focusing attention on child sexual abuse, giving voice in particular to adult female survivors of abuse, and generating a significant reform of the child welfare system (Andrew 2006; Mangold 2003; Stemple 2009; Todd 2004; E. Wilson 2003).

The reasons why child sexual abuse, and more generally child abuse, was ignored are linked to the traditional treatment of children and families by the legal system. Children were considered the property of their families, and that concept along with strong deference to parents and respect for family privacy kept much abuse out of public view (Mangold 2003). The doctrine of parent-child immunity also shielded parents from tort suits by children until relatively recently, and the requirement of fulfilling statutes of limitations caused problems as well for adult victims (E. Wilson 2003). Nineteenth-century intervention in families was framed as the state standing in the shoes of parents, under the parens patriae doctrine, to deal with incompetent or inadequate parents. Intervention was not based on children's rights or children's harm but rather on the value of children, consistent with their characterization as property (Andrew 2006).

Another factor was the evolution of psychology and the influence of psychological concepts on the law's concept of harm (or lack of it). Particularly influential was a very specific turn in Freud's work that recharacterized reports of abuse. In his early work based on his therapy with female patients, Freud reported that his patients' symptoms indicated they had been sexually traumatized as children. Freud abandoned this interpretation, however, when his peers and mentors reacted with disdain and silence. The implications of his conclusions would have suggested that many respectable men were abusing their daughters. Instead, Freud reinterpreted the statements of his female patients as evidence of sexual fantasies based on incestuous desire. Because of Freud's enormous impact on psychology, this interpretation was adopted by many psychologists. Alfred Kinsey, for example, in his groundbreaking research on sexuality in the 1950s, collected data indicating the presence of child sexual abuse but dismissed the reports as false, following the classic Freudian interpretation (Phipps 1997). A shift in the psychological literature did not come until the 1980s; the impetus for change in the legal treatment of abuse came instead from medicine.

The emergence of a new legal framework for child welfare began with medical doctors in the 1950s. Pediatric radiologists began to gather information about long bone fractures, culminating in the seminal article by C. Henry Kempe and colleagues in 1962 describing and naming "battered child syndrome." With remarkable speed, within four years every state and the District of Columbia enacted legislation mandating the reporting of child battering. Also during the 1960s advocates for women's rights and children's rights pressed for legislation to recognize the harm of child abuse and specifically sexual abuse, since girls disproportionately were the victims. In 1974 Congress enacted the Child Abuse Prevention and Treatment Act (CAPTA), which reinforced the reporting model by encouraging further state legislation and also funding research and demonstration projects (E. Wilson 2003).

The recognition of child sexual abuse emerged within this general movement to recognize child abuse. Recognizing the harm of child sexual abuse was the work of feminist analysis and critique beginning in the 1970s (Mangold 2003; E. Wilson 2003). This originated from aggregating the experiences of adult women, first articulated in consciousness-raising groups. These stories emerged as feminists began to focus on rape, and feminists saw the linkages in a broad pattern of the sexual victimization of girls and women. "Father-daughter incest emerged as a paradigm of male power, a literal expression of the patriarchal organization of society" (E. Wilson 2003, 160). The surfacing of women's stories of incest merged with feminist critical analysis of psychology. Feminist analysis of male-centered psychological concepts eventually led to the exposure of Freud's shift from reporting data to constructing the theory of female fantasies, which was dubbed the "Freudian cover-up" (ibid.). In feminists' search for other psychological approaches to help female victims, their inquiry intersected with research on trauma to aid the disorders of (virtually all male) veterans in the wake of the Vietnam War. A contemporary of Freud's, Pierre Janet, had done groundbreaking work on trauma which led to modern work on post-traumatic stress disorder (PTSD). This work was resurrected and fused with feminist goals to address adult women's needs for dealing with the consequences of their sexual abuse as children (ibid.; Leibowitz 2003). A major assumption of feminist activists, consistent with this connection, was that the suffering of adult women was linked to widespread sexual victimization as children (E. Wilson 2003). Judith Herman identified common threads between World War I "battle fatigue" (which could not be recognized as a psychological war wound because real men were not supposed to be emotionally vulnerable), the recognition of this syndrome as "PTSD" after the Vietnam War, and the sufferings of incest survivors (Herman 1992).

As a result of feminist activism, therefore, child sexual abuse was brought to public attention. This resulted in increased reporting, prosecution and incarceration, and strengthening of state legislation, particularly in the area of criminal law reform. At the same time, much of the sentencing was oriented around treatment and rehabilitation, reflecting the dominant pattern of offenses within families and the belief that offenders (particularly incest offenders) could be rehabilitated. A second wave of legislative effort in the 1990s focused on sexual predators, and constructed a much more punitive model of dealing with sex offenders, including the requirement of lifetime registration (Lieb, Quinsey, and Berliner 1998). These reforms responded to less typical and common forms of abuse, particularly the most violent offenders and those with assumed high recidivism, but affected all offenders. By 1996 all fifty states had registration laws, and community notification became part of these laws. Another reform of the 1990s was the reevaluation of whether victims of abuse and neglect could be reunited with their families. Legislation passed in the late 1990s made it easier to remove children from abusive homes and more quickly terminate parental rights and facilitate adoption (Mangold 2003).

One of the consequences of this evolution and activism was the emergence of efforts to provide criminal and civil remedies for adult victims. This occurred both domestically and in international law from the 1970s to the 1990s (Stemple 2009; E. Wilson 2003). Again, these developments were linked to the efforts of feminists and reflect their advocacy on behalf of adult women struggling as adults with the impact of childhood abuse. Remedies for adults rested on an understanding and justification for why these harms should be dealt with so long after they occurred. In particular, remedies assumed the likelihood that the trauma associated with child sexual abuse would be resolved by many victims by repression of the memory of abuse. The understanding that child sexual abuse could trigger the repression of memory became a challenge for the legal system in several respects. Statutes of limitations, unless revised, could bar any claim because the victim had waited too long to seek redress (E. Wilson 2003). Exceptions, such as the discovery rules (which allow the time to seek a remedy to be tolled if the victim did not know or have reason to know of the harm) did not always work for all victims, particularly those who remembered the abuse but did not connect it to harms they suffered until they were adults, as opposed to victims who repressed the memory totally until some triggering event in adulthood. In addition, the reliability of the memory was questioned. Indeed, the phenomenon of repressed memories of childhood sexual abuse became a matter of considerable controversy (Alison, Kebbell, and Lewis 2006; M. Donaldson 1993; Leibowitz 2003; E. Wilson 2003). Expert testimony to validate recovered memory, according to one set of researchers, cannot be generalized but rather must rely on the specifics of particular cases and probably should require supporting evidence (Alison, Kebbell, and Lewis 2006). Even basic assumptions are contested: for example, "a fundamental question exists concerning whether trauma enhances or inhibits memory" (424).

The difficulties experienced by adult survivors expose the range of consequences of sexual abuse. These include depression, anxiety, sleeping difficulties, eating disorders, low self-esteem, difficulty with interpersonal relationships, dissociation, and multiple personality disorder (Whitcombe 2001). Clinical findings confirm that adult survivors often suffer from underlying mistrust that affects their relationships and often have particularly difficult relationships with parents and other family members (Todd 2004). At the same time, not all children manifest the same responses to sexual abuse, either immediately or long term. It is also difficult to isolate abuse as the sole factor triggering particular psychological difficulties (Phipps 1997; E. Wilson 2003). The empirical data on this subject as elsewhere reflect the challenges of framing our understanding, including how recently this area has been taken seriously and how strongly it has been affected by the beliefs of advocates.

There are also distinctive issues with sexual abuse cases when children do report. Children's testimony always creates difficulties, and the younger the children are, the more challenging it is to hear their voices while also protecting the rights of defendants. In an effort to validate children's testimony, some experts proposed the existence of child sexual abuse accommodation syndrome, suggesting a pattern of how children respond to sexual abuse (London et al. 2005). But critics have found that there simply is no pattern (ibid.; Gitlin 2008). Sexual abuse cases remain difficult to prosecute.

One ironic consequence of the feminist roots of the current structure of the legal response to child sexual abuse is that it has defined the legal response in ways that also limit its effectiveness. As Elizabeth Wilson (2003) points out, the link between feminist grassroots organizing, the analysis of psychological bias against listening to women's voices, and the widespread ignoring of sexual assaults for children and adults converged to make child sexual abuse, especially incest, a powerful focus of feminist activists. The result was to give much needed focus to sexual abuse but with two significant limitations. First, the focus was entirely on female victims (see also Phipps 1997). Kay Levine (2006) points out the same pattern in statutory rape statutes, which were gendered at their inception to protect females and, even when modified to become gender neutral-statutes, have been used almost exclusively for the benefit of female victims. Similarly, as Lara Stemple (2009) points out, the human rights framework assumes a female victim, so much so that even language focusing on gender violence is commonly understood as only encompassing female victims. If boys and men are included at all, it is within an implicit hierarchy that puts the victimization of girls and women as primary.

Second, the feminist focus on sexual abuse drew attention away from other forms of child abuse, rather than directing attention to this broader subject. Of particular concern to boys and men, physical child abuse is disproportionate and more severe for boys and may have an impact on the rate of adult male violence (E. Wilson 2003). In addition, for both boys and girls, the feminist focus ignores the role of women as the predominant perpetrators of abuse and neglect. Masculinities analysis might lead us to deepen and enrich our analysis not only to include boys and men but to consider the complex role of gender in the widespread problem of child abuse generally and sexual abuse specifically.

The Impact of Sexual Abuse on Adult Men

Because sexual abuse of boys, and its impact on adult men, has remained hidden, it is important to explore what we know about the effects of sexual abuse on men. First we must consider the fact that the impact and consequences of sexual abuse for boys as well as girls begins immediately and continues through the remainder of their childhood, into adolescence and ultimately into adulthood. Initial reaction to sexual abuse can be severely traumatic, or when it combines pleasure and trauma, it can be confusing, leaving lasting memories that trigger fear and guilt. These symptoms often meet criteria for diagnosing post-traumatic stress disorder (PTSD), particularly when the abuse has been violent and/or threatening. In a study using autobiographical interviews with twenty-six male survivors, David Lisak (1994) found evidence of fifteen recurring psychological themes related to the abuse: anger, betrayal, fear, homosexuality issues, helplessness, isolation and alienation, legitimacy, loss, masculinity issues, negative childhood peer relations, negative schemas about people, negative schemas about the self, problems with sexuality, self-blame/guilt, and shame/humiliation. Although some of the sequelae to sexual abuse for boys are similar to those for girls, including sexual promiscuity, social and sexual anxiety, and depression, unlike girls, boys have been found to be more likely to engage in aggressive and criminal behaviors, drug and alcohol use, suicide attempts, and truancy in response to sexual trauma (Sorsoli, Kia-Keating, and Grossman 2008). They tend to suffer emotional trauma including depression and anxiety; behavioral issues including aggression, delinquency, and substance abuse; and personality issues including avoidance, passive-aggressiveness, and hostility (Larson et al. 2007).

Clearly what emerges from the literature is that men are traumatized by child sexual abuse in a way similar to women when considering the intensity of the trauma, but male survivors' symptoms tend to operationalize externally with various forms and degrees of acting out. Ketring and Feinauer (1999) found in a study of male and female sexual abuse survivors that there was no statistically significant difference for trauma based on gender when each was mildly or moderately abused. As the intensity of the abuse increased for women, their internalized symptoms increased. This was not true for the much smaller male sample. Here again for men the recommendation was to focus intervention on "externalized symptoms such as drug use, antisocial behavior and sexual acting out" (119).

Issues for male survivors of abuse begin with the experience itself and are often exacerbated by the dilemma of disclosure (Sorsoli, Kia-Keating, and Grossman 2008). As one author puts it, "Psychological responses to abuse such as anxiety, denial, self-hypnosis, dissociation, and self-mutilation are common. Coping strategies may include being the angry avenger, the passive victim, rescuer, daredevil, or conformist. Sexual abuse may precipitate runaway behavior, chronic use of sick days, poor school or job performance" (Valente 2005, 10). When male survivors disclose, the reaction is not always positive or supportive. While the experience of disclosure may lead to personal growth and ultimately to interventions for the trauma, male survivors clearly experience issues related to disclosure which may be personal, relational, or sociocultural (Sorsoli, Kia-Keating, and Grossman 2008). They are often confronted with skepticism and doubt and may be accused of inviting the abuse. The fact that boys are significantly more likely to be sexually abused by a male suggests that the boys may incur some degree of sexual identity confusion or embarrassment, and it is not uncommon for victims to leave out explicit details of their abuse. Experience with male child molesters has shown that they frequently pleasure the victim prior to meeting their own needs in order to gain the complicity of the victim and to make it more difficult for the victim to report the abuse because of feelings of guilt and shame.

Adolescent and adult survivors have been found to have more difficulty dating and engaging in consensual sex as a result of childhood sexual trauma than do nonabused males (Larson et al. 2007). Interviews of older adults molested as children confirm that the trauma of this abuse for boys can be debilitating throughout adulthood and is not simple to resolve. Even with the use of various therapeutic interventions, long-term and intrusive issues of intimacy, trust, and dysfunctional sexuality appear to last throughout the lifespan for many survivors (Andersen 2008).

Masculinities Analysis and Male Victims of Child Sexual Abuse

What might feminist analysis, infused by masculinities analysis, offer to this highly gendered and very socially sensitive area of law? Feminists have identified sex and sexuality as critical aspects of subordination. Catharine MacKinnon has been particularly strongly identified with analysis that identifies sex as a major site of domination and hegemony where the complicity of the dominated is part of what is constructed as desire. Feminists thus bring to the topic enormous insight on sex and sexuality, although this has also been a place of significant disagreement. So feminist analysis has the potential to bring a great deal to the subject of men's victimization once masculinities analysis opens up men's harm from child sexual abuse.

For girls, feminists have analyzed child sexual abuse as a setup for domination by men as an adult and for further risks of sexual assault as adults. For boys, child sexual abuse violates the norms of manhood. Or, alternatively, it represents the norms of manhood in a way feminists have not previously recognized: it is a form of imposing hierarchy between men, or a perverse way to teach the importance of domination, lest you be dominated. Sexual abuse has a powerful impact on identity as a man and on sexuality (just as it does on women), and again, it is gender specific. So the harm done and the need for support, healing, and care is gender specific.

At the same time, there may be critical interactions between men and women, as well as between men and men, that are linked to the consequences of child sexual abuse. Considering the connections, along with differences and similarities in the consequences for adults, has the potential to elaborate a richer picture that might have an impact on our policies and practices for prevention and both criminal and civil consequences, including effective treatment of both offenders and victims.

The gender-specific aspects of abuse might also illuminate places that we find particularly uncomfortable to confront. For example, as the data on adult male victims indicate, one particularly challenging part of support and intervention is dealing with the link between sexual abuse and pleasure. Our paradigm of sexual abuse is brute force; the reality is that many offenders use persuasion and pleasuring as part of the offense. This creates a particularly challenging place of healing for victims, to get past their feelings of shame and guilt.

Masculinities analysis also points to the critical impact of sexual orientation on this issue, requiring that not all men be viewed as the same. For those boys who identify as gay, abuse remains a violation of the core right to control one's sexuality and sexual partners. The silencing and refusal to deal with the specific harms of abuse for gay men require the articulation of that harm and its recognition in both domestic and international law. Moreover, the identification of that harm clearly delineates the affirmative rights of sexuality for boys and girls and men and women. Those affirmative rights require imagining sex and sexuality in the absence of subordination.

Masculinities analysis also causes us to think about the implications of strong feminist analysis that has been largely gender specific. Without reducing the powerful and necessary light that has illuminated girls' and women's harm, what has been missed? What if we ask the other question? By asking the man (and boy) question with respect to child sexual abuse, we expose connections that suggest additional ways to understand harm, as well as widening what we identify as harm. For both boys and girls, a core connection with respect to child sexual abuse that is not gender specific is the violation of the rights of childhood and core developmental freedom. Sexual abuse interferes with necessary relationships of trust and care and with critical stages of development from child to adult. Those injuries to children may be addressed and healed while they are still children, given the remarkable resilience of youth. But for some, the trauma and implications of child sexual abuse have the potential to generate significant scars that are carried into adulthood. This developmental harm is even more clearly underscored with the addition of masculinities analysis. This suggests a significant mental health issue that is at present not addressed in the same way as other widespread public health harms that we recognize and deal with in the open.

In addition, asking other questions and examining the impact of prior feminist advocacy exposes how the focus on child sexual abuse has unintentionally meant that other forms of abuse have been given less attention. The negative consequences of that focus are disproportionate for boys. In addition, this focus has avoided the reality that women constitute the majority of offenders. The dynamic of that pattern of maltreatment and abuse is a critical part of understanding motherhood that must be addressed.

Where this analysis might lead ultimately is toward interventions that would proactively reduce the rate of child sexual abuse and other forms of child abuse, as well as more effectively support victims. Particularly with respect to child sexual abuse, it might well lead toward constructing and challenging what healthy masculinity is. This is where the treatment of offenders and support of victims in some ways, ironically, seem to intersect. One of the challenges with respect to victims is that so much of child sexual abuse comes from family members or persons in a position of trust, which necessitates educating and empowering children with a vision of what is positive and healthy. That leads toward a reconstruction of masculinities that has been, according to masculinities scholars, one of the most challenging goals of masculinities analysis. It is a place where classic feminist analysis may have the most to offer masculinities and where the interaction of feminism and masculinities analysis may yield significant results. By coming at this issue from the context of abuse and the harm done to adult men, and indirectly to all those with whom they have relationships, there might be a different way to challenge and change masculinity and, more broadly, to imagine sexual equality.

9

Conclusion

Masculinities analysis has much to add to feminist analysis. By focusing on boys we begin to reexamine the dynamics of gender socialization and how it reproduces gender inequality. The psychological data expose fundamental similarities between girls and boys and how those similarities are affected by concepts of gender role that are not limited to families but are also strongly reinforced in the structure of education. In the ecology of childhood, education is one of the most influential systems, along with family, peers, and community. As chapter 5 demonstrates, for both boys and girls, education remains a highly gendered structure and culture that perpetuates gender inequality rather than achieving gender justice. The example of education is one in which a historically male-only structure evolved into a structure embedded with gender hierarchy and difference and then was challenged to remove artificial barriers and reexamine its assumptions and thus to reorient its culture and structure to accommodate girls as formally equal students. To some degree that challenge has been successful. What the masculinities perspective uncovers, in the guise of examining the place of boys and education, is that the system remains gendered in ways that disserve boys as well as continuing to disserve girls. Thus although the gender-bias tilt has equalized to a certain degree, because the examination of the system has approached the bias issue only from a limited perspective, much work remains to be done. It requires simultaneous attention to boys and girls, gender specific and gender connected without reinforcing a binary, heterosexual norm.

A central premise of prior gender analysis, it seems, has been that the education system serves boys while disserving girls. Masculinities analysis exposes that education does not, in several respects, serve boys. It disserves boys in relation to their academic goals because it remains limited to learning styles and developmental assumptions that serve only a narrow class of learners which may disproportionately clash with boys' socialization and development. It also reinforces a culture of gender assumptions that are based in gender hierarchies, between boys and girls and between some boys and other boys. Masculinities analysis also suggests that boys come to school differently socialized with respect to school and as gendered beings. School is not a neutral structure or culture with respect to the boys and girls that come to its doors, nor are boys and girls ungendered subjects, simply "children." By ignoring the complex ways that gender functions at school, education tends to reinforce traditional socialization. If socialization tends toward limits and restrictions on both boys and girls, then schools act either to open up the limits or to reaffirm them. Masculinities analysis of the "hidden curriculum" of school exposes how school tends to reinforce the gender hierarchy that for boys means hierarchy over all girls and hierarchy among boys. It exposes how as children grow older, and particularly as they reach adolescence, the hidden curriculum reinforces the most traditional gender norms.

The education example challenges gender analysis to think of boys and girls simultaneously, rather than approach gender equity in education from the perspective of one group or the other. It also points to how easily discourse can become confrontational and either/or. The claim of a "crisis" regarding boys and education reads largely as a backlash to feminist gains. While it might lead in the direction of a more inclusive look at gender bias, in gender-specific ways that stay connected to the ultimate goal of justice, it has the tendency to displace gains for girls. The potential for patriarchy to reassert itself is very obvious in this example, where the concern for boys is a thin façade over resistance and reaction against gains for girls. The education example is one in which it is essential that feminists remain vigilant but not resistant, opening the analysis to a richer, more complex approach to equity in education. One of the other benefits to exposing the issue of boys' development as it relates to education is to question how the caring, empathetic side of boys and men can be nurtured instead of being repressed. This is an issue that is not limited to education, but it is one that is very evident in this area.

The education example, then, suggests that equity requires asking the other question, the man question. Doing so takes us away from gender or feminism "unmodified" to the intersection of gender with other critical characteristics. It reminds us that in considering justice, gender cannot be isolated from other forms of subordination. Considering the controversy between the needs of boys and girls leads not only to demanding that both be considered but also to recognizing this issue is secondary to the needs of educational equality based on race and class. This challenges gender analysis to embrace and take on race as a feminist issue, because it is a deeper, broader, and more entrenched form of discrimination that must be uprooted if meaningful gender equity for both boys and girls is ultimately to be meaningful for *all* boys and *all* girls.

The second example of applying masculinities theory, the juvenile justice system, has a different set of lessons to suggest for the usefulness of masculinities analysis. It particularly reinforces the limits of the concept of gender neutrality, especially in systems that disproportionately deal with either boys or girls. Indeed, it shows how gendered systems often render gender invisible. When that pattern is present, however, it should trigger strong inquiry into why the gender-disproportionate pattern exists, as well as a consideration of the implications for both the overrepresented group and the underrepresented group. The juvenile justice system was originally designed, and remains structured, for boys. Indeed, juvenile justice might more accurately be called the "boys' justice" system (to which some girls are also subject). Why are boys disproportionately its subjects? Why do we accept this pattern as given, as taken for granted? Moreover, when we measure the effectiveness of the system, what lessons it teaches, and its outcomes, we might call it the "boys' *injustice*" system. Why injustice? The system has lost much of its rehabilitative focus, and boys come out worse, not better, after intersecting with the system; the system turns many boys over to the adult criminal justice system, which is expressly punitive and just as disproportionately male; it disregards core developmental empirical data that are inconsistent with imposing punishments premised on concepts of judgment and culpability; and it fails to serve either children's or society's best interests. If this is all true, why have we treated boys this way? What are our assumptions and goals? And when girls come into this system and structure, are we exacerbating their consequences (and in what ways?) by imposing on them this strongly gendered system?

Masculinities analysis suggests that the framework and culture of the juvenile justice system reflects our unvarnished view of boys. If we use that analysis to question the assumptions of the system, then what is reflected back suggests several powerful themes. First, we think boys are violent and unmanageable; we fear them and want to control them. Second, the juvenile justice system (and the adult system and prisons) is not a departure from masculinity but simply an expression of masculinity. We expect boys to be here, as we expect men to be in our adult system. The maleness of these systems perpetuates an essentialist assumption about men that feeds male hierarchy over women and the hierarchies among men. The message for all of us is that male violence is a danger that is very present. That creates a patriarchal dividend for boys and men and subordination for women. This becomes a system that tells boys that they have exceeded the limits of acceptable masculinity, but at the same time it reinforces the most traditional masculinity. It reminds those outside the system of the configuration of danger, and it is male.

And not only is it male; it is black male. Masculinities analysis reminds us of the intersection of race and gender in the juvenile justice system. Race again emerges as a feminist issue, one that it is essential for feminism to embrace. With the pattern in both the juvenile and adult criminal justice systems, the incarceration and connection of black males with these systems is nothing short of epidemic. It is a gender issue that should not be ignored.

The juvenile justice system should remind us to remain concerned about girls, since we know the system was not constructed for them. But that very concern should have led advocates to ask, then what about the boys? Does this system serve them? If not, then there are several gender issues that need resolution in order to reform the juvenile justice system. At the same time, we must be cautious that this discussion does not lead away from considering the position of girls. The combination of masculinities analysis with feminist analysis can ensure this dual focus.

The juvenile justice example thus suggests that when the gender positions are asymmetric—women in the welfare system; men in highly sex-segregated jobs; differentiated use by men and women of parts of the health care system, especially mental health; the disproportion of maternal child custody—gender analysis must take into account that asymmetry. It should be questioned, understood, and part of the analysis. Particularly when it is a system of disadvantage or harm (such as juvenile justice or adult criminal justice), we should question and explore why the disproportion exists and its implications for gender justice. When it is a system of advantage (such as political power, wealth, or high-income employment positions), we should similarly challenge the asymmetry. We must ask about the group that has not been welcome or has been shut out or denied; but we must also look at the group that has dominated.

In the application of masculinities analysis to fathers, we are confronted with an exclusively male category. It is akin to the juvenile justice example to some extent but different because the category does not trigger the question of why disproportion exists, since the category is male by definition. At the same time, there is a similar failure to address or consider gender. Much of the work on fathers does not include consideration of masculinities and therefore misses the cultural challenge to reorienting fatherhood to a nurturing father standard.

Fatherhood exposes a combination of advantage and disadvantage, with some parallels to boys and education. It is an example of the combination of privilege with a price for privilege. Systemically, fathers have historically benefited from a patriarchal norm, much as boys historically have benefited from a presumption that only they merited or needed an education or were capable of learning. Patriarchal power rested on legally enforced rights of discipline and control, as well as responsibilities of care increasingly defined as economic. The consignment of mothers to the domestic sphere also drew a boundary for fathers and constructed a father as a successful breadwinner. Under the challenge of feminists, men in theory have embraced the idea of egalitarian relationships that include parenting in a way more like mothers, as mothers also have increasingly engaged in wage work akin to breadwinner fathers. At the same time, fathers continue to disengage from their children in significant numbers and to have great difficulty functioning in an equal relationship. Unraveling the classic and modern patterns of fathers exposes the pull of hegemonic masculinity at its most harmful and confounding. It is here that the negative commands of masculinity translate into barriers to caregiving and, with that, a conflict with the idea of a different norm of fatherhood. If empowered men as a group were to embrace care, we might assume that this would provoke a significant shift in policy with respect to work and family. The push-pull between ideal and reality of fathering exposes a core conflict in masculinity.

The shift in ideals, and in some lived realities, of fatherhood also suggests that masculinity can change, indeed has changed. On the other hand, it demonstrates how deeply embedded is the command not to embrace or emulate anything associated with women. The reconfiguring of care as manly and masculine is challenging, as it raises the concern that it is being bent to serve a hierarchical concept of being, rather than an egalitarian or collaborative one. Can men and women form alliances to achieve more equity in work and family? To do so, coming from the masculinities perspective, requires a gender-specific approach that must connect fatherhood to motherhood and not assert "rights" based on status that is disconnected to relationship. Masculinities analysis would connect the patterns of fatherhood, both its reconceptualization as nurture and its frequent practice as disconnection, to concepts of masculinities, both positive and negative. Masculinities analysis reinforces the difficulties of recasting manhood, even where the benefits seem so tangible and significant. Is it possible to envision care-based, child-focused masculinity that incorporates collaborative partnering, as opposed to needing to masculinize care in a way that sustains male-female and male-male hierarchies?

The last focus of analysis, adult male survivors of child sexual abuse, returns again to the value of masculinities analysis in simply identifying gender harms, without making assumptions that render men invisible as victims. In addition, it reminds us that we cannot assume that women never cause harm. In expanding and reconceptualizing child sexual abuse, and its implications for adults, it reminds us of the pervasiveness of sexual abuse and its connection to the broad categories of child abuse and neglect. It also tells us that even when harm to girls and women is predominant, we should ask if boys are harmed as well. The man question is not to solidify the value of the claim but rather to ensure its accuracy. It is to ensure that all victims are heard, to understand the pattern of harm, and to deal more effectively, both proactively and reactively, with victims. One of the powerful claims of feminist theory has been to give voice to those who previously had not been heard or believed, including the victims of domestic violence, sexual assault, and child abuse. Gender had rendered them silent, unacknowledged, or as not suffering any cognizable harm. Feminists brought attention to child sexual abuse when it was a harm that went largely unrecognized. Masculinities analysis as a further infusion in that analysis adds further depth and complexity to the analysis. Up to this point, male victims have simply not been imagined, have been discouraged from disclosing, and have been unsupported as adults in their efforts to deal with the consequences of abuse. This is not because feminists have silenced them; rather it is because they have not been acknowledged, by feminists or others.

Sexual abuse has been a core concern for feminists because it is such a common and deeply harmful experience for women. It is a core practice of subordination. Sexuality, more generally, has also been a concern: whether sexuality can be imagined as infused with equality and liberty, instead of intertwining pleasure with domination. Masculinities analysis not only adds to this particular area the recognition of men as victims and women as offenders but also challenges us to think about the implications of victimization in a gendered culture, with gendered subjects. Masculinities analysis suggests that sexual abuse may be experienced and dealt with differently by a man, particularly if that man senses that telling his story and sharing his feelings and responses will not be welcomed or understood. Indeed, telling his story may lead others to question his manhood. It may only make the lifelong struggle of proving oneself to be a man, a common thread of masculinity, that much more difficult.

Ultimately the addition of adult male child abuse survivors to our understanding and our strategies to prevent such abuse may contribute to identifying a healthy sexuality and how to promote it within an unequal and sexually violent culture. Masculinities analysis reminds us that this goal is as critical for men as it is for women and that as we think of those in need of change we must include women who victimize men as well as men who are victims. This need not take any focus or concern from female victims or male perpetrators. But our vision and scope need to be clear, and truthful, if we are to continue to describe what justice would mean. The expansion of the scope of our understanding of sexuality and violence, then, by using this perspective, is essential to deal with the issues of men's violence against women and the high rate of sexual assault.

Although these chapters have focused on boys and men, it is clear that masculinities analysis is not simply an area of gender-specific benefit. Adding masculinities analysis clearly does mean that gender issues of boys and men come into view to replace the unidimensional picture of men that has heretofore dominated much feminist theory. Thus, for example, we might also look at the military obligations of men and their sacrifice in war and the gendered pattern of prison rape and the imposition of the death penalty. Or we might examine boys' victimization from violent crime or their victimization from physical child abuse. Clearly we also have to recognize the differential patterns of privilege and the places where other factors, such as race and class, completely trump male privilege as compared to other men and even to women.

But masculinities analysis goes further, just as feminist analysis is not inherently limited to women. Masculinities analysis might further inform efforts to achieve gender equality where women are the dominant subjects or where women's needs create priorities for strategies. For example, workplace discrimination has been a core concern of feminists. Identifying structures and cultures at work as "male," even articulating what it means to call something "male," continues to be challenging, despite ongoing development of discrimination theory, particularly the expansion of the concept of sexual harassment. Masculinities scholarship is helpful in unraveling how employment cultures and structures function and how they are coded "male." It also should remind us that "male" is not unitary and that the culture of work contains multiple masculinities that create a hierarchy within "male" rules and culture. This provides a strong argument to identify and label rules and policies, such as evaluation standards or promotion criteria, as biased and unfair, on the basis that men (or men disproportionately) can more easily achieve them because they have been socialized in those norms and are accepted and valued when they conform or perform according to those values and expectations. Women, on the other hand, may find it more difficult to achieve the same result, or, perversely, they will be criticized for behaving in a way that would be valued in a man (for example, by being brusque or aggressive) if they step too far out of prescribed gender roles. At the same time, the insight that men also are subordinated in "male" work codes and culture helps to defend against the simplistic argument that if men are also discriminated against, then this is not gender inequality.

The concept of gender policing at work is also more understandable from the perspective of masculinities scholarship. Gender policing affects how welcome women are in male-dominated workplaces. Among the core concepts of masculinities is that it is important not to be female or female identified. The presence of women raises the specter that the work will be tainted by the presence of women and will be given less value. If a woman can do the job, then it loses its social as well as economic value. Discouraging women preserves turf, value, and hegemony. Gender policing also reinforces hierarchies among men, defining male work as requiring adherence to very traditional male constructions of masculinities. Masculinities scholarship focuses attention on both the male-female and male-male dynamic of gender policing and might add to efforts to identify the practice more clearly, as well as identify ways to disrupt and change workplace culture toward embracing the value of equality, rather than identifying equality as threat.

Another example of an area where masculinities insights might be helpful is in the area of reproductive rights and responsibilities. This has been an area of presumed woman-only focus or woman-primary focus. Control of women's bodies has been a critical issue for feminists, as has honoring their decision-making. At the same time, this focus has arguably burdened women with taking total reproductive responsibility, in addition to bearing all the health implications of birth control, pregnancy, abortion, and miscarriage. Masculinities analysis might contribute toward bringing men into the analysis to reconceptualize their role, and responsibilities, and to strengthen a relational, egalitarian relationship with women. It also reminds us that men often feel powerless, not powerful. In areas identified as women's choices and concerns, which should not be dictated or directed by men, men may especially see themselves as powerless. Instead of an analysis of competing claims of rights, when women and men are unequally situated, we might construct a different analysis. As part of the analysis, whenever women are the presumed objects, we might ask the man question: what are we assuming about men when we implement this policy or rule? In what ways might the hierarchy among men or of men over women be affected? Can you accomplish greater freedom for women and also greater responsibility for men? The critical point is that masculinities perspectives are not limited to subjects that we identify as "male," just as feminism is not limited to women.

Masculinities scholarship, as an infusion to feminist analysis, is consistent with feminists' dedication to unraveling and diminishing (or ending) gender inequality. Asking the man question will remind us to bring this perspective in. At the same time, inherent in the man question must be the recognition of the asymmetric places of women and men.

Masculinities analysis not only should lead to understanding and identifying with men, to seeing their harms as well as their privileges, but should also more strongly work toward the redefining of masculinity and the end of hegemony. Here feminist analysis, in collaboration with masculinities analysis, has much to offer. Feminists may, so to speak, hold masculinities scholars' feet to the fire. While incorporating masculinities analysis, feminists will remain skeptical, and that skepticism will translate into asking that girls and women always be kept in view, even when boys or men are the primary, justified focus. Feminists might well suggest to masculinities scholars that the most critical question to ask, in most situations, is whether men have power in a situation. Is it power over other men or women, that is, is it *power over* versus *empowerment*? If it is gender power (or gender combined with race, class, etc.), then that kind of power is unjustified because it is inconsistent with equality and justice. Powerlessness of the individual has to be taken into account but does not remove the reality of power—and maybe advantage or privilege—for the group as a whole. Institutions, structures, and practices that reinforce such arbitrary gender power should be the focus of law. Feminist analysis can remind masculinities scholarship that a focus on power and material advantage is critical.

Finally, infusing feminist analysis with the perspectives of masculinities scholarship benefits feminist analysis by reinforcing the core lesson of anti-essentialism and encouraging feminists to take on race as a feminist issue. Masculinities analysis reveals how male hierarchy is racialized. The consequence is that in many areas gender gets pitted against race in a way that benefits (mostly white, mostly middle-class) women over men of color. To continue to orient to male/female hierarchy when the racialized gender hierarchy is more commonly characterized by white men and white women over women of color and men of color is to ignore the skin privilege of white women and ignore the gender subordination of black men and other men of color, along with women of color. It might indeed be argued that race is such a primary, deep, primordial system of subordination that feminists should take the position that this system of oppression must take primacy in struggles for equality. At the very least, it requires a strongly proactive stance from feminists that holds the potential for interesting and fruitful collaboration. Asking the man question, then, in these many ways, is another step toward the goal of justice.

References

Abelove, Henry, Michele Aina Barale, and David M. Halperin, eds. 1993. *The Lesbian and Gay Studies Reader*. New York: Routledge.

Abrams, Laura S., Ben Anderson-Nathe, and Jemel Aguilar. 2008. Constructing Masculinities in Juvenile Corrections. *Men and Masculinities* 11(1):22–41.

Abu-Jamal, Mumia. 2001. Caged and Celibate. In *Prison Masculinities*, edited by Don Sabo, Terry A. Kupers, and Willie London. Philadelphia: Temple University Press, pp. 139–42.

Adams, Rachel, and David Savran. 2002a. Introduction to *The Masculinity Studies Reader*, edited by Rachel Adams and David Savran. Malden, MA: Blackwell, pp. 1–8.

Adams, Rachel, and David Savran, eds. 2002b. *The Masculinity Studies Reader*. Malden, MA: Blackwell.

Addis, Michael, and Geoffrey H. Cohane. 2005. Social Scientific Paradigms of Masculinity and Their Implications for Research and Practice in Men's Mental Health. *Journal of Clinical Psychology* 61(6):633–47.

Adu-Poku, Samuel. 2001. Envisioning (Black) Male Feminism: A Cross-Cultural Perspective. *Journal of Gender Studies* 10(2):157–67.

Alaggia, Ramona, and Graeme Millington. 2008. Male Child Sexual Abuse: A Phenomenology of Betrayal. *Clinical Social Work Journal* 36(3):265–75.

Albiston, Catherine. 2005. Anti-essentialism and the Work/Family Dilemma. *Berkeley Journal of Gender Law and Justice* 20:30–49.

Alison, Laurence, Mark Kebbell, and Penney Lewis. 2006. Considerations for Experts in Assessing the Credibility of Recovered Memories of Child Sexual Abuse. *Psychology, Public Policy and Law* 12(4):419–41.

Allen, Walter R. 1999. Missing in Action: Race, Gender, and Black Students' Educational Opportunities. In *Black Men on Race, Gender and Sexuality: A Critical Reader*, edited by Devon Carbado. New York: New York University Press, pp. 194–211.

Almqvist, Anna-Lena. 2008. Why Most Swedish Fathers and Few French Fathers Use Paid Parental Leave: An Exploratory Qualitative Study of Parents. *Fathering* 6(2):192–200.

American Association of University Women. 1992. *How Schools Shortchange Girls*. Washington, DC: American Association of University Women Educational Foundation.

American Bar Association and National Bar Association. 2001. Justice by Gender: The Lack of Appropriate Prevention, Diversion and Treatment Alternatives for Girls in the Justice System.

Andersen, Torbgjorn Herlof. 2008. Men Dealing with Memories of Childhood Sexual Abuse: Conditions and Possibilities of "Positive Deviance." *Journal of Social Work Practice* 22(1): 51–65.

Andrew, Ruby. 2006. Child Sexual Abuse and the State: Applying Critical Outsider Methodologies to Legislative Policymaking. *U.C. Davis Law Review* 39:1851–90.

Annie E. Casey Foundation. 2008. A Road Map for Juvenile Justice Reform, 2008 Kids Count Data Book. http://www.aecf.org/.

Anonymous. 2001. The Story of a Black Punk. In *Prison Masculinities,* edited by Don Sabo, Terry A. Kupers, and Willie London. Philadelphia: Temple University Press, pp. 127–32.

Arredondo, David E. 2003. Child Development, Children's Mental Health and the Juvenile Justice System: Principles for Effective Decision-Making. *Stanford Law and Policy Review* 14(1):13–28.

Ashe, Fidelma. 2004. Deconstructing the Experiential Bar: Male Experience and Feminist Resistance. *Men and Masculinities* 7(2):187–204.

Atkins, Gary L. 2005. My Man Fridae: Re-producing Asian Masculinity. *Seattle Journal for Social Justice* 4:61–96.

Awkward, Michael. 2002. Black Male Trouble: The Challenges of Rethinking Masculine Differences. In *Masculinity Studies and Feminist Theory: New Directions,* edited by Judith Kegan Gardiner. New York: Columbia University Press, pp. 290–304.

Awkward, Michael. 1999. A Black Man's Place in Black Feminist Criticism. In *Black Men on Race, Gender, and Sexuality: A Reader,* edited by Devon Carbado. New York: New York University Press, pp. 362–82.

Bach, Michael. 1993. Uncovering the Institutionalized Masculine: Notes for a Sociology of Masculinity. In *Men and Masculinities: A Critical Anthology,* edited by Tony Haddad. Toronto: Canadian Scholars Press, pp. 37–55.

Back, Les. 1996. The "White Negro" Revisited: Race and Masculinities in South London. In *Dislocating Masculinity: Comparative Ethnographies,* edited by Andrea Cornwall and Nancy Lindisfarne. New York: Routledge, pp. 172–83.

Backer, Larry C. 2005. Emasculated Men, Effeminate Law in the United States, Zimbabwe and Malaysia. *Yale Journal of Law and Feminism* 17:1–63.

Badinter, Elisabeth. 1995. *XY and Masculine Identity.* New York: Columbia University Press.

Balbus, Isaac D. 2002. Masculinity and the (M)other: Toward A Synthesis of Feminist Mothering Theory and Psychoanalytic Theories of Narcissism. In *Masculinity Studies and Feminist Theory: New Directions,* edited by Judith Kegan Gardiner. New York: Columbia University Press, pp. 210–34.

Ball, Carlos A. 2001. Essentialism and Universalism in Gay Rights Philosophy: Liberalism Meets Queer Theory. *Law and Social Inquiry* 26:271–93.

Bankart, C. Peter. 2005. Review of *Men and Masculinities: Theory, Research and Social Practice,* by C. Haywood and M. Mac an Ghaill; *Men and Gender Relations,* by B. Pease; *Men and Masculinities: Key Themes and New Directions,* by S.M. Whitehead; and *The Masculinities Reader,* edited by S.M. Whitehead and Frank J. Barrett. *Men and Masculinities* 7(4):434–36.

Barlow, Anne. 2006. Cohabitation Law Reform—Messages from Research. *Feminist Legal Studies* 14:167–80.

Barnard, George, A. Kenneth Fuller, Lynn Robbins, and Theodore Shaw. 1990. *The Child Molester: An Integrated Approach to Evaluation and Treatment.* New York: Bruner/Mazel.

Barnickol, Laura A. 2000. Note: The Disparate Treatment of Males and Females within the Juvenile Justice System. *Washington University Journal of Law and Policy* 2:429–58.

Barrett, Frank J. 2001. The Organizational Construction of Hegemonic Masculinity: The Case of the U.S. Navy. In *The Masculinities Reader,* edited by Stephen M. Whitehead and Frank J. Barrett. Cambridge, UK: Polity, pp. 77–99.

Bartlett, Peter. 2007. Killing Gay Men. *British Journal of Criminology* 47(4):573–95.

Bennett, Gerald, and Rosalind Jones. 2006. Men, Masculinity, and Mental Health. *Issues in Mental Health Nursing* 27(4):333–36.

Bereska, Tami M. 2003. The Changing Boys' World in the 20th Century: Reality and "Fiction." *Journal of Men's Studies* 11(2):157–74.

Berger, Maurice, Brian Wallis, and Simon Watson, eds. 1995a. *Constructing Masculinity.* New York: Routledge.

Berger, Maurice, Brian Wallis, and Simon Watson. 1995b. Introduction to *Constructing Masculinity,* edited by Maurice Berger, Brian Wallis, and Simon Watson. New York: Routledge, pp. 1–7.

Bergman, Helena, and Barbara Hobson. 2002. Compulsory Fatherhood: The Coding of Fatherhood in the Swedish Welfare State. In *Making Men into Fathers: Men, Masculinities and the Social Politics of Fatherhood,* edited by Barbara Hobson. New York: Cambridge University Press, pp. 92–124.

Bergman, Stephen J. 1995. Men's Psychological Development: A Relational Perspective. In *A New Psychology of Men,* edited by Ronald F. Levant and William S. Pollack. New York: Basic Books, pp. 68–89.

Berkheiser, Mary. 2002. The Fiction of Juvenile Right to Counsel: Waiver in the Juvenile Courts. *Florida Law Review* 54:577–682.

Bernard, Thomas J. 2007. *Serious Delinquency: An Anthology.* Los Angeles: Roxbury.

Beyer, Margaret. 1998. Mental Health Care for Children in Corrections. *Children's Legal Rights Journal* 18:18–35.

Beyer, Marty. 2000. Immaturity, Culpability and Competency in Juveniles: A Study of 17 Cases. *Criminal Justice* 15(27):27–35.

Beyer, Marty 1999. Recognizing the Child in the Delinquent. *Kentucky Children's Rights Journal* 7:16–31.

Beynon, John. 2002. *Masculinities and Culture.* Buckingham, UK: Open University Press.

Biden, Joseph R. 2003. What about the Girls? The Role of the Federal Government in Addressing the Rise in Female Juvenile Offenders. *Stanford Law and Policy Review* 14:29–44.

Bienen, Leigh B. 1998. Defining Incest. *Northwestern Law Review* 92:1501–80.

Bishop, Donna M., and Charles E. Frazier. 1992. Gender Bias in Juvenile Justice Processing: Implications of the JJDP Act. *Journal of Criminal Law and Criminology* 82(4):1162–86.

Black, Derek W. 2008. The Mysteriously Reappearing Cause of Action: The Court's Expanded Concept of Intentional Gender and Race Discrimination in Federally Funded Programs. *Maryland Law Review* 67:358–424.

Blazina, Christopher. 2004. Gender Role Conflict and the Disidentification Process: Two Case Studies on Fragile Masculine Self. *Journal of Men's Studies* 12(2):151–61.

Blazina, Chris, et al. 2007. The Relationship between Masculinity Ideology, Loneliness, and Separation-Individuation Difficulties. *Journal of Men's Studies* 15(1): 101–9.

Bly, Robert. 1990. *Iron John: A Book about Men.* Reading, MA: Addison-Wesley.

Bookser, Susanne M. 2004. Making *Gault* Meaningful: Access to Counsel and Quality of Representation in Delinquency Proceedings for Indigent Youth. *Whittier Journal of Child and Family Advocacy* 3:297–328.

Boon, Kevin A. 2005. Heroes, Metanarratives, and the Paradox of Masculinity in Contemporary Western Culture. *Journal of Men's Studies* 13(3):301–12.

Bouchard, Genevieve, Catherine M. Lee, Veronica Asgary, and Lue Pelletier. 2007. Fathers' Motivation for Involvement with Their Children: A Self-Determination Theory Perspective. *Fathering* 5(1):25–41.

Bourdieu, Pierre. 2001. *Masculine Domination.* Translated by Richard Nice. Stanford, CA: Stanford University Press.

Bowe, John. 2006. Gay Donor or Gay Dad? *New York Times,* November 19.

Bowker, Lee H., ed. 1988. *Masculinities and Violence.* Thousand Oaks, CA: Sage.

Brake, Deborah L. 2008. The Invisible Pregnant Athlete and the Promise of Title IX. *Harvard Journal of Law and Gender* 31:323–66.

Brake, Deborah L. 2007. Title IX as Pragmatic Feminism: Symposium: Celebrating Thirty-Five Years of Sport and Title IX. *Cleveland State Law Review* 55(4):513–46.

Brandth, Berit, and Elin Kvande. 1998. Masculinity and Child Care: The Reconstruction of Fathering. *Sociological Review* 26(2):293–313.

Brannon, Robert. 1976. The Male Sex Role: Our Culture's Blueprint of Manhood and What It's Done for Us Lately. In *The Forty-Nine Percent Majority: The Male Sex Role,* edited by Deborah S. David and Robert Brannon. Reading, MA: Addison-Wesley, pp. 1–45.

Breines, Ingeborg, Robert Connell, and Ingrid Eide. 2000a. Introduction to *Male Roles, Masculinities and Violence: A Culture of Peace Perspective,* edited by Ingeborg Breines, Robert Connell, and Ingrid Eide. Paris: UNESCO, pp. 1–10.

Breines, Ingeborg, Robert Connell, and Ingrid Eide, eds. 2000b. *Male Roles, Masculinities and Violence: A Culture of Peace Perspective.* Paris: UNESCO.

Brickell, Chris. 2005. Masculinities, Performativity, and Subversion: A Sociological Reappraisal. *Men and Masculinities* 8(1):24–43.

Brittan, Arthur. 1989. *Masculinity and Power.* New York: Blackwell.

Brod, Harry. 2002. Studying Masculinities as Superordinate Studies. In *Masculinity Studies and Feminist Theory: New Directions,* edited by Judith Kegan Gardiner. New York: Columbia University Press, pp. 161–75.

Brod, Harry. 2001. Male Pride and Antisexism. *Men and Masculinities* 3(4):405–10.

Brod, Harry. 1994. Some Thoughts on Some Histories of Some Masculinities: Jews and Other Others. In *Theorizing Masculinities,* edited by Harry Brod and Michael Kaufman. Thousand Oaks, CA: Sage, pp. 82–96.

Brod, Harry, ed. 1987 *The Making of Masculinities: The New Men's Studies.* New York: Routledge.

Brod, Harry, and Michael Kaufman. 1994a. Introduction to *Theorizing Masculinities,* edited by Harry Brod and Michael Kaufman. Thousand Oaks, CA: Sage, pp. 1–10.

Brod, Harry, and Michael Kaufman, eds. 1994b. *Theorizing Masculinities.* Thousand Oaks, CA: Sage.

Brooks, Kim, and Debra Parkes. 2004. Queering Legal Education: A Project of Theoretical Discovery. *Harvard Women's Law Journal* 27:89–136.

Brown v. Board of Education, 347 U.S. 483 (1954).

Brown, Laura S. 1997. New Voices, New Visions: Toward a Lesbian/Gay Paradigm for Psychology. In *Toward a New Psychology of Gender,* edited by Mary M. Gergen and Sara N. Davis. New York: Routledge, pp. 295–310.

Browne, Kath. 2005. Stages and Streets, Reading and (Mis)reading Female Masculinities. In *Spaces of Masculinities,* edited by Bettina van Hoven and Kathrin Horschelmann. London: Routledge, pp. 237–48.

Brownwell, Susan, and Jeffrey N. Wasserstrom, eds. 2002. *Chinese Femininities/Chinese Masculinities: A Reader.* Berkeley: University of California Press.

Brunson, Rod K., and Jody Miller. 2006. Young Black Men and Urban Policing in the United States. *British Journal of Criminology* 46:613–40.

Buchbinder, David. 1994. *Masculinities and Identities.* Carlton, Victoria: Melbourne University Press.

Burgess, Susan. 2006. Queer (Theory) Eye for the Straight (Legal) Guy: *Lawrence v. Texas'* Makeover of *Bowers v. Hardwick. Political Research Quarterly* 59(3):401–14.

Butler, Judith. 1997. *The Psychic Life of Power: Theories of Subjection.* Stanford, CA: Stanford University Press.

Butler, Judith. 1990. *Gender Trouble: Feminism and the Subversion of Identity.* New York: Routledge.

Byrne, Jeffrey S. 1993. Affirmative Action for Lesbians and Gay Men: A Proposal for True Equality of Opportunity and Workforce Diversity. *Yale Law and Policy Review* 11:47–108.

Calhoun, Cheshire. 1995. Sexuality Injustice. *Notre Dame Journal of Law, Ethics and Public Policy* 9:241–74.

Canaan, Joyce E. 1998. Is Doing Nothing Just Boys' Play? Integrating Feminist and Cultural Studies Perspectives on Working-Class Young Men's Masculinity. In *Criminology at the Crossroads: Feminist Readings in Crime and Justice,* edited by Kathleen Daly and Lisa Maher. New York: Oxford University Press, pp. 172–87.

Canaan, Joyce E., and Christine Griffin. 1990. The New Men's Studies: Part of the Problem or Part of the Solution? In *Men, Masculinities and Social Theory,* edited by Jeff Hearn and David Morgan. London: Unwin Hyman, pp. 206–14.

Carbado, Devon W. 2006. Men in Black. *Journal of Gender, Race and Justice* 3:427–88.

Carbado, Devon, ed. 1999a. *Black Men on Race, Gender and Sexuality: A Critical Reader.* New York: New York University Press.

Carbado, Devon. 1999b. Epilogue to *Black Men on Race, Gender and Sexuality: A Critical Reader,* edited by Devon Carbado. New York: New York University Press, pp. 417–67.

Carbado, Devon. 1999c. Introduction to *Black Men on Race, Gender and Sexuality: A Critical Reader,* edited by Devon Carbado. New York: New York University Press, pp. 1–18.

Carbone, June. 2000. *From Partners to Parents: The Second Revolution in Family Law.* New York: Columbia University Press.

Carby, Hazel V. 1987. *Reconstructing Womanhood: The Emergence of the Afro-American Woman Novelist.* New York: Oxford University Press.

Carlson, Marcia, Sara McLanahan, and Paula England. 2004. Union Formation in Fragile Families. *Demography* 41(2):237–61.

Carr, Benjamin. 2007. Note, Can Separate Be Equal? Single-Sex Classrooms, the Constitution, and Title IX. *Notre Dame Law Review* 83:409–42.

Carrigan, T., R.W. Connell, and J. Lee. 1985. Toward a New Sociology of Masculinity. *Theory and Society* 14(5):551–604.

Carrington, Kerry. 1998. Postmodernism and Feminist Criminologies: Disconnecting Discourses? In *Criminology at the Crossroads: Feminist Readings in Crime and Justice,* edited by Kathleen Daly and Lisa Maher. New York: Oxford University Press, pp. 69–84.

Carroll, Bret E., ed. 2003. *American Masculinities: A Historical Encyclopedia.* Thousand Oaks, CA: Sage.

Catalano, Richard F., Rolf Loeber, and Kay McKinney. 1999. School and Community Interventions to Prevent Serious and Violent Offending. Office of Juvenile Justice, Juvenile Justice Bulletin (October 1999), www.ncjrs.gov/pdffiles1/ojjdp/177624.pdf.

Catlett, Beth S., and Patrick C. McKenry. 2004. Class-Based Masculinities: Divorce, Fatherhood, and the Hegemonic Ideal. *Fathering* 2(2):165–90.

Centers for Disease Control. 2008. Child Maltreatment: Facts at a Glance. http://www.cdc.gov/violenceprevention/pdf/CM-DataSheet-a.pdf (accessed July 31, 2009).

Chalk Talk. 2003. "No Child Left Behind" and the Promotion of Single-Sex Public Education in Primary and Secondary Schools: Shattering the Glass Ceilings Perpetuated by Coeducation. *Journal of Law and Education* 32:291–96.

Cheng, Cliff. 1999. Marginalized Masculinities and Hegemonic Masculinity: An Introduction. *Journal of Men's Studies* 7(3):295–314.

Cheung, King-Kok. 2002a. Art, Spirituality, and the Ethic of Care: Alternative Masculinities in Chinese American Literature. In *Masculinity Studies and Feminist Theory: New Directions,* edited by Judith Kegan Gardiner. New York: Columbia University Press, pp. 261–89.

Cheung, King-Kok. 2002b. The Woman Warrior versus the Chinaman Pacific: Must a Chinese American Critic Choose between Feminism and Heroism? In *The Masculinity Studies Reader,* edited by Rachel Adams and David Savran. Malden, MA: Blackwell, pp. 175–87.

Children's Bureau, U.S. Department of Health and Human Services. 2007. Child Maltreatment. www.acf.hhs.gov/programs/ch/pubs/cm07/index.htm.

Chodorow, Nancy J. 2002. The Enemy Outside: Thoughts on the Psychodynamics of Extreme Violence with Special Attention to Men and Masculinity. In *Masculinity Studies and Feminist Theory: New Directions,* edited by Judith Kegan Gardiner. New York: Columbia University Press, pp. 235–60.

Chu, Judy Y. 2004. A Relational Perspective on Adolescent Boys' Identity Development. In *Adolescent Boys: Exploring Diverse Cultures of Boyhood,* edited by Niobe Way and Judy Y. Chu. New York: New York University Press, pp. 78–104.

Chu, Judy Y., Michelle V. Porche, and Deborah L. Tolman. 2005. The Adolescent Masculinity Ideology in Relationships Scale: Development and Validation of a New Measure for Boys. *Men and Masculinities* 8(1):93–115.

Clapp, Elizabeth. 1998. *Mothers of All Children: Women Reformers and the Rise of Juvenile Courts in Progressive-Era America.* University Park: Pennsylvania State University Press.

Cleaver, Frances, ed. 2002a. *Masculinities Matter! Men, Gender and Development.* New York: Zed Books.

Cleaver, Frances. 2002b. Men and Masculinities: New Directions in Gender and Development. In *Masculinities Matter! Men, Gender and Development,* edited by Frances Cleaver. New York: Zed Books, pp. 1–27.

Cloke, Paul. 2005. Masculinity and Rurality. In *Spaces of Masculinities,* edited by Bettina van Hoven and Kathrin Horschelmann. London: Routledge, pp. 45–62.

Cohen, Jeffrey W., and Patrick J. Harvey. 2006. Misconceptions of Gender: Sex, Masculinity, and the Measurement of Crime. *Journal of Men's Studies* 14(2):223–33.

Cohen, Michele. 1998. "A Habit of Healthy Idleness": Boys' Underachievement in Historical Perspective. In *Failing Boys? Issues in Gender and Achievement,* edited by Debbie Epstein, Jannette Elwood, Virginia Hey, and Janet Maw. Buckingham, UK: Open University Press, pp. 19–34.

Cohn, Carol. 1998. Gays in the Military: Texts and Subtexts. In *The "Man" Question in International Relations,* edited by Marysia Zalewski and Jane Parpart. Boulder, CO: Westview, pp. 129–49.

Cohn, Carol, and Cynthia Enloe. 2003. A Conversation with Cynthia Enloe: Feminists Look at Masculinity and the Men Who Wage War. *Signs: Journal of Women in Culture and Society* 28(4):1187–1207.

Collier, Richard. 2009. The Fathers' Rights Movement, Law Reform and the New Politics of Fatherhood: Some Reflections on the UK Experience. *University of Florida Journal of Law and Public Policy* 20:65–110.

Collier, Richard. 1998. *Masculinities, Crime and Criminology: Men, Heterosexuality and the Criminal(ised) Other.* London: Sage.

Collier, Richard, and Sally Sheldon. 2008. *Fragmenting Fatherhood: A Socio-legal Study.* London: Hart.

Collinson, David, and Jeff Hearn. 2001. Naming Men as Men. In *The Masculinities Reader,* edited by Stephen Whitehead and Frank Barrett. Cambridge, UK: Polity, pp. 144–69.

Coltrane, Scott. 2006. Book Review. *Men and Masculinities* 8(3):380–81.

Coltrane, Scott. 2004. Comment: Elite Careers and Family Commitment: It's (Still) about Gender. *Annals of the American Academy of Political and Social Science* 596:214–20.

Coltrane, Scott. 2000. Research on Household Labor: Modeling and Measuring the Social Embeddedness of Routine Family Work. *Journal of Marriage and the Family* 62:1208–33.

Coltrane, Scott. 1994. Theorizing Masculinities in Contemporary Social Science. In *Theorizing Masculinities,* edited by Harry Brod and Michael Kaufman. Thousand Oaks, CA: Sage, pp. 39–60.

Conn, Kathleen. 2005. Bullying, Harassment, and Student Threats: Are Schools and the Courts Working Together? *Education Law Reporter* 203:1–6.

Connell, R.W. 2005a. Globalization, Imperialism, and Masculinities. In *Handbook of Studies on Men and Masculinities,* edited by Michael S. Kimmel, Jeff Hearn, and R.W. Connell. Thousand Oaks, CA: Sage, pp. 71–89.

Connell, R.W. 2005b. *Masculinities,* 2d ed. Berkeley: University of California Press.

Connell, R.W. 2002a. *Gender.* London: Polity.

Connell, R.W. 2002b. The History of Masculinity. In *The Masculinity Studies Reader,* edited by Rachel Adams and David Savran. Malden, MA: Blackwell, pp. 245–61.

Connell, R.W. 2000a. Arms and the Man: Using the New Research on Masculinity to Understand Violence and Promote Peace in the Contemporary World. In *Male Roles, Masculinities and Violence: A Culture of Peace Perspective,* edited by Ingeborg Breines, Robert Connell, and Ingrid Eide. Paris: UNESCO, pp. 21–33.

Connell, R.W. 2000b. *The Men and the Boys.* Berkeley: University of California Press.

Connell, R.W. 1994. Psychoanalysis on Masculinity. In *Theorizing Masculinities,* edited by Harry Brod and Michael Kaufman. Thousand Oaks, CA: Sage, pp. 11–38.

Connell, R.W. 1992. A Very Straight Gay: Masculinity, Homosexual Experience, and the Dynamics of Gender. *American Sociological Review* 57(6):735–51.

Connell, R.W., and James W. Messerschmidt. 2005. Hegemonic Masculinity: Rethinking the Concept. *Gender and Society* 19(6):829–59.

Connell, R.W., and Julian Wood. 2005. Globalization and Business Masculinities. *Men and Masculinities* 7(4):347–64.

Cook, Philip J., and John H. Laub. 1998. The Unprecedented Epidemic in Youth Violence. *Crime and Justice* 24:27–64.

Cooper, Frank R. 2006. Against Bipolar Black Masculinity: Intersectionality, Assimilation, Identity Performance, and Hierarchy. *U.C. Davis Law Review* 39:853–903.

Cornish, Peter A. 1999. Men Engaging Feminism: A Model of Personal Change and Social Transformation. *Journal of Men's Studies* 7(2):173–99.

Cornwall, Andrea. 1996. Gendered Identities and Gender Ambiguity among Travestis in Salvador, Brazil. In *Dislocating Masculinity: Comparative Ethnographies,* edited by Andrea Cornwall and Nancy Lindisfarne. New York: Routledge, pp. 111–32.

Cornwall, Andrea, and Nancy Lindisfarne, eds. 1996a. *Dislocating Masculinity: Comparative Ethnographies.* New York: Routledge.

Cornwall, Andrea, and Nancy Lindisfarne. 1996b. Dislocating Masculinity: Gender, Power and Anthropology. In *Dislocating Masculinity: Comparative Ethnographies,* edited by Andrea Cornwall and Nancy Lindisfarne. New York: Routledge, pp. 11–47.

Cornwall, Andrea, and Nancy Lindisfarne. 1996c. Introduction to *Dislocating Masculinity: Comparative Ethnographies,* edited by Andrea Cornwall and Nancy Lindisfarne. New York: Routledge, pp. 1–10.

Coughlin, Chris, and Samuel Vuchinich. 1996. Family Experience in Preadolescence and the Development of Male Delinquency. *Journal of Marriage and the Family* 58(2):491–501.

Coupet, Sacha M. 2000. What to Do with the Sheep in Wolf's Clothing: The Role of Rhetoric and Reality about Youth Offenders in the Constructive Dismantling of the Juvenile Justice System. *University of Pennsylvania Law Review* 148:1303–46.

Crozier, Patience W. 2001. Forcing Boys to Be Boys: The Persecution of Gender Nonconforming Youth: Book Review. *B.C. Third World Law Journal* 21:123–44.

Cunneen, Chris, and Rob White. 1996. Masculinity and Juvenile Justice. *Australian and New Zealand Journal of Criminology* 29:1–14.

Currah, Paisley. 2001. Queer Theory, Lesbian and Gay Rights, and Transsexual Marriages. In *Sexual Identities, Queer Politics,* edited by Mark Blasius. Princeton, NJ: Princeton University Press, pp. 178–99.

Dalley-Trim, Leanne. 2007. The Boys Present . . . Hegemonic Masculinity: A Performance of Multiple Acts. *Gender and Education* 19(2):199–217.

Dalley-Trim, Leanne. 2006. Just Boys Being Boys? *Youth Studies Australia* 25(3): 26–33.

Daly, Kathleen, and Lisa Maher, eds. 1998a. *Criminology at the Crossroads: Feminist Readings in Crime and Justice.* New York: Oxford University Press.

Daly, Kathleen, and Lisa Maher. 1998b. Introduction to *Criminology at the Crossroads: Feminist Readings in Crime and Justice,* edited by Kathleen Daly and Lisa Maher. New York: Oxford University Press.

Danziger, Gloria. 2003. Delinquency Jurisdiction in a Unified Family Court: Balancing Intervention, Prevention, and Adjudication. *Family Law Quarterly* 37:381–402.

Dasgupta, Romit. 2003. Creating Corporate Warriors: The "Salaryman" and Masculinity in Japan. In *Asian Masculinities: The Meaning and Practice of Manhood in China and Japan,* edited by Kam Louie and Morris Low. New York: Routledge, pp. 118–34.

Datesman, Susan K., and Frank R Scarpitti, eds. 1980. *Women, Crime, and Justice.* New York: Oxford University Press.

Davies, Julie A., and Lisa M. Bohon. 2007. Re-imagining Public Enforcement of Title IX. *Brigham Young University Education and Law Journal* 2007:25–81.

Davis, Angela Y. 2001. Race, Gender, and Prison History: From the Convict Lease System to the Supermax Prison. In *Prison Masculinities,* edited by Don Sabo, Terry A. Kupers, and Willie London. Philadelphia: Temple University Press, pp. 35–45.

Davis, James Earl. 2006. Research at the Margin: Mapping Masculinity and Mobility of African-American High School Dropouts. *International Journal of Qualitative Studies in Education* 19(3):289–304.

Day, R.D., and M.E. Lamb. 2004. *Conceptualizing and Measuring Father Involvement.* Mahwah, NJ: Erlbaum.

Delgado, Richard, and Jean Stefancic. 1995. Minority Men, Misery, and the Marketplace of Ideas. In *Constructing Masculinity,* edited by Maurice Berger, Brian Wallis, and Simon Watson. New York: Routledge, pp. 211–20.

Demetriou, Demetrakis Z. 2001. Connell's Concept of Hegemonic Masculinity: A Critique. *Theory and Society* 30:337–61.

Dines, Gail. 2006. The White Man's Burden: Gonzo Pornography and the Construction of Black Masculinity. *Yale Journal of Law and Feminism* 18:283–97.

Donaldson, Mike. 1993. What Is Hegemonic Masculinity? *Theory and Society* 22(5):643–57.

Donaldson, Stephen "Donny." 2001. A Million Jockers, Punks, and Queens. In *Prison Masculinities,* edited by Don Sabo, Terry A. Kupers, and Willie London. Philadelphia: Temple University Press, pp. 118–26.

Doucet, Andrea. 2006. *Do Men Mother? Fathering, Care and Domestic Responsibility.* Toronto: University of Toronto Press.

Doucet, Andrea. 2004. "It's Almost Like I Have a Job, but I Don't Get Paid": Fathers at Home Reconfiguring Work, Care, and Masculinity. *Fathering* 2(3):277–303.

Dowd, Nancy E. 2007. Multiple Parents/Multiple Fathers. *Journal of Law and Family Studies* 9:231–63.

Dowd, Nancy E. 2006. Introduction to *Handbook: Children, Culture and Violence,* edited by Nancy Dowd, Dorothy Singer, and Robin Wilson. Thousand Oaks, CA: Sage, pp. ix–xxvi.

Dowd, Nancy E. 2005. Fathers and the Supreme Court: Founding Fathers and Nurturing Fathers. *Emory Law Journal* 54:1271–1333.

Dowd, Nancy E. 2000. *Redefining Fatherhood.* New York: New York University Press.

Dowd, Nancy E. 1990. Work and Family: Restructuring the Workplace. *Arizona Law Review* 32:431–500.

Dowd, Nancy E. 1989. Envisioning Work and Family: A Critical Perspective on International Models. *Harvard Journal on Legislation* 26:311–48.

Downey, Erin. 2001. Federal Child Access Prevention Laws: An Exercise in Futility or a Feasible Means of Curbing Juvenile Violence? *Journal of Law in Society* 2:148–82.

Edley, Nigel. 2006. Never the Twain Shall Meet: A Critical Appraisal of the Combination of Discourse and Psychoanalytic Theory in Studies of Men and Masculinity. *Sex Roles* 55:601–8.

Edwards, Tim. 2006. *Cultures of Masculinity.* New York: Routledge.

Edwards, Tim. 2005. Queering the Pitch? In *Handbook of Studies on Men and Masculinities,* edited by Michael S. Kimmel, Jeff Hearn, and R.W. Connell. Thousand Oaks, CA: Sage, pp. 51–68.

Ehrenreich, Nancy. 2005. Disguising Empire: Racialized Masculinity and the "Civilizing" of Iraq. *Cleveland State Law Review* 52:131–38.

Ehrenreich, Nancy. 2002. Subordination and Symbiosis: Mechanisms of Mutual Support between Subordinating Systems. *University of Missouri–Kansas City Law Review* 71:251–79.

Ellman, Ira Mark. 1989. The Theory of Alimony. *California Law Review* 77:1–80.

Eng, David L. *Racial Castration: Managing Masculinity in Asian America.* Durham, NC: Duke University Press, 2001.

Epstein, Debbie. 1998. Real Boys Don't Work: "Underachievement," Masculinity and the Harassment of "Sissies." In *Failing Boys? Issues in Gender and Achievement,* edited by Debbie Epstein, Jannette Elwood, Valerie Hey, and Janet Maw. Buckingham, UK: Open University Press, pp. 96–108.

Epstein, Debbie, Jannette Elwood, Valerie Hey, and Janet Maw, eds. 1998a. *Failing Boys? Issues in Gender and Achievement.* Buckingham, UK: Open University Press.

Epstein, Debbie, Jannette Elwood, Valerie Hey, and Janet Maw. 1998b. Schoolboy Frictions: Feminism and "Failing" Boys. In *Failing Boys? Issues in Gender and Achievement,* edited by Debbie Epstein, Jannette Elwood, Valerie Hey, and Janet Maw. Buckingham, UK: Open University Press, pp. 3–18.

Epstein, Debbie, and Máirtín Mac an Ghaill. 2001. Series editors' introduction to *Schooling the Boys: Masculinities and Primary Education,* by Christine Skelton. Philadelphia: Open University Press, pp. ix–xi.

Equal Justice Initiative. 2007. Cruel and Unusual: Sentencing 13- and 14-Year Old Children to Die in Prison. Available at http://eji.org/eji/files/20071017cruelandunusual.pdf.

Eskridge, William N., Jr. 1999. *Gaylaw: Challenging the Apartheid of the Closet.* Cambridge, MA: Harvard University Press.

Eskridge, William N., Jr., and Nan Hunter, eds. 2004. *Sexuality, Gender, and the Law,* 2d ed. New York: Foundation Press.

Eskridge, William N., Jr., and Darren R. Spedale. 2006. *Gay Marriage: For Better or for Worse? What We've Learned from the Evidence.* New York: Oxford University Press.

Estrada, Rudy, and Jody Marksamer. 2008. Lesbian, Gay, Bisexual, and Transgender Young People in State Custody: Making the Child Welfare and Juvenile Justice Systems Safe for All Youth through Litigation, Advocacy, and Education. *Temple Law Review* 79:415–38.

Evans, Lorraine, and Kimberly Davies. 2000. No Sissy Boys Here: A Content Analysis of the Representation of Masculinity in Elementary School Reading Textbooks. *Sex Roles* 42:255–70.

Fagan, Jeffrey. 2008. Juvenile Crime and Criminal Justice: Resolving Border Disputes. *Future of Children* 18(2):81–118.

Fagan, Jeffrey. 2003. Atkins, Adolescence, and the Maturity Heuristic: Rationales for a Categorical Exemption for Juveniles from Capital Punishment. *New Mexico Law Review* 33:207–54.

Fagan, Jeffrey. 2002. This Will Hurt Me More Than It Hurts You. *Notre Dame Journal of Law, Ethics and Public Policy* 16:101–49.

Fagan, Jeffrey, and Franklin E. Zimring, eds. 2000. *The Changing Borders of Juvenile Justice: Transfer of Adolescents to the Criminal Court.* Chicago: University of Chicago Press.

Faludi, Susan. 1999. *Stiffed: The Betrayal of the American Man.* New York: Morrow.

Farough, Steven D. 2006. Believing Is Seeing: The Matrix of Vision and White Masculinities. *Journal of Contemporary Ethnography* 35(1):51–83.

Fausto-Sterling, Anne. 1995. How to Build a Man. In *Constructing Masculinity,* edited by Maurice Berger, Brian Wallis, and Simon Watson. New York: Routledge, pp. 127–34.

Feld, Barry C. 2007. A Century of Juvenile Justice: A Work in Progress or a Revolution That Failed? *Northern Kentucky Law Review* 34:189–256.

Feld, Barry C. 2006. Police Interrogation of Juveniles: An Empirical Study of Policy and Practice. *Journal of Criminal Law and Criminology* 97:219–313.

Feld, Barry C. 2003a. Competence, Culpability, and Punishment: Implications of Atkins for Executing and Sentencing Adolescents. *Hofstra Law Review* 32:463–552.

Feld, Barry C. 2003b. Race, Politics, and Juvenile Justice: The Warren Court and the Conservative "Backlash." *Minnesota Law Review* 87:1447–1577.

Feld, Barry C. 1999. *Bad Kids: Race and the Transformation of the Juvenile Court.* New York: Oxford University Press.

Ferguson, Ann Arnett. 2000. *Bad Boys: Public Schools in the Making of Black Masculinity.* Ann Arbor: University of Michigan Press.

Fineman, Martha Albertson. 2005. *The Autonomy Myth: A Theory of Dependency.* New York: New Press.

Fineman, Martha Albertson. 1995. *The Neutered Mother, The Sexual Family and Other Twentieth-Century Tragedies.* New York: Routledge.

Fineman, Martha Albertson. 1994. *The Illusion of Equality: The Rhetoric and Reality of Divorce Reform.* Chicago: University of Chicago Press.

Finkelhor, David, Gerald Hotaling, I.A. Lewis, and Christine Smith. 1990. Sexual Abuse in a National Survey of Adult Men and Women: Prevalence, Characteristics, and Risk Factors. *Child Abuse and Neglect* 14(1):19–28.

Finkelhor, David, and Lisa Jones. 2006. Why Have Child Maltreatment and Child Victimization Declined? *Journal of Social Issues* 62(4):685–716.

Finley, Gordon E., and Seth J. Schwartz. 2006. Parsons and Bales Revisited: Young Adult Children's Characterization of the Fathering Role. *Psychology of Men and Masculinity* 7(1):42–55.

Flood, Michael. 2005. Men's Collective Struggles for Gender Justice: The Case of Antiviolence Activism. In *Handbook of Studies on Men and Masculinities,* edited by Michael S. Kimmel, Jeff Hearn, and R.W. Connell. Thousand Oaks, CA: Sage, pp. 458–66.

Foels, Rob, and Christopher J. Pappas. 2004. Learning and Unlearning the Myths We Are Taught: Gender and Social Dominance Orientation. *Sex Roles* 50:743–57.

Fondacaro, Mark R., Christopher Slobogin, and Tricia Cross. 2006. Reconceptualizing Due Process in Juvenile Justice: Contributions from Law and Social Science. *Hastings Law Journal* 57(5):955–89.

Forrest, David. 1996. "We're Here, We're Queer, and We're Not Going Shopping": Changing Gay Male Identities in Contemporary Britain. In *Dislocating Masculinity: Comparative Ethnographies,* edited by Andrea Cornwall and Nancy Lindisfarne. New York: Routledge, pp. 97–110.

Foucault, Michael. 1980 [1976]. *The History of Sexuality, Volume 1: An Introduction.* Translated by Robert Hurley. New York: Vintage Books.

Fox, John. 2004. How Men's Movement Participants View Each Other. *Journal of Men's Studies* 12(2):103–18.

Fox, Sanford J. 1996. The Early History of the Court. *Future of Children* 6(3): 29–39.

Fragile Families Research Team. 2005. Fragile Families and Child Wellbeing Study, http://www.researchforum.org/project_printable_28.html.

Francis, Becky, and Christine Skelton. 2005. *Reassessing Gender and Achievement: Questioning Contemporary Key Debates.* London: Routledge.

Frank, Blye, Michael Kehler, Trudy Lovell, and Kevin Davison. 2003. A Tangle of Trouble: Boys, Masculinity and Schooling—Future Directions. *Educational Review* 55(2):119–33.

Freel, Mike. 2003. Child Sexual Abuse and the Male Monopoly: An Empirical Exploration of Gender and a Sexual Interest in Children. *British Journal of Social Work* 33:481–98.

Freeman-Longo, Robert E., and Geral T. Blanchard. 1998. *Sexual Abuse in America: Epidemic of the 21st Century.* Brandon, VT: Safer Society.

Freyd, Jennifer J., Frank W. Putnam, Thomas D. Lyon, Kathryn A. Becker-Blease, Ross E. Cheit, Nancy B. Siegel, and Kathy Pezdek. 2005. The Science of Child Sexual Abuse, http://dynamic.uoregon.edu/~jjf/articles/science05.htm.

Fuchs, Cynthia. 1996. "Beat Me Outta Me": Alternative Masculinities. In *Boys: Masculinities in Contemporary Culture,* edited by Paul Smith. Boulder, CO: Westview, pp. 171–97.

Gardiner, Judith Kegan. 2005a. Men, Masculinities, and Feminist Theory. In *Handbook of Studies on Men and Masculinities,* edited by Michael S. Kimmel, Jeff Hearn, and R.W. Connell. Thousand Oaks, CA: Sage, pp. 35–50.

Gardiner, Judith Kegan. 2005b. Why Saddam Is Gay: Masculinity Politics in South Park—Bigger, Longer, and Uncut. *Quarterly Review of Film and Video* 22(1):51–62.

Gardiner, Judith Kegan. 2003. Gender and Masculinity Texts: Consensus and Concerns for Feminist Classrooms. *National Women's Studies Association* 15(1): 147–57.

Gardiner, Judith Kegan. 2002a. Introduction to *Masculinity Studies and Feminist Theory: New Directions,* edited by Judith Kegan Gardiner. New York: Columbia University Press, pp. 1–29.

Gardiner, Judith Kegan. 2002b. Theorizing Age with Gender: Bly's Boys, Feminism, and Maturity Masculinity. In *Masculinity Studies and Feminist Theory: New Directions,* edited by Judith Kegan Gardiner. New York: Columbia University Press, pp. 90–118.

Gardiner, Judith Kegan, ed. 2002c. *Masculinity Studies and Feminist Theory: New Directions.* New York: Columbia University Press.

Gardiner, Judith Kegan. 2000a. Masculinity, the Teening of America, and Empathic Targeting. *Signs: Journal of Women in Culture and Society* 25(4):1257–61.

Gardiner, Judith Kegan. 2000b. South Park, Blue Men, Anality, and Market Masculinity. *Men and Masculinities* 2(3):251–71.

Garrison, Marsha. 2005. Is Consent Necessary? An Evaluation of the Emerging Law of Cohabitant Obligation. *UCLA Law Review* 52:885–97.

Gavanas, Anna. 2004. Domesticating Masculinity and Masculinizing Domesticity in Contemporary U.S. Fatherhood Politics. *Social Politics* 11(2):247–66.

Gavanas, Anna. 2002. The Fatherhood Responsibility Movement: The Centrality of Marriage, Work and Male Sexuality in Reconstructions of Masculinity and Fatherhood. In *Making Men into Fathers: Men, Masculinities and the Social Politics of Fatherhood,* edited by Barbara Hobson. New York: Cambridge University Press, pp. 213–42.

Gergen, Mary M., and Sara N. Davis, eds. 1997. *Toward a New Psychology of Gender.* New York: Routledge.

Gher, Jaime M. 2008. Polygamy and Same-Sex Marriage—Allies or Adversaries within the Same-Sex Marriage Movement. *William and Mary Journal of Women and the Law* 14:559–603.

Giller, Olga. 2004. Notes and Comments: Patriarchy on Lockdown: Deliberate Indifference and Male Prison Rape. *Cardozo Women's Law Journal* 10:659–89.

Gilmore, David. 1990. *Manhood in the Making: Cultural Concepts of Masculinity.* New Haven, CT: Yale University Press.

Gitlin, Cara. 2008. Expert Testimony on Child Sexual Abuse Accommodation Syndrome: How Proper Screening Should Severely Limit Its Admission. *Quinnipiac Law Review* 26:497–549.

Glennon, Lisa. 2008. Obligations between Adult Partners: Moving from Form to Function? *International Journal of Law Policy and Family* 22:22–57.

Glennon, Theresa. 2002. Evaluating Institutional Practice and the African American Boy. *Journal of Health Care Law and Policy* 5:10–67.

Godenzi, Alberto. 2000. Determinants of Culture: Men and Economic Power. In *Male Roles, Masculinities and Violence: A Culture of Peace Perspective,* edited by Ingeborg Breines, Robert Connell, and Ingrid Eide. Paris: UNESCO, pp. 35–51.

Goldrick-Jones, Amanda. 2001. Pessimism, Paralysis, and Possibility: Crisis-Points in Profeminism. *Journal of Men's Studies* 9(3):323–39.

Goldscheider, Frances K. 2000. Men, Children and the Future of the Family in the Third Millennium. *Futures* 32(6):525–38.

Good, Glenn E., and Tiffany S. Borst. 1994. Masculinity Research: A Review and Critique. *Applied and Preventive Psychology* 3:3–14.

Goodkind, Sara. 2005. Gender-Specific Services in the Juvenile Justice System: A Critical Examination. *AFFILIA* 20(1):52–70.

Gough, Brendan. 2004. Psychoanalysis as a Resource for Understanding Emotional Ruptures in the Text: The Case of Defensive Masculinities. *British Journal of Social Psychology* 43(2):245–67.

Grall, Timothy S. 2007. Custodial Mothers and Fathers and Their Child Support: 2005. U.S. Census Bureau, Current Population Reports, pp. 60–234. http://www.2010census.biz/prod/2007/pubs.

Green, Adam Isaiah. 2007. Queer Theory and Sociology: Locating the Subject and the Self in Sexuality Studies. *Sociological Theory* 25(1):26–45.

Green, Beatrice. 2005. Homosexual Signification: A Moral Construct in Social Contexts. *Journal of Homosexuality* 49(2):119–34.

Guarino-Ghezzi, Susan, and Edward J. Loughran. 2004. *Balancing Juvenile Justice,* exp. and rev. 2d ed. New Brunswick, NJ: Transaction.

Gunn, Raymond. 2004. Inner-City "Schoolboy" Life. *Annals of the American Academy of Political and Social Science* 595:63–79.

Gurian, Michael, and Patricia Henley. 2001. *Boys and Girls Learn Differently!* San Francisco: Jossey-Bass.

Gurian, Michael, and Kathy Stevens. 2005. *The Minds of Boys: Saving Our Sons from Falling Behind in School and Life.* San Francisco: Jossey-Bass.

Haas, Linda P., C. Philip Hwang, and Graeme Russell. 2000. Programs and Politics Promoting Women's Economic Equality and Men's Sharing of Child Care in Sweden. In *Organizational Change and Gender Equity: International Perspectives on Fathers and Mothers in the Workplace,* edited by Linda P. Haas, C. Philip Hwang, and Graeme Russell. Thousand Oaks, CA: Sage.

Haddad, Tony. 1993a. Introduction to *Men and Masculinities: A Critical Anthology,* edited by Tony Haddad. Toronto: Canadian Scholars Press , pp. xi–xxi.

Haddad, Tony, ed. 1993b. *Men and Masculinities: A Critical Anthology.* Toronto: Canadian Scholars Press.

Haenfler, Ross. 2004. Manhood in Contradiction: The Two Faces of Straight Edge. *Men and Masculinities* 7(1):77–99.

Halberstam, Judith. 2002. The Good, The Bad, and the Ugly: Men, Women and Masculinity. In *Masculinity Studies and Feminist Theory: New Directions,* edited by Judith Kegan Gardiner. New York: Columbia University Press, pp. 344–67.

Halberstam, Judith. 1998. *Female Masculinity.* Durham, NC: Duke University Press.

Hall, C. Michael. 2005. Shifting Spaces of Masculinity. In *Spaces of Masculinities,* edited by Bettina van Hoven and Kathrin Horschelmann. London: Routledge.

Halley, Ian. 2004. Queer Theory by Men. *Duke Journal of Gender Law and Policy* 11:7–52.

Hammond, Wizdom P., Kira H. Banks, and Jacqueline S. Mattis. 2006. Masculinity Ideology and Forgiveness of Racial Discrimination among African American Men: Direct and Interactive Relationships. *Sex Roles* 55:679–92.

Hammond, Wizdom P., and Jacqueline S. Mattis. 2005. Being a Man about It: Manhood Meaning among African American Men. *Psychology of Men and Masculinity* 6(2): 114–26.

Hanmer, Jalna. 1990. Men, Power and the Exploitation of Women. In *Men, Masculinities and Social Theory,* edited by Jeff Hearn and David Morgan. London: Unwin Hyman, pp. 21–42.

Hanna, Fadi, 2005. Punishing Masculinity in Gay Asylum Claims. *Yale Law Journal* 114:913–20.

Hanson, R. Karl, and Monique T. Bussiere. 1998. Predicting Relapse: A Meta-analysis of Sexual Offender Recidivism Studies. *Journal of Consulting and Clinical Psychology* 66(2):348–62.

Harris, Angela P. 2000. Gender, Violence, Race, and Criminal Justice. *Stanford Law Review* 52:777–807.

Harris, Luke Charles. 1999. The Challenge and Possibility for Black Males to Embrace Feminism. In *Black Men on Race, Gender and Sexuality: A Critical Reader,* edited by Devon Carbado. New York: New York University Press, pp. 383–86.

Hart, Angie. 1996. Missing Masculinity? Prostitutes' Clients in Alicante, Spain. In *Dislocating Masculinity: Comparative Ethnographies,* edited by Andrea Cornwall and Nancy Lindisfarne. New York: Routledge, pp. 48–65.

Hatty, Suzanne E. 2000. *Masculinities, Violence, and Culture.* Thousand Oaks, CA: Sage.

Hawkins, A.J., and Rob Palkovitz. 1999. Beyond Ticks and Clicks: The Need for More Diverse and Broader Conceptualizations and Measures of Father Involvement. *Journal of Men's Studies* 8:11–12.

Hearn, Jeff. 2004. From Hegemonic Masculinity to the Hegemony of Men. *Feminist Theory* 5(1):49–72.

Hearn, Jeff. 2002. Men, Fathers and the State: National and Global Relations. In *Making Men into Fathers: Men, Masculinities and the Social Politics of Fatherhood,* edited by Barbara Hobson. New York: Cambridge University Press, pp. 245–72.

Hearn, Jeff. 1996. Is Masculinity Dead? A Critique of the Concept of Masculinity/Masculinities. In *Understanding Masculinities: Social Relations and Cultural Arenas,* edited by Máirtín Mac an Ghaill. Philadelphia: Open University Press, pp. 202–17.

Hearn, Jeff, and David L. Collinson. 1994. Theorizing Unities and Differences between Men and between Masculinities. In *Theorizing Masculinities,* edited by Harry Brod and Michael Kaufman. Thousand Oaks, CA: Sage, pp. 97–118.

Hearn, Jeff, and David H.J. Morgan. 1990a. The Critique of Men. In *Men, Masculinities and Social Theory,* edited by Jeff Hearn and David Morgan. London: Unwin Hyman, pp. 203–5.

Hearn, Jeff, and David H.J. Morgan. 1990b. Men, Masculinities and Social Theory. In *Men, Masculinities and Social Theory,* edited by Jeff Hearn and David Morgan. London: Unwin Hyman, pp. 1–18.

Hearn, Jeff, and David H.J. Morgan, eds. 1990c. *Men, Masculinities and Social Theory.* London: Unwin Hyman.

Hegarty, Peter, and Sean Massey. 2006. Anti-homosexual Prejudice . . . as Opposed to What? Queer Theory and the Social Psychology of Anti-homosexual Attitudes. *Journal of Homosexuality* 52:47–71.

Heise, Michael. 2004. Are Single-Sex Schools Inherently Unequal? *Michigan Law Review* 102:1219–44.

Herek, Gregory M. 2009. Hate Crimes and Stigma-Related Experiences among Sexual Minority Adults in the United States: Prevalence Estimates from a National Probability Sample. *Journal of Interpersonal Violence* 24(1):54–74.

Herek, Gregory M. 2007. Confronting Sexual Stigma and Prejudice: Theory and Practice. *Journal of Social Issues* 63(4):905–25.

Herek, Gregory M., and Kevin T. Berrill, eds. 1992. Hate Crimes Confronting Violence against Lesbians and Gay Men. London: Sage.

Herman, Judith. 1992. *Trauma and Recovery.* New York: Basic Books.

Hobson, Barbara, ed. 2002. *Making Men into Fathers: Men, Masculinities and the Social Politics of Fatherhood.* New York: Cambridge University Press.

Hobson, Barbara, and David Morgan. 2002. Introduction to *Making Men into Fathers: Men, Masculinities and the Social Politics of Fatherhood,* edited by Barbara Hobson. New York: Cambridge University Press, pp. 1–21.

Hoffman, Rose M. 2001. The Measurement of Masculinity and Femininity: Historical Perspective and Implications for Counseling. *Journal of Counseling and Development* 79(4):472–85.

Hoge, Robert D., Nancy G. Guerra, and Paul Boxer, eds. 2008. *Treating the Juvenile Offender.* New York: Guilford.

Holter, Øystein Gullvåg. 2007. Men's Work and Family Reconciliation in Europe. *Men and Masculinities* 9(4):425–56.

Holter, Øystein Gullvåg. 2005. Social Theories for Researching Men and Masculinities: Direct Gender Hierarchy and Structural Inequality. In *Handbook of Studies on Men and Masculinities*, edited by Michael S. Kimmel, Jeff Hearn, and R.W. Connell. Thousand Oaks, CA: Sage, pp. 15–34.

Holter, Øystein Gullvåg. 2000. Masculinities in Context: On Peace Issues and Patriarchal Orders. In *Male Roles, Masculinities and Violence: A Culture of Peace Perspective*, edited by Ingeborg Breines, Robert Connell and Ingrid Eide. Paris: UNESCO, pp. 61–83.

Hondagneu-Sotelo, Pierrette, and Michael A. Messner. 1994. Gender Displays and Men's Power: The "New Man" and the Mexican Immigrant Man. In *Theorizing Masculinities*, edited by Harry Brod and Michael Kaufman. Thousand Oaks, CA: Sage, pp. 200–218.

Hostetler, Andrew J., and Gilbert H. Herdt. 1998. Culture, Sexual Lifeways, and Developmental Subjectivities: Rethinking Sexual Taxonomies. *Social Research* 65(2):249–90.

Howarth, Joan W. 2002. Executing White Masculinities: Learning from Karla Faye Tucker. *Oregon Law Review* 81:184–229.

Howell, James C. 2003. *Preventing and Reducing Juvenile Delinquency: A Comprehensive Framework*. Thousand Oaks, CA: Sage.

Hudson, Annie. 1987. Boys Will Be Boys: Masculinism and the Juvenile Justice System. *Critical Social Policy* 7(30):30–48.

Humphrey, Alecia. 2003. Introduction: Girls in the Juvenile Justice System: The Intersection of Gender, Age and Crime. *Wisconsin Women's Law Journal* 18:1–5.

Hutchinson, Darren Lenard. 1997. Out yet Unseen: A Racial Critique of Gay and Lesbian Legal Theory and Political Disclosure. *Connecticut Law Review* 29:561–645.

In re Gault, 387 U.S. 1 (1967).

In re Winship, 397 U.S. 358 (1970).

Jackson, Chantelle, and Mark Perlaky. 2008. Problems for Females in the Juvenile Justice System: What Is Happening and What Can Be Done? *DCBA Brief* 20:31–40.

Jackson, David. 1998. Breaking Out of the Binary Trap: Boys' Underachievement, Schooling and Gender Relations. In *Failing Boys? Issues in Gender and Achievement*, edited by Debbie Epstein, Jannette Elwood, Virginia Hey, and Janet Maw. Buckingham, UK: Open University Press, pp. 77–95.

Jacobs, Jerry A., and Kathleen Gerson. 1998. Toward a Family-Friendly, Gender-Equitable Work Week. *University of Pennsylvania Journal of Labor and Employment Law* 1:457–72.

Jacobs, Melanie. 2007. Why Just Two? Disaggregating Traditional Parental Rights and Responsibilities to Recognize Multiple Parents. *Journal of Law and Family Studies* 9:309–39.

Jagose, Annamarie. 1996. *Queer Theory: An Introduction*. New York: New York University Press.

Jeffries, Elena D. 2004. Experiences of Trust with Parents: A Qualitative Investigation of African American, Latino, and Asian American Boys from Low-Income Families. In *Adolescent Boys: Exploring Diverse Cultures of Boyhood*, edited by Niobe Way and Judy Y. Chu. New York: New York University Press, pp. 107–28.

Jenkins, Kimberly J. 2006. Constitutional Lessons for the Next Generation of Public Single Sex Elementary and Secondary Schools. *William and Mary Law Review* 47:1953–2043.

Jewkes, Yvonne. 2005. Men Behind Bars: "Doing" Masculinity as an Adaptation to Imprisonment. *Men and Masculinities* 8(1):44–63.

Joseph, Lauren. 2006. Book Review. *Men and Masculinities* 8(4):528–39.

Kaminer, Debbie. 2007. The Child Care Crisis and the Work-Family Conflict: A Policy Rationale for Federal Legislation. *Berkeley Journal of Employment and Labor Law* 28:495–540.

Kann, Mark E. 2001. Penitence for the Privileged: Manhood, Race, and Penitentiaries in Early America. In *Prison Masculinities,* edited by Don Sabo, Terry A. Kupers, and Willie London. Philadelphia: Temple University Press, pp. 21–34.

Katz, Jackson. 2000. Violence Prevention Education. In *Masculinities at School,* edited by Nancy Lesko. Thousand Oaks, CA: Sage, pp. 283–304.

Katz, Jackson. 1995. Reconstructing Masculinity in the Locker Room: The Mentors in Violence Prevention Project. *Harvard Educational Review* 65(2):163–74.

Kaufman, Michael. 2005. Beyond Presumptions and Peafowl: Reconciling the Legal Principle of Equality with the Pedagogical Benefits of Gender Differentiation. *Buffalo Law Review* 53:1059–1109.

Kaufman, Michael. 2000. Working with Men and Boys to Challenge Sexism and End Men's Violence. In *Male Roles, Masculinities and Violence: A Culture of Peace Perspective,* edited by Ingeborg Breines, Robert Connell, and Ingrid Eide. Paris: UNESCO, pp. 213–22.

Kaufman, Michael. 1994. Men, Feminism, and Men's Contradictory Experiences of Power. In *Theorizing Masculinities,* edited by Harry Brod and Michael Kaufman. Thousand Oaks, CA: Sage, pp. 142–63.

Kempf-Leonard, Kimberly, and Lisa L. Sample. 2000. Disparity Based on Sex: Is Gender-Specific Treatment Warranted? *Justice Quarterly* 17(1):89–128.

Kennedy, Kathleen. 2004. Manhood and Subversion during World War I: The Cases of Eugene Debs and Alexander Berkman. *North Carolina Law Review* 82:1661–1703.

Kent v. United States, 383 U.S. 541 (1966).

Kepros, Laurie Rose. 1999–2000. Queer Theory: Weed or Seed in the Garden of Legal Theory? *Law and Sexuality* 9:279–310.

Kerrigan, Jennifer L. 2008. "It's Not World Peace, but . . ." Restorative Justice: Analysis of Recidivism Rates in Campbell Law School's Juvenile Justice Project. *Campbell Law Review* 30:339–61.

Kessler, Laura T. 2007. Keeping Discrimination Theory Front and Center in the Discourse over Work and Family Conflict. *Pepperdine Law Review* 34:313–31.

Kessler, Laura T. 2005. Transgressive Caregiving. *Florida State University Law Review* 33:1–87.

Ketring, Scott A., and Leslie L. Feinauer. 1999. Perpetrator-Victim Relationship: Long-Term Effects of Sexual Abuse for Men and Women. *Journal of Family Therapy* 27:109–20.

Kilianski, Stephanen E. 2003. Explaining Heterosexual Men's Attitudes toward Women and Gay Men: The Theory of Exclusively Masculine Identity. *Psychology of Men and Masculinity* 4(1):37–56.

Kilmartin, Christopher. 2000. *The Masculine Self.* 2d ed. Boston: McGraw Hill.

Kimmel, Michael S. 2004. *The Gendered Society.* New York: Oxford University Press.

Kimmel, Michael S. 2002a. Foreword to *Masculinities Matter! Men, Gender and Development,* edited by Frances Cleaver. New York: Zed Books, pp. xi–xiv.

Kimmel, Michael S. 2002b. Foreword to *Masculinity Studies and Feminist Theory: New Directions,* edited by Judith Kegan Gardiner. New York: Columbia University Press, pp. ix–xi.

Kimmel, Michael S. 2001. Global Masculinities: Restoration and Resistance. In *A Man's World? Changing Men's Practices in a Globalized World,* edited by Bob Pease and Keith Pringle. New York: Zed Books, pp. 21–37.

Kimmel, Michael S. 2000. Reducing Men's Violence: The Personal Meets the Political. In *Male Roles, Masculinities and Violence: A Culture of Peace Perspective,* edited by Ingeborg Breines, Robert Connell, and Ingrid Eide. Paris: UNESCO, pp. 239–47.

Kimmel, Michael S. 1997a. Integrating Men into the Classroom. *Duke Journal of Gender Law and Policy* 4:181–95.

Kimmel, Michael S. 1997b. Masculinity as Homophobia: Fear, Shame, and Silence in the Construction of Gender Identity. In *Toward a New Psychology of Gender,* edited by Mary M. Gergen and Sara N. Davis. New York: Routledge, pp. 223–43.

Kimmel, Michael S. 1994. Masculinity as Homophobia: Fear, Shame, and Silence in the Construction of Gender Identity. In *Theorizing Masculinities,* edited by Harry Brod and Michael Kaufman. Thousand Oaks, CA: Sage, pp. 119–41.

Kimmel, Michael S., Jeff Hearn, and R.W. Connell. 2005a. Introduction. In *Handbook of Studies on Men and Masculinities,* edited by Michael S. Kimmel, Jeff Hearn, and R.W. Connell. Thousand Oaks, CA: Sage, pp. 1–12.

Kimmel, Michael S., Jeff Hearn, and R.W. Connell, eds. 2005b. *Handbook of Studies on Men and Masculinities.* Thousand Oaks, CA: Sage.

Kimmel, Michael S., and Michael Kaufman. 1994. Weekend Warriors: The New Men's Movement. In *Theorizing Masculinities,* edited by Harry Brod and Michael Kaufman. Thousand Oaks, CA: Sage, pp. 259–88.

Kimmel, Michael S., and Michael A. Messner, eds. 2001. *Men's Lives.* Boston: Allyn and Bacon.

Kimmel, Michael S., and Amy Traver. 2005. Mentoring Masculinities: Race and Class in the (Re-)construction of Gender in the USA and the UK. *Irish Journal of Sociology* 14(2):213–30.

Kindlon, Dan, and Michael Thomson, with Tersa Barker. 1999. *Raising Cain: Protecting the Emotional Life of Boys.* New York: Ballantine Books.

King, James R. 2000. The Problem(s) of Men in Early Education. In *Masculinities at School,* edited by Nancy Lesko. Thousand Oaks, CA: Sage, pp. 3–26.

Kirsch, Max H. 2000. *Queer Theory and Social Change.* New York: Routledge.

Kirsta, Alix. 1994. *Deadlier Than the Male: Violence and Aggression in Women.* London: HarperCollins.

Kisthardt, Elizabeth S. 2007. Singling Them Out: The Influence of the "Boy Crisis" on the New Title IX Regulations. *Wisconsin Women's Law Journal* 22:13–336.

Klinth, Roger. 2008. The Best of Both Worlds? Fatherhood and Gender Equality in Swedish Paternity Leave Campaigns 1976–2006. *Fathering* 6(1):20–38.

Klomsten, Anne Torhild, Herb W. Marsh, and Einar M. Skaalvik. 2005. Adolescents' Perceptions of Masculine and Feminine Values in Sport and Physical Education: A Study of Gender Differences. *Sex Roles* 52(9–10): 25–36.

Knijn, Trudie, and Peter Selten. 2002. Transformations of Fatherhood: The Netherlands. In *Making Men into Fathers: Men, Masculinities and the Social Politics of Fatherhood,* edited by Barbara Hobson. New York: Cambridge University Press, pp. 168–87.

Korobov, Neill. 2005. Ironizing Masculinity: How Adolescent Boys Negotiate Hetero-nor-mative Dilemmas in Conversational Interaction. *Journal of Men's Studies* 13(2):225–46.

Kozol, Jonathan. 2005. *The Shame of the Nation: The Restoration of Apartheid Schooling in America*. New York: Crown.

Krisberg, Barry. 2005. *Juvenile Justice: Redeeming Our Children*. Thousand Oaks, CA: Sage.

Krishnaswamy, Revathi. 2002. The Economy of Colonial Desire. In *The Masculinity Studies Reader*, edited by Rachel Adams and David Savran. Malden, MA: Blackwell, pp. 292–317.

Kuzmic, Jeffrey J. 2000. Textbooks, Knowledge and Masculinity: Examining Patriarchy from Within. In *Masculinities at School*, edited by Nancy Lesko. Thousand Oaks, CA: Sage, pp. 105–20.

Lamb, Michael. 1997. *The Role of the Father in Child Development*. New York: Wiley.

Larsen, Thomas R. 2001. The War against Boys: Justified Retribution. *Journal of Law and Family Studies* 3:29–143.

Larson, Jeffrey H., Kenneth E. Newell, Thomas B. Holman, and Ian D. Feinauer. 2007. The Role of Family Environment in the Dating Relationships and Readiness for Marriage of Young Adult Male Survivors of Non-familial Childhood Sexual Abuse. *American Journal of Family Therapy* 35:73–86.

Law, Sylvia A. 1988. Homosexuality and the Social Meaning of Gender. *Wisconsin Law Review* 1988:187–235.

Lawrence, Charles R., III. 1999. The Message of the Verdict: A Three-Act Morality Play Starring Clarence Thomas, Willie Smith, and Mike Tyson. In *Black Men on Race, Gender and Sexuality: A Critical Reader*, edited by Devon Carbado. New York: New York University Press, pp. 212–36.

Lazur, Richard F., and Richard Majors. 1995. Men of Color: Ethnocultural Variations of Male Gender Role Strain. In *A New Psychology of Men*, edited by Ronald F. Levant and William S. Pollack. New York: Basic Books, pp. 337–58.

Lee, Stacey J. 2004. Hmong American Masculinities: Creating New Identities in the United States. In *Adolescent Boys: Exploring Diverse Cultures of Boyhood*, edited by Niobe Way and Judy Y. Chu. New York: New York University Press, pp. 13–30.

Leibowitz, Jodi. 2003. Criminal Statutes of Limitations: An Obstacle to the Prosecution and Punishment of Child Sexual Abuse. *Cardozo Law Review* 25:907–45.

Lesko, Nancy, ed. 2000. *Masculinities at School*. Thousand Oaks, CA: Sage.

Levant, Ronald F., and William S. Pollack. 1995a. Introduction to *A New Psychology of Men*, edited by Ronald F. Levant and William S. Pollack. New York: Basic Books, pp. 1–10.

Levant, Ronald F., and William S. Pollack, eds. 1995b. *A New Psychology of Men*. New York: Basic Books.

Levant, Ronald F., and Katherine Richmond. 2007. A Review of Research on Masculinity Ideologies Using the Male Role Norms Inventory. *Journal of Men's Studies* 15(2):130–46.

Leverenz, David. 1986. Manhood, Humiliation, and Public Life: Some Stories. *Southwest Review* 71:442–62.

Levine, Kay. 2006. No Penis, No Problem. *Fordham Urban Law Journal* 33:357–404.

Levit, Nancy. 2005. Embracing Segregation: The Jurisprudence of Choice and Diversity in Race and Sex Separatism in Schools. *University of Illinois Law Review* 2005:455–512.

Levit, Nancy. 2001. Male Prisoners: Privacy, Suffering, and the Legal Construction of Masculinity. In *Prison Masculinities*, edited by Don Sabo, Terry A. Kupers, and Willie London. Philadelphia: Temple University Press, pp. 93–102.

Lewis, Joan. 2002. The Problem of Fathers: Policy and Behavior in Britain. In *Making Men into Fathers: Men, Masculinities and the Social Politics of Fatherhood,* edited by Barbara Hobson. New York: Cambridge University Press, pp. 125–49.

Lieb, Roxanne, Vernon Quinsey, and Lucy Berliner. 1998. Sexual Predators and Social Policy. *Crime and Justice* 23:43–73.

Lingard, Bob, and Peter Douglas. 1999. *Men Engaging Feminisms: Pro-feminism, Backlashes and Schooling.* Buckingham, UK: Open University Press.

Lisak, David. 1994. The Psychological Impact of Sexual Abuse: Content Analysis of Interviews with Male Survivors. *Journal of Traumatic Stress* 7(4):525–48.

Locke, John. 1692. *Some Thoughts Concerning Education.* Available at www.fordham.edu/halsall/mod/1692locke-education.html.

Lockie, Adrienne Jennings. 2009. Multiple Families, Multiple Goals, Multiple Failures: The Need for "Limited Equalization" as a Theory of Child Support. *Harvard Journal of Law and Gender* 32:109–63.

London, Kamala, Maggie Bruck, Stephen J. Ceci, and Daniel W. Shuman. 2005. Disclosure of Child Sexual Abuse: What Does Research Tell Us about the Ways That Children Tell? *Psychology, Public Policy, and Law* 11(1):194–226.

Louie, Kam. 2003. Chinese, Japanese and Global Masculine Identities. In *Asian Masculinities: The Meaning and Practice of Manhood in China and Japan,* edited by Kam Louie and Morris Low. New York: Routledge Curzon, pp. 1–15.

Louie, Kam, and Morris Low, eds. 2003. *Asian Masculinities: The Meaning and Practice of Manhood in China and Japan.* New York: Routledge Curzon.

Ludeke, Brian W. 2007. Malibu Locals Only: "Boys Will Be Boys," or Dangerous Street Gang? Why the Criminal Justice System's Failure to Properly Identify Suburban Gangs Hurts Efforts to Fight Gangs. *California Western Law Review* 34:309–62.

Lumsden, Malvern. 2000. Engendering Peace: Creative Arts Approaches to Transforming Domestic and Communal Violence. In *Male Roles, Masculinities and Violence: A Culture of Peace Perspective,* edited by Ingeborg Breines, Robert Connell, and Ingrid Eide. Paris: UNESCO, pp. 257–70.

Lunbeck, Elizabeth. 1994. *The Psychiatric Persuasion: Knowledge, Gender, and Power in Modern America.* Princeton, NJ: Princeton University Press.

Luxton, Meg. 1993. Dreams and Dilemmas: Feminist Musings on "The Man Question." In *Men and Masculinities: A Critical Anthology,* edited by Tony Haddad. Toronto: Canadian Scholars Press, pp. 347–74.

Mac an Ghaill, Máirtín, ed. 1996. *Understanding Masculinities: Social Relations and Cultural Arenas.* Philadelphia: Open University Press.

Mac an Ghaill, Máirtín. 1994. *The Making of Men: Masculinities, Sexualities and Schooling.* Buckingham, UK: Open University Press.

MacDonald, John M., and Meda Chesney-Lind. 2001. Gender Bias and Juvenile Justice Revisited: A Multiyear Analysis. *Crime and Delinquency* 47(2):173–95.

MacInnes, John. 2001. The Crisis of Masculinity and the Politics of Identity. In *The Masculinities Reader,* edited by Stephen M. Whitehead and Frank J. Barrett. Cambridge, UK: Polity, pp. 311–29.

MacInnes, John. 1998. *The End of Masculinity: The Confusion of Sexual Genesis and Sexual Difference in Modern Society.* Philadelphia: Open University Press.

Mahini, Robert. 2000. There's No Place Like Home: The Availability of Judicial Review over Certification Decisions Invoking Federal Jurisdiction under the Juvenile Justice and Delinquency Prevention Act. *Vanderbilt Law Review* 53:1311–53.

Mahoney, Pat. 1998. Girls Will Be Girls and Boys Will Be First. In *Failing Boys? Issues in Gender and Achievement*, edited by Debbie Epstein, Jannette Elwood, Virginia Hey, and Janet Maw. Buckingham, UK: Open University Press, pp. 37–55.

Majors, Richard. 2001. Cool Pose: Black Masculinity and Sports. In *The Masculinities Reader*, edited by Stephen Whitehead and Frank J. Barrett. Cambridge, UK: Polity, pp. 209–17.

Majors, Richard, and Janet Mancini Billson. 1992. *Cool Pose: The Dilemmas of Black Manhood in America*. New York: Simon and Schuster.

Maldonado, Solange. 2006. Deadbeat or Deadbroke: Redefining Child Support for Poor Fathers. *U.C. Davis Law Review* 39:991–1021.

Mallett, Christopher. 2007. Death Is Not Different: The Transfer of Juvenile Offenders to Adult Criminal Courts. *Criminal Law Bulletin* 43(4):3–20.

Man, Christopher D., and John P. Cronan. 2002. Forecasting Sexual Abuse in Prison: The Prison Subculture of Masculinity as a Backdrop for "Deliberate Indifference." *Journal of Criminal Law and Criminology* 92:127–84.

Mandel, Laurie, and Charol Shakeshaft. 2000. Heterosexism in Middle Schools. In *Masculinities at School*, edited by Nancy Lesko. Thousand Oaks, CA: Sage, pp. 73–103.

Mangold, Susan Vivian. 2003. Reforming Child Protection in Response to the Catholic Church Child Sexual Abuse Scandal. *University of Florida Journal of Law and Public Policy* 14:55–178.

Mariani, Philomena. 1995. Law-and-Order Science. In *Constructing Masculinity*, edited by Maurice Berger, Brian Wallis, and Simon Watson. New York: Routledge, pp. 135–56.

Marks, L.D., and Rob Palkovitz. 2004. American Fatherhood Types: The Good, the Bad, and the Uninterested. *Fathering* 2:113–29.

Martin, Patricia Y. 2003. "Said and Done" versus "Saying and Doing": Gendering Practices, Practicing Gender at Work. *Gender and Society* 17(3):342–66.

Martin, Sonia Renee. 1996. A Child's Right to Be Gay: Addressing the Emotional Maltreatment of Queer Youth. *Hastings Law Journal* 48:167–96.

Martino, Wayne. 2003. Boys, Masculinities and Literacy: Addressing the Issues. *Australian Journal of Language and Literacy* 26(3):9–27.

Martino, Wayne, and Deborah Berrill. 2003. Boys, Schooling and Masculinities: Interrogating the "Right" Way to Educate Boys. *Educational Review* 55(2):99–117.

Martino, Wayne, and Blye Frank. 2006. The Tyranny of Surveillance: Male Teachers and the Policing of Masculinities in a Single Sex School. *Gender and Education* 18(1):17–33.

Martino, Wayne, and Bob Meyenn. 2001a. Preface to *What about the Boys?* Buckingham, UK: Open University Press, x–xii.

Martino, Wayne, and Bob Meyenn, eds. 2001b. *What about the Boys?* Buckingham, UK: Open University Press.

Martino, Wayne, and Maria Pallotta-Chiarolli. 2003. *So What's a Boy? Addressing Issues of Masculinity and Schooling*. Berkshire, UK: Open University Press.

Masciadrelli, Brian P., Joseph H. Pleck, and Jeffrey L. Stueve. 2006. Fathers' Role Model Perceptions: Themes and Linkages with Involvement. *Men and Masculinities* 9(1):23–34.

Mathis, J.L. 1972. *Clear Thinking about Sexual Deviations: A New Look at an Old Problem.* Chicago: Nelson-Holt.

Matsuda, Mari. 1993. Beside My Sister, Facing the Enemy: Legal Theory Out of Coalition. *Stanford Law Review* 43:1183–92.

Maurer, Trent W., and Joseph H. Pleck. 2006. Fathers' Caregiving and Breadwinning: A Gender Congruence Analysis. *Psychology of Men and Masculinity* 7(2):101–12.

Mayeri, Serena. 2006. The Strange Career of Jane Crow: Sex Segregation and the Transformation of Anti-discrimination Discourse. *Yale Journal of Law and the Humanities* 18:187–272.

McCaffery, Edward. 1997. *Taxing Women.* Chicago: University of Chicago Press.

McClain, Linda C. 2001. The Domain of Civic Virtue in a Good Society: Families, Schools, and Sex Equality. *Fordham Law Review* 69:1617–66.

McCord, Joan, Cathy Spatz Widom, and Nancy A. Crowell, eds. 2001. *Juvenile Crime, Juvenile Justice.* Washington, DC: National Academy Press.

McCune, Jeffrey Q. 2007. Book Review: *New Black Man* by Mark Anthony Neal (New York: Routledge, 2005). *Men and Masculinities* 9(3):401–3.

McGinley, Ann C. 2007. Babes and Beefcake: Exclusive Hiring Arrangements and Sexy Dress Codes. *Duke Journal of Gender Law and Policy* 14:257–83.

McGinley, Ann C. 2004. Masculinities at Work. *Oregon Law Review* 83:359–433.

McKeiver v. Pennsylvania, 403 U.S. 528 (1971).

McLaughlin, Janice, Mark E. Casey, and Diane Richardson. 2006. At the Intersections of Feminist and Queer Debates. In *Intersections between Feminist and Queer Theory*, edited by Diane Richardson, Janice McLaughlin, and Mark E. Casey. New York: Palgrave Macmillan, pp. 1–18.

Meis-Knupfer, Anne. 2001. *Reform and Resistance: Delinquency, Gender and America's First Juvenile Court.* New York: Routledge.

Meissner, W.W. 2005. Gender Identity and the Self: I. Gender Formation in General and in Masculinity. *Psychoanalytic Review* 92(1):1–27.

Mendenhall, Lawrence Kent. 1995. Misters Korematsu and Steffan: The Japanese Internment and the Military's Ban on Gays in the Armed Forces. *New York University Law Review* 70:196–232.

Messerschmidt, James W. 2001. Masculinities, Crime, and Prison. In *Prison Masculinities*, edited by Don Sabo, Terry A. Kupers, and Willie London. Philadelphia: Temple University Press, pp. 67–72.

Messerschmidt, James W. 2000a. Becoming "Real Men": Adolescent Masculinity Challenges and Sexual Violence. *Men and Masculinities* 2(3):286–307.

Messerschmidt, James W. 2000b. *Nine Lives: Adolescent Masculinities, The Body, and Violence.* Boulder, CO: Westview.

Messerschmidt, James W. 1993. *Masculinities and Crime: Critique and Reconceptualization of Theory.* Lanham, MD: Rowman and Littlefield.

Messerschmidt, James W. 1998. Men Victimizing Men: The Case of Lynching, 1865–1900. In *Masculinities and Violence*, edited by Lee H. Bowker. Thousand Oaks, CA: Sage, pp. 125–51.

Messner, Michael A. 1997. Like Family Power, Intimacy, and Sexuality in Male Athletes' Friendships. In *Toward a New Psychology of Gender*, edited by Mary M. Gergen and Sara N. Davis. New York: Routledge, pp. 341–60.

Migliaccio, Todd A. 2001. Marginalizing the Battered Male. *Journal of Men's Studies* 9(2):205–26.

Miles, Sharrolyn Jackson. 2003. The Administration of Justice: Disparate Treatment and Effect on Black Male Youth in Louisiana's Juvenile Justice System. *Southern University Law Review* 30:373–92.

Millar, Kathleen. 2007. Book Review. *Men and Masculinities* 9:399–401.

Miller, Geoffrey P. 2000. Custody and Couvade: The Importance of Paternal Bonding in the Law of Family Relations. *Indiana Law Review* 33:691–736.

Mills, Martin. 2001. *Challenging Violence in Schools: An Issue of Masculinities.* Buckingham, UK: Open University Press.

Mingo, Jeffery C. 1998. More Colors Than the Rainbow: Gay Men of Color Speak about Their Identities and Legal Choices. *Law and Sexuality* 8:561–610.

Mirsky, Seth. 1996. Three Arguments for the Elimination of Masculinity. In *Men's Bodies, Men's Gods: Male Identities in a (Post-)Christian Culture,* edited by B. Krondorfer. New York: New York University Press, pp. 27–37.

Möller-Leimkühler, Anne M. 2003. The Gender Gap in Suicide and Premature Death; or, Why Are Men So Vulnerable? *European Archives of Psychiatry and Clinical Neuroscience* 253(1):1–8.

Morgan, David H.J. 1994. Theater of War: Combat, the Military, and Masculinities. In *Theorizing Masculinities,* edited by Harry Brod and Michael Kaufman. Thousand Oaks, CA: Sage, pp. 165–82.

Mota, Sue Ann. 2006. Title IX after Thirty-Four Years—Retaliation Is Not Allowed According to the Supreme Court in *Jackson v. Birmingham Board of Education. Villanova Sports and Entertainment Law Journal* 13:245–70.

Murphy, Jane C. 2005. Legal Images of Fatherhood: Welfare Reform, Child Support Enforcement, and Fatherless Children. *Notre Dame Law Review* 81:325–86.

Murphy, Patricia, and Jannette Elwood. 1998. Gendered Learning outside and inside School: Influences on Achievement. In *Failing Boys? Issues in Gender and Achievement,* edited by Debbie Epstein, Jannette Elwood, Virginia Hey, and Janet Maw. Buckingham, UK: Open University Press, pp. 163–81.

Murphy, Peter Francis. 2001. *Studs, Tools and the Family Jewels: Metaphors Men Live By.* Madison: University of Wisconsin Press.

Murray, Melissa. 2008. The Networked Family: Reframing the Legal Understanding of Caregiving and Caregivers. *Virginia Law Review* 94:385–455.

Myers, Tamara. 2005. Embodying Delinquency: Boys' Bodies, Sexuality, and Juvenile Justice History in Early-Twentieth-Century Quebec. *Journal of the History of Sexuality* 14(4):383–414.

Naffine, Ngaire. 1996. *Feminism and Criminology.* Philadelphia: Temple University Press.

Najcevska, Mirjana. 2000. Education, Masculinity and Violence. In *Male Roles, Masculinities and Violence: A Culture of Peace Perspective,* edited by Ingeborg Breines, Robert Connell, and Ingrid Eide. Paris: UNESCO, pp. 181–87.

National Center for Children in Poverty, Mailman School of Public Health, Columbia University. 2008. Poverty Statistics for Poor and Low Income Children. Last updated September 2008. Available at www.nccp.org (accessed June 4, 2009).

Neal, Mark Anthony. 2005. *New Black Men.* New York: Routledge.

Nespor, Jan. 2000. Topologies of Masculinity: Gendered Spatialities of Preadolescent Boys. In *Masculinities at School*, edited by Nancy Lesko. Thousand Oaks, CA: Sage, pp. 27–48.

Newberger, Eli H. 1999. *The Men They Will Become: The Nature and Nurture of Male Character*. Cambridge, MA: Perseus Books.

Newkirk, Thomas. 2002. *Misreading Masculinity: Boys, Literacy and Popular Culture*. Portsmouth, NH: Heinemann.

Newton, Judith. 2002. Masculinity Studies: The Longed for Profeminist Movement for Academic Men? In *Masculinity Studies and Feminist Theory: New Directions*, edited by Judith Kegan Gardiner. New York: Columbia University Press, pp. 176–92.

Niva, Steve. 1998. Tough and Tender: New World Order Masculinity and the Gulf War. In *The "Man" Question in International Relations*, edited by Marysia Zalewski and Jane Parpart. Boulder, CO: Westview, pp. 109–28.

Noble, Colin, and Wendy Bradford. 2000. *Getting It Right for Boys . . . and Girls*. London: Routledge.

Noble, Jean Bobby. 2004. *Masculinities without Men? Female Masculinities in Twentieth Century Fiction*. Vancouver: University of British Columbia Press.

No Child Left Behind. 2008. Public Law 107-110, 20 USC section 6319.

Novkov, Julie. 2008. The Miscegenation/Same-Sex Marriage Analogy: What Can We Learn from Legal History? *Law and Social Inquiry* 33:345–86.

Nunn, Kenneth B. 2002. The Child as Other: Race and Differential Treatment in the Juvenile Justice System. *De Paul Law Review* 51:679–714.

Nye, Robert A. 2005. Locating Masculinity: Some Recent Work on Men. *Signs: Journal of Women in Culture and Society* 30(3):1937–62.

O'Donnell, Mike, and Sue Sharpe. 2000. *Uncertain Masculinities: Youth, Ethnicity and Class in Contemporary Britain*. New York: Routledge.

Oftung, Knut. 2000. Men and Gender Equality in the Nordic Countries. In *Male Roles, Masculinities and Violence: A Culture of Peace Perspective*, edited by Ingeborg Breines, Robert Connell, and Ingrid Eide. Paris: UNESCO, pp. 143–62.

Oláh, Livia Sz., Eva M. Bernhardt, and Frances K. Goldscheider. 2002. Coresidential Paternal Roles in Industrialized Countries: Sweden, Hungary and the United States. In *Making Men into Fathers: Men, Masculinities and the Social Politics of Fatherhood*, edited by Barbara Hobson. New York: Cambridge University Press, pp. 25–57.

Orfield, Gary, ed. 2004. *Dropouts in America: Confronting the Graduation Rate Crisis*. Cambridge, MA: Harvard University Press.

Orloff, Ann Shola, and Renee A. Monson. 2002. Citizens, Workers or Fathers? Men in the History of U.S. Social Policy. In *Making Men into Fathers: Men, Masculinities and the Social Politics of Fatherhood*, edited by Barbara Hobson. New York: Cambridge University Press, pp. 61–91.

Osborne, Allan G., and Ralph D. Mawdsley. 2008. Investigating Complaints of Peer-to-Peer Sexual Harassment under Title IX: The Implications of *Fitzgerald v. Barnstable School Committee*. *Education Law Reporter* 226:21–26.

Palkovitz, Rob. 2002. *Involved Fathering and Men's Adult Development: Provisional Balances*. Mahwah, NJ: Erlbaum.

Palkovitz, Rob, Marcella A. Copes, and Tara N. Woolfolk. 2001. "It's Like . . . You Discover a New Sense of Being": Involved Fathering as an Evoker of Adult Development. *Men and Masculinities* 4(1):49–69.

Parenti, Christian. 2001. Rehabilitating Prison Labor: The Uses of Imprisoned Masculinity. In *Prison Masculinities*, edited by Don Sabo, Terry A. Kupers, and Willie London. Philadelphia: Temple University Press, pp. 247–54.

Parness, Jeffrey A. 2005–2006. Adoption Notices to Genetic Fathers: No to Scarlet Letters, Yes to Good-Faith Cooperation. *Cumberland Law Review* 36:63–81.

Pascoe, C.J. 2007. *Dude You're a Fag: Masculinity and Sexuality in High School*. Berkeley: University of California Press.

Pascoe, C.J. 2003. Multiple Masculinities? Teenage Boys Talk about Jocks and Gender. *American Behavioral Scientist* 46(10):1423–37.

PBS Frontline website. 2009a. Juvenile Justice: Basic Statistics. http://www.pbs.org/wgbh/pages/frontline/shows/juvenile/stats/basic.html (accessed July 26, 2009).

PBS Frontline website. 2009b. Juvenile Justice: Child or Adult? A Century Long View. http://www.pbs.org/wgbh/pages/frontline/shows/juvenile/stats/childadult.html (accessed July 26, 2009).

Pease, Bob. 2002 (Re)Constructing Men's Interests. *Men and Masculinities* 5(2):165–77.

Pease, Bob, and Keith Pringle, eds. 2001. *A Man's World? Changing Men's Practices in a Globalized World*. New York: Zed Books.

Perry, Twila L. 2003. The "Essentials of Marriage": Reconsidering the Duty of Support and Services. *Yale Journal of Law and Feminism* 15:1–49.

Pershing, Jana L. 2006. Men and Women's Experiences with Hazing in a Male-Dominated Elite Military Institution. *Men and Masculinities* 8(4):470–92.

Petersen, Alan. 2003. Research on Men and Masculinities: Some Implications of Recent Theory for Future Work. *Men and Masculinities* 6(1):54–69.

Phillips, Debby A. 2007. Punking and Bullying: Strategies in Middle School, High School, and Beyond. *Journal of Interpersonal Violence* 22(2):158–78.

Phillips, Debby A. 2006. Masculinity, Male Development, Gender, and Identity: Modern and Postmodern Meanings. *Issues in Mental Health Nursing* 27(4):403–23.

Phipps, Charles A. 1997. Children, Adults, Sex and the Criminal Law: In Search of Reason. *Seton Hall Legislative Journal* 22:1–138.

Phoenix, Ann. 2003. Neoliberalism and Masculinity: Racialization and the Contradictions of Schooling for 11- to 14-Year-Olds. *Youth and Society* 36(2):227–46.

Pieronek, Catherine. 2005. Title IX and Gender Equity in Science, Technology, Engineering and Mathematics Education: No Longer an Overlooked Application of the Law. *Journal of College and University Law* 31:291–350.

Pinzler, Isabelle Katz. 2004–5. Separate but Equal Education in the Context of Gender. *New York Law School Law Review* 49:785–807.

Pipher, Mary. 1994. *Reviving Ophelia: Saving the Lives of Adolescent Girls*. New York: Ballantine Books.

Plantin, Lars, Swen-Axel Mansson, and Jeremy Kearney. 2003. Talking and Doing Fatherhood: On Fatherhood and Masculinity in Sweden and England. *Fathering* 1(1):3–26.

Pleck, Joseph. 1995. The Gender Role Strain Paradigm: An Update. In *A New Psychology of Men*, edited by Ronald F. Levant and William S. Pollack. New York: Basic Books, pp. 11–32.

Pleck, Joseph. 1981. *The Myth of Masculinity*. Cambridge, MA: MIT Press.

Pleck, Joseph, and Elizabeth Pleck, eds. 1980. *The American Man*. Englewood Cliffs, NJ: Prentice Hall.

Pleck, Joseph, and Jack Sawyer, eds. 1974. *Men and Masculinity.* Englewood Cliffs, NJ: Prentice Hall.

Poe-Yamagata, Eileen, and Jeffery A. Butts. 1996. *Female Offenders in the Juvenile Justice System: Statistics Summary.* Office of Juvenile Justice and Delinquency Prevention (OJJDP), U.S. Department of Justice, Office of Justice Programs. Pittsburgh: National Center for Juvenile Justice.

Poe-Yamagata, Eileen, and Michael A. Jones. 2000. *And Justice for Some—Differential Treatment of Minority Youth in the Justice System.* Building Blocks for Youth Initiative. Washington, DC: Justice Policy Institute.

Poirier, Marc R. 2003. Hastening the Kulturkampt: *Boy Scouts of America v. Dale* and the Politics of American Masculinity. *Law and Sexuality* 12:271–336.

Polakow, Valerie. 2000. *The Public Assault on America's Children: Poverty, Violence, and Juvenile Justice.* New York: Teachers College Press.

Polikoff, Nancy. 2004. Making Marriage Matter Less: The ALI Domestic Partner Principles Are One Step in the Right Direction. *University of Chicago Legal Forum* 2004:353–79.

Polk, Kenneth. 1998. Masculinity, Honour, and Confrontational Homicide. In *Criminology at the Crossroads: Feminist Readings in Crime and Justice,* edited by Kathleen Daly and Lisa Maher. New York: Oxford University Press, pp. 188–205.

Pollack, William S. 2006. The "War" for Boys: Hearing "Real Boys'" Voices, Healing Their Pain. *Professional Psychology, Research and Practice* 37(2):190–95.

Pollack, William S. 2000. *Real Boys' Voices.* New York: Random House.

Pollack, William S. 1998. *Real Boys: Rescuing Our Sons from the Myths of Boyhood.* New York: Random House.

Pollack, William S. 1995. No Man Is an Island: Toward a New Psychoanalytic Psychology of Men. In *A New Psychology of Men,* edited by Ronald F. Levant and William S. Pollack. New York: Basic Books, pp. 33–67.

Pope, Carl E., and William H. Feyerherm. 1983. Gender Bias in Juvenile Court Dispositions. *Journal of Social Science Research* 6:1–16.

Poulin, Anne Bowen. 1996. Symposium: Juvenile Justice System Reform: Article: Female Delinquents: Defining Their Place in the Justice System. *Wisconsin Law Review* 1996:541–75.

Provine, Doris Marie. 1998. Too Many Black Men: The Sentencing Judge's Dilemma. *Law and Social Inquiry* 23:823–56.

Putnam, Frank W. 2003. Ten-Year Research Update Review: Child Sexual Abuse. *Journal of the American Academy of Child Adolescent Psychiatry* 42(3):269–78.

Raag, Tarja. 2004. Book review: *A Sex and Gender Text That Is Shaping and Defining Our Discipline. Psychology of Women Quarterly* 28(3):266–72.

Ramsay, Christine. 1996. Male Horror: On David Cronenberg. In *Boys: Masculinities in Contemporary Culture,* edited by Paul Smith. Boulder, CO: Westview, pp. 81–95.

Ranson, Gillian. 2001. Men at Work: Change—or No Change?—in the Era of the "New Father." *Men and Masculinities* 4(1):3–26.

Rayburn, Corey. 2003. Why Are YOU Taking Gender and the Law? Deconstructing the Norms That Keep Men Out of the Law School's "Pink Ghetto." *Hastings Women's Law Journal* 14:71–88.

Raymond, Sara. 2000. From Playpens to Prisons: What the Gang Violence and Juvenile Crime Prevention Act of 1998 Does to California's Juvenile Justice System and Reasons to Repeal It. *Golden Gate University Law Review* 30:233–84.

Razack, Sherene. 2002. "Outwhiting the White Guys": Men of Colour and Peacekeeping Violence. *University of Missouri–Kansas City Law Review* 71:331–54.

Redman, Peter. 1996. "Empowering Men to Disempower Themselves": Heterosexual Masculinities, HIV and the Contradictions of Anti-Oppressive Education. In *Understanding Masculinities: Social Relations and Cultural Arenas*, edited by Máirtín Mac an Ghaill. Philadelphia: Open University Press, pp. 168–79.

Reinheimer, Justin. 2006. Same-Sex Marriage through the Equal Protection Clause: A Gender-Conscious Analysis. *Berkeley Journal of Gender, Law and Justice* 21:213–40.

Remy, John. 1990. Patriarchy and Fratriarchy as Forms of Androcracy. In *Men, Masculinities and Social Theory*, edited by Jeff Hearn and David Morgan. London: Unwin Hyman, pp. 43–54.

Renold, Emma. 2007. Primary School "Studs": (De)constructing Young Boys' Heterosexual Masculinities. *Men and Masculinities* 9(3):275–97.

Rich, John A. 2000. The Health of African American Men. *Annals of the American Academy of Political and Social Science* 569:149–59.

Richards, Barry. 1990. Masculinity, Identification, and Political Culture. In *Men, Masculinities and Social Theory*, edited by Jeff Hearn and David Morgan. London: Unwin Hyman, pp. 160–69.

Richardson, Diane, Janice McLaughlin, and Mark E. Casey, eds. 2006. *Intersections Between Feminist and Queer Theory*. New York: Palgrave Macmillan.

Rigdon, Amy R. 2008. Dangerous Data: How Disputed Research Legalized Public Single-Sex Education. *Stetson Law Review* 37:527–77.

Risman, Barbara J. 1998. *Gender Vertigo: American Families in Transition*. New Haven, CT: Yale University Press.

Roberts, Dorothy. 2004. The Social and Moral Cost of Mass Incarceration in African American Communities. *Stanford Law Review* 56:1271–1305.

Roberts, Jessica L. 2005. Comment: Conclusions from the Body: Coerced Fatherhood and Caregiving as Child Support. *Yale Journal of Law and Feminism* 17:501–16.

Robertson, James E. 2003. A Clean Heart and an Empty Head: The Supreme Court and Sexual Terrorism in Prison. *North Carolina Law Review* 81:433–81.

Robinson, Sally. 2002. Pedagogy of the Opaque: Teaching Masculinity Studies. In *Masculinity Studies and Feminist Theory: New Directions*, edited by Judith Kegan Gardiner. New York: Columbia University Press, pp. 141–60.

Roper v. Simmons, 543 U.S. 551 (2005).

Rose, Elizabeth. 2002. Review of *Mothers of All Children: Women Reformers and the Rise of Juvenile Courts in Progressive Era America*, by Elizabeth Clapp. *Law and History Review* 20:217–18.

Rosenblum, Darren. 1994. Queer Intersectionality and the Failure of Recent Lesbian and Gay "Victories." *Law and Sexuality: A Review of Lesbian and Gay Legal Issues* 4:83–122.

Ross, Marlon B. 2004. *Manning the Race: Reforming Black Men in the Jim Crow Era*. New York: New York University Press.

Ross, Marlon B. 2002. Race, Rape, Castration: Feminist Theories of Sexual Violence and Masculine Strategies of Black Protest. In *Masculinity Studies and Feminist Theory: New Directions*, edited by Judith Kegan Gardiner. New York: Columbia University Press, pp. 305–43.

Roussel, Jean-Francois, and Christian Downs. 2007. Epistemological Perspectives on Concepts of Gender and Masculinity/Masculinities. *Journal of Men's Studies* 15(2):178–96.

Royster, Deirdre A. 2007. What Happens to Potential Discouraged? Masculinity Norms and the Contrasting Institutional and Labor Market Experiences of Less Affluent Black and White Men. *Annals of the American Academy of Political and Social Science* 609:153–80.

Runner, Amy D. 2000. Women Who Dance on the Professional Track: Custody and the Red Shoes. *Harvard Women's Law Journal* 23:173–217.

Ryan, Megan. 2008. Comments from the Spring 2007 Harvard Journal of Law and Gender Conference—Opening Remarks by Conference Organizers, Alexis Kuznick and Megan Ryan. *Harvard Journal of Law and Gender* 31:378–406.

Ryan Report. 2009. Child Abuse Commission (Ireland) Executive Summary. www.childabusecommission.com/rpt/execsummary.php.

Sabo, Don, Terry A. Kupers, and Willie London. 2001a. Gender and the Politics of Punishment. In *Prison Masculinities*, edited by Don Sabo, Terry A. Kupers, and Willie London. Philadelphia: Temple University Press, pp. 3–18.

Sabo, Don, Terry A. Kupers, and Willie London, eds. 2001b. *Prison Masculinities*. Philadelphia: Temple University Press.

Sadker, David, and Myra Sadker. 1994. *Failing at Fairness: How America's Schools Cheat Girls*. New York: Simon and Schuster.

Safilios-Rothschild, Constantina. 2000. The Negative Side of Development Interventions and Gender Transitions: Impoverished Male Roles Threaten Peace. In *Male Roles, Masculinities and Violence: A Culture of Peace Perspective*, edited by Ingeborg Breines, Robert Connell, and Ingrid Eide. Paris: UNESCO, pp. 85–93.

Salomone, Rosemary C. 2004. Feminist Voices in the Debate over Single-Sex Schooling: Finding Common Ground. *Michigan Journal of Gender and Law* 11:63–95.

Salter, Daniel, Dean McMillan, Mark Richards, Tiffany Talbot, Jill Hodges, Arnon Bentovim, Richard Hastings, Jim Stephenson, and David Skuse. 2003. Development of Sexually Abusive Behaviour in Sexually Victimised Males: Longitudinal Study. *Lancet* 361(9356):471–76.

Sargent, Paul. 2005. The Gendering of Men in Early Childhood Education. *Sex Roles* 52(3–4):251–60.

Schlichter, Annette. 2004. Queer at Last? Straight Intellectuals and the Desire for Transgression. *GLQ: A Journal of Lesbian and Gay Studies* 10(4):543–64.

Schmitt, Richard. 2001. Proud to Be a Man? *Men and Masculinities* 3(4):393–404.

Schroeder, Theodore A. 1998. Fables of the Deconstruction: The Practical Failures of Gay and Lesbian Theory in the Realm of Employment Discrimination. *American University Journal of Gender and Law* 6:333–67.

Schultz, Vicki. 2000. Life's Work. *Columbia Law Review* 100:1881–1964.

Schwalbe, Michael, and Michelle Wolkomir. 2001. The Masculine Self as Problem and Resource in Interview Studies of Men. *Men and Masculinities* 4(1):90–103.

Scott, Elizabeth S., and Thomas Grisso. 1997. The Evolution of Adolescence: A Developmental Perspective on Juvenile Justice Reform. *Journal of Criminal Law and Criminology* 88:137–89.

Scott, Elizabeth S., and Robert E. Scott. 1998. Marriage as Relational Contract. *Virginia Law Review* 84:1225–1334.

Scott, Elizabeth S., and Laurence Steinberg. 2008. *Rethinking Juvenile Justice.* Cambridge, MA: Harvard University Press.

Scourfield, Jonathan B. 2001. Constructing Men in Child Protection Work. *Men and Masculinities* 4(1):70–89.

Seaman, Julie A. 2007. The Peahen's Tale, or Dressing Our Parts at Work. *Duke Journal of Gender Law and Policy* 14:423–66.

Secunda, Paul M. 2005. At the Crossroads of Title IX and a New "Idea": Why Bullying Need Not Be "a Normal Part of Growing Up" for Special Education Children. *Duke Journal of Gender Law and Policy* 12:1–32.

Segal, Lynne. 1990. *Slow Motion: Changing Masculinities, Changing Men.* London: Virago.

Seidler, Victor J. 2007. Masculinities, Bodies, and Emotional Life. *Men and Masculinities* 10(1):9–21.

Seidler, Victor J. 1990. Men, Feminism and Power. In *Men, Masculinities and Social Theory*, edited by Jeff Hearn and David Morgan. London: Unwin Hyman, pp. 215–28.

Selmi, Michael. 2007. The Work-Family Conflict: An Essay on Employers, Men and Responsibility. *University of St. Thomas Law Journal* 4:573–98.

Selmi, Michael. 2005. Sex Discrimination in the Nineties, Seventies Style: Case Studies in the Preservation of Male Workplace Norms. *Employee Rights and Employment Policy Journal* 9:1–49.

Selmi, Michael. 2001. Care, Work and the Road to Equality: A Commentary on Fineman and Williams. *Chicago-Kent Law Review* 76:1557–68.

Selmi, Michael. 2000. Family Leave and the Gender Wage Gap. *North Carolina Law Review* 78:707–82.

Selmi, Michael, and Naomi Cahn. 2006. Women in the Workplace: Which Women, Which Agenda? *Duke Journal of Gender Law and Policy* 13:7–30.

Selmi, Michael, and Naomi Cahn. 2003. Caretaking and the Contradictions of Contemporary Policy. *Maine Law Review* 55:289–312.

Seward, Rudy R., Dale E. Yeatts, Iftekhar Amin, and Amy DeWitt. 2006. Employment Leave and Fathers' Involvement with Children. *Men and Masculinities* 8(4):405–27.

Sewell, Tony. 1998. Loose Canons: Exploding the Myth of the "Black Macho" Lad. In *Failing Boys? Issues in Gender and Achievement*, edited by Debbie Epstein, Jannette Elwood, Virginia Hey, and Janet Maw. Buckingham, UK: Open University Press, pp. 111–27.

Sewell, Tony. 1997. *Black Masculinities and Schooling: How Black Boys Survive Modern Schooling.* Oakhill, UK: Trentham Books.

Shek, Yen Ling. 2006. Asian American Masculinity: A Review of the Literature. *Journal of Men's Studies* 14(3):379–91.

Shepherd, Robert E., Jr. 2008. Evidence Mounts on Wisdom of Trying Juveniles as Adults. *WTR Criminal Justice* 22:42–45.

Sherwin, Galen. 2005. Single-Sex Schools and the Antisegregation Principle. *New York University Review of Law and Social Change* 30:35–87.

Silbaugh, Katherine. 2007. Women's Place: Urban Planning, Housing Design, and Work-Family Balance. *Fordham Law Review* 76:1797–1851.

Silbaugh, Katherine. 2001. Gender and Nonfinancial Matters in the ALI Principles of the Law of Family Dissolution. *Duke Journal of Gender Law and Policy* 8:203–12.

Simmons, Ron. 1999. Baraka's Dilemma: To Be or Not to Be? In *Black Men on Race, Gender and Sexuality: A Critical Reader,* edited by Devon Carbado. New York: New York University Press, pp. 317–23.

Singley, Susan G., and Kathryn Hynes. 2005. Transitions to Parenthood: Work-Family Policies, Gender and the Couple Context. *Gender and Society* 19(3):376–97.

Skelton, Christine. 2001. *Schooling the Boys: Masculinities and Primary Education.* Philadelphia: Open University Press, 2001.

Smiler, Andrew P. 2006a. Introduction to Manifestations of Masculinity. *Sex Roles* 55(9–10):585–87.

Smiler, Andrew P. 2006b. Living the Image: A Quantitative Approach to Delineating Masculinities. *Sex Roles* 55(9–10):621–32.

Smiler, Andrew P. 2004. Thirty Years after the Discovery of Gender: Psychological Concepts and Measures of Masculinity. *Sex Roles* 50(1–2):15–26.

Smith, George P., II. 1998. Civil Liberties, Sexuality and the Law. *New York University Review of Law and Social Change* 24:333–37.

Smith, Jeffrey. 2007. "Ye've Got to 'Ave Balls to Play This Game Sir!" Boys, Peers and Fears: The Negative Influence of School-Based "Cultural Accomplices" in Constructing Hegemonic Masculinities. *Gender and Education* 19(2):179–98.

Smith, Pamela J. 1999a. Looking beyond Traditional Educational Paradigms: When Old Victims Become New Victimizers. *Hamline Law Review* 23:101–74.

Smith, Pamela J. 1999b. Part II—Romantic Paternalism—The Ties That Bind: Hierarchies of Economic Oppression That Reveal Judicial Disaffinity for Black Women and Men. *Journal of Gender, Race and Justice* 3(1):181–256.

Smith, Paul, ed. 1996. *Boys: Masculinities in Contemporary Culture.* Boulder, CO: Westview.

Smith, Tyson, and Michael Kimmel. 2005. The Hidden Discourse of Masculinity in Gender Discrimination Law. *Signs: Journal of Women in Culture and Society* 30(3):1827–49.

Snyder, Howard N. 1999. *Juvenile Arrests 1998.* Washington, DC: U.S. Department of Justice, Office of Juvenile Justice and Delinquency Prevention.

Snyder, Howard N. 1996. *Juvenile Arrests 1996.* Washington, DC: U.S. Department of Justice, Office of Juvenile Justice and Delinquency Prevention.

Snyder, Howard N., and Melissa Sickmund. 2006. *Juvenile Offenders and Victims: 2006 National Report.* Washington, DC: U.S. Department of Justice, Office of Justice Programs, Office of Juvenile Justice and Delinquency Prevention.

Soban, Catherine. 2006. What about the Boys? Addressing Issues of Masculinity within Male Anorexia Nervosa in a Feminist Therapeutic Environment. *International Journal of Men's Health* 5(3):225–27.

Sommers, Christina Hoff. 2000. *The War against Boys: How Misguided Feminism Is Harming Our Young Men.* New York: Simon and Schuster.

Sorenson, Elaine, and Chara Zebman. 2001. *Poor Dads Who Don't Pay Child Support: Deadbeats or Disadvantaged.* Washington, DC: Urban Institute. Available at http://www.urbasn.org/ur/cfm?ID=310334.

Sorsoli, Lynn, Maryam Kia-Keating, and Frances K. Grossman. 2008. "I Keep That Hush-Hush": Male Survivors of Sexual Abuse and the Challenges of Disclosure. *Journal of Counseling Psychology* 55(3):333–45.

Spain, Daphne. 1993. Gendered Spaces and Women's Status. *Sociological Theory* 11(2):137–51.

Spector-Mersel, Gabriela. 2006. Never-Aging Stories: Western Hegemonic Masculinity Scripts. *Journal of Gender Studies* 15(1):67–82.

Speer, Susan A. 2001. Reconsidering the Concept of Hegemonic Masculinity: Discursive Psychology, Conversation Analysis and Participants' Orientations. *Feminism and Psychology* 11(1):107–35.

Spindelman, Marc. 2005. Homosexuality's Horizon. *Emory Law Journal* 54:1361–1406.

Spitko, E. Gary. 2005. From Queer to Paternity: How Primary Gay Fathers Are Changing Fatherhood and Gay Identity. *St. Louis Public University Law Review* 24:195–20.

Stemple, Lara. 2009. Male Rape and Human Rights. *Hastings Law Journal* 60:605–45.

Stevenson, Howard C. 2004. Boys in Men's Clothing: Racial Socialization and Neighborhood Safety as Buffers to Hypervulnerability in African American Adolescent Males. In *Adolescent Boys: Exploring Diverse Cultures of Boyhood*, edited by Niobe Way and Judy Y. Chu. New York: New York University Press, pp. 59–77.

Stogner v. California. 123 S.Ct. 2446 (2003).

Stoudt, Brett G. 2006. "You're Either In or You're Out": School Violence, Peer Discipline, and the (Re)Production of Hegemonic Masculinity. *Men and Masculinities* 8(3):273–87.

Stough, O'Neil. 2001. A Moment. In *Prison Masculinities*, edited by Don Sabo, Terry A. Kupers, and Willie London. Philadelphia: Temple University Press, pp. 137–38.

Streib, Victor L. 2002. Gendering the Death Penalty: Countering Sex Bias in a Masculine Sanctuary. *Ohio State Law Journal* 63:433–72.

Suárez-Orozco, Carola, and Desirée Baolian Qin-Hilliard. 2004. Immigrant Boys' Experiences in U.S. Schools. In *Adolescent Boys: Exploring Diverse Cultures of Boyhood*, edited by Niobe Way and Judy Y. Chu. New York: New York University Press, pp. 295–316.

Swann, Joan. 1998. Language and Gender: Who, If Anyone, Is Disadvantaged by What? In *Failing Boys? Issues in Gender and Achievement*, edited by Debbie Epstein, Jannette Elwood, Virginia Hey, and Janet Maw. Buckingham, UK: Open University Press, pp. 147–61.

Tager, David, and Glenn E. Good. 2005. Italian and American Masculinities: A Comparison of Masculine Gender Role Norms. *Psychology of Men and Masculinity* 6(4):264–74.

Tamis-LeMonda, Catherine S., and Natasha Cabrera. 2002. *Handbook of Father Involvement: Multidisciplinary Perspectives.* Mahwah, NJ: Erlbaum.

Taylor, Lindsay. 2008. Family Care Commitment Discrimination: Bridging the Gap between Work and Family. *Family Court Review* 46:558–67.

Teilmann, Katherine S., and Pierre H. Landry, Jr. 1981. Gender Bias in Juvenile Justice. *Journal of Research in Crime and Delinquency* 47–80.

Thompson, Damian. 2009. The Latest Child Abuse Scandal Is as Irish as It Is Catholic. Telegraph.co.uk blogs, http://blogs.telegraph.co.uk/damian_thompson/blog/2009/05/28.

Thompson, Edward H., Jr. 2006. Images of Old Men's Masculinity: Still a Man? *Sex Roles* 55:633–48.

Thompson, Edward H., Jr., and Joseph H. Pleck. 1995. Masculinity Ideologies: A Review of Research Instrumentation on Men and Masculinities. In *A New Psychology of Men*, edited by Ronald F. Levant and William S. Pollack. New York: Basic Books, pp. 129–225.

Thorne, Barrie. 1993. *Gender Play: Girls and Boys in School*. New Brunswick, NJ: Rutgers University Press.

Thro, William E. 2003. Judicial Paradigms of Educational Equality. *Education Law Reporter* 174:1–42.

Tillner, George. 2000. The Identity of Dominance: Masculinity and Xenophobia. In *Male Roles, Masculinities and Violence: A Culture of Peace Perspective*, edited by Ingeborg Breines, Robert Connell, and Ingrid Eide. Paris: UNESCO, pp. 53–60.

Title IX. 2008. Public Law 103-382, 20 USC sections 1681–99.

Todd, Debra. 2004. Sentencing of Adult Offenders in Cases Involving Sexual Abuse of Children: Too Little, Too Late? A View from the Pennsylvania Bench. *Pennsylvania State Law Review* 109:487–564.

Toker, Rachel L. 1999. Multiple Masculinities: A New Vision for Same-Sex Harassment Law. *Harvard Civil Rights–Civil Liberties Law Review* 34:577–602.

Townsend, Nicholas W. 2002. *The Package Deal: Marriage, Work and Fatherhood in Men's Lives*. Philadelphia: Temple University Press.

Trickett, Penelope, Frank Putnam, and Jennie Noll. 2005. Longitudinal Study Survey, Longitudinal Survey of Childhood Sexual Abuse. Available at http://www.cincinnat-ichildrens.org/svc/alpha/c/child-abuse/publications.htm#articles.

Tsolidis, Georgina, and Ian R. Dobson. 2006. Single-Sex Schooling: Is It Simply a "Class Act"? *Gender and Education* 18(2):213–28.

U.S. Department of Education, Institute of Education Sciences. 2004. *Trends in Educational Equity of Girls and Women: 2004*. Available at http://nces.ed.gov/pubs2005/equity/.

U.S. Department of Health and Human Services, Office of the Assistant Secretary for Planning and Evaluation (ASPE). 2008. ASPE Fact Sheet: Juvenile Delinquency. Available at http://aspe.hhs.gov/hsp/08/boys/FactSheets/jd/index.shtml (accessed July 27, 2009).

Valdes, Francisco. 1998. Beyond Sexual Orientation in Queer Legal Theory: Majoritarianism, Multidisciplinary, and Responsibility in Social Justice Scholarship or Legal Scholars as Cultural Warriors. *Denver University Law Review* 75:1409–64.

Valdes, Francisco. 1995. Queers, Sissies, Dykes, and Tomboys: Deconstructing the Conflation of "Sex," "Gender," and "Sexual Orientation" in Euro-American Law and Society. *California Law Review* 83:1–343.

Valente, Sharon M. 2005. Sexual Abuse of Boys. *Journal of Child and Adolescent Psychiatric Nursing* 18(1):10–16.

van Hoven, Bettina, and Kathrin Horschelmann. 2005a. Introduction to *Spaces of Masculinities*, edited by Bettina van Hoven and Kathrin Horschelmann. London: Routledge, pp. 1–15.

van Hoven, Bettina, and Kathrin Horschelmann, eds. 2005b. *Spaces of Masculinities*. London: Routledge.

Ventura, Stephanie J. 2009. *Changing Patterns of Nonmarital Childbearing in the United States*. NCHS Data Brief 18. Centers for Disease Control. Available at http://www.cdc.gov/nchs/data/databriefs/db18.htm.

Vojdik, Valorie K. 2002. Gender Outlaws: Challenging Masculinity in Traditionally Male Institutions. *Berkeley Women's Law Journal* 17:68–121.

Walby, Sylvia. 1990. *Theorizing Patriarchy*. Oxford, UK: Blackwell.

Walker, Barbara M. 2004. Frames of Self: Capturing Working-Class British Boys' Identities through Photographs. In *Adolescent Boys: Exploring Diverse Cultures of Boyhood*, edited by Niobe Way and Judy Y. Chu. New York: New York University Press, pp. 31–58.

Walker, Gregory W. 2006. Disciplining Protest Masculinity. *Men and Masculinities* 9(1):5–22.

Walklate, Sandra. 2004. *Gender, Crime and Criminal Justice*. Portland, OR: Willan.

Ward, Elijah. 2005. Homophobia, Hypermasculinity and the U.S. Black Church. *Culture, Health and Sexuality* 7(5):493–504.

Warren, Marguerite Q., ed. 1981. *Comparing Female and Male Offenders*. London: Sage.

Warrington, Molly, and Mike Younger. 2006. *Raising Boys' Achievement in Primary Schools: Toward a Holistic Approach*. Berkshire, UK: Open University Press.

Way, Niobe, and Judy Y. Chu, eds. 2004a. *Adolescent Boys: Exploring Diverse Cultures of Boyhood*. New York: New York University Press.

Way, Niobe, and Judy Y. Chu. 2004b. Introduction to *Adolescent Boys: Exploring Diverse Cultures of Boyhood*, edited by Niobe Way and Judy Y. Chu. New York: New York University Press, pp. 1–10.

Weaver-Hightower, Marcus. 2003. The "Boy Turn" in Research on Gender and Education. *Review of Educational Research* 73(4):471–98.

Webb, Stephen H. 2001. Defending All-Male Education: A New Cultural Moment for a Renewed Debate. *Fordham Urban Law Journal* 29:601–10.

Weber, Cynthia. 1998. Something's Missing: Male Hysteria and the U.S. Invasion of Panama. In *The "Man" Question in International Relations*, edited by Marysia Zalewski and Jane Parpart. Boulder, CO: Westview, pp. 150–68.

Weisberg, D. Kelly. 1995. Professional Women and the Professionalization of Motherhood: Marcia Clark's Double Bind. *Hastings Women's Law Journal* 6:295–338.

Wencelblat, Patricia. 2004. Note: Boys Will Be Boys? An Analysis of Male-on-Male Heterosexual Sexual Violence. *Columbia Journal of Law and Social Problems* 38:37–66.

West, Cornel. 1993. *Race Matters*. Boston: Beacon.

Wester, Stephen R., David R. Pionke, and David L. Vogel. 2005. Male Gender Role Conflict, Gay Men, and Same-Sex Romantic Relationships. *Psychology of Men and Masculinity* 6(3):195–208.

Westwood, Sallie. 1996. "Feckless Fathers": Masculinities and the British State. In *Understanding Masculinities: Social Relations and Cultural Arenas*, edited by Máirtín Mac an Ghaill. Philadelphia: Open University Press, pp. 21–34.

Wexler, David B. 2000. Just Some Juvenile Thinking about Delinquent Behavior: A Therapeutic Jurisprudence Approach to Relapse Prevention Planning and Youth Advisory Juries. *University of Missouri–Kansas City Law Review* 69:93–105.

Whitcombe, Rebecca J. 2001. Child Sexual Abuse: Adult Survivors, Repressed Memories, and Stories Finally Told. *UCLA Women's Law Journal* 11:255–79.

Whitehead, Stephen M. 2002. *Men and Masculinities: Key Themes and New Directions*. Cambridge, UK: Polity.

Whitehead, Stephen M. 1999. Review article: Hegemonic Masculinity Revisited. *Gender, Work and Organization* 6(1):58–62.

Whitehead, Stephen M., and Frank J. Barrett, eds. 2001. *The Masculinities Reader.* Cambridge, UK: Polity.

Whorley, MySha R., and Michael E. Addis. 2006. Ten Years of Psychological Research on Men and Masculinity in the United States: Dominant Methodological Trends. *Sex Roles* 55:649–58.

Wible, Brent. 2005. Achieving the Promise of Girls' Education: Strategies to Overcome Gender-Based Violence in Beninese Schools. *Columbia Human Rights Law Review* 36:513–59.

Wilkinson, Wayne W. 2004. Authoritarian Hegemony, Dimensions of Masculinity, and Male Antigay Attitudes. *Psychology of Men and Masculinity* 5(2):121–31.

Williams, Joan. 2001. *Unbending Gender: Why Family and Work Conflict and What to Do about It.* New York: Oxford University Press.

Williams, Joan C., and Elizabeth S. Westfall. 2006. Deconstructing the Maternal Wall: Strategies for Vindicating the Civil Rights of "Careers" in the Workplace. *Duke Journal of Gender Law and Policy* 13:31–53.

Williams, Verna L. 2006. Private Choices, Public Consequences: Public Education Reform and Feminist Legal Theory. *William and Mary Journal of Women and the Law* 12:563–601.

Willott, Sara, and Christine Griffin. 1996. Men, Masculinity and the Challenge of Long-Term Unemployment. In *Understanding Masculinities: Social Relations and Cultural Arenas,* edited by Máirtín Mac an Ghaill. Philadelphia: Open University Press, pp. 75–92.

Wilson, Elizabeth A. 2003. Suing for Lost Childhood: Child Sexual Abuse, the Delayed Discovery Rule, and the Problem of Finding Justice for Adult-Survivors of Child Abuse. *UCLA Women's Law Journal* 12:145–250.

Wilson, Gary. 2006. *Breaking through Barriers to Boys' Achievement: Developing a Caring Masculinity.* London: Network Continuum Education.

Woodhouse, Barbara Bennett. 2008. *Hidden in Plain Sight: The Tragedy of Children's Rights from Ben Franklin to Lionel Tate.* Princeton, NJ: Princeton University Press.

Wooster, Ann K. 1999. Sex Discrimination in Public Education under Title IX—Supreme Court Cases. *American Law Reports, Federal* 158:563–610.

Yoshino, Kenji. 2002. Covering. *Yale Law Journal* 111:769–939.

Young, Josephine Peyton. 2001. Displaying Practices of Masculinity: Critical Literacy and Social Contexts. *Journal of Adolescent and Adult Literacy* 45(1):4–14.

Young, Robert, and Helen Sweeting. 2004. Adolescent Bullying, Relationships, Psychological Well-Being, and Gender-Atypical Behavior: A Gender Diagnosticity Approach. *Sex Roles* 50(7–8):525–37.

Zalewski, Marysia. 1998. Introduction: From the "Woman" Question to the "Man" Question in International Relations. In *The "Man" Question in International Relations,* edited by Marysia Zalewski and Jane Parpart. Boulder, CO: Westview, pp. 1–13.

Zalewski, Marysia, and Jane Parpart, eds. 1998. *The "Man" Question in International Relations.* Boulder, CO: Westview.

Zeidan, Sami. 2006. The Limits of Queer Theory in LGBT Litigation and the International Human Rights Discourse. *Boston University International Law Journal* 24:313–48.

Index

About the Author

NANCY E. DOWD is the director of the Center on Children and Families at the University of Florida Fredric G. Levin College of Law and holds the David H. Levin Chair in Family Law. She is the author of several books, including *Redefining Fatherhood* (NYU Press, 2000).